NEW FORMATIONS

EDITOR:
Judith Squires

CONSULTING EDITORS:
James Donald
Erica Carter

GUEST EDITOR:
Simon Frith

EDITORIAL BOARD:
Homi Bhabha
Lesley Caldwell
Tony Davies
Simon Frith
Jim Grealy
Stuart Hall
Dick Hebdige
Maria Lauret
Kobena Mercer
Graham Murdock
Ali Rattansi
Denise Riley
Jenny Bourne Taylor
Valerie Walkerdine

OVERSEAS EDITORS:
Ien Ang
Angelika Bammer
Tony Bennett
Jody Berland
Victor Burgin
Hazel Carby
Iain Chambers
Joan Copjec
Lidia Curti
Ian Hunter
Cora Kaplan
Noel King
Colin Mercer
Edward Said
Renata Salecl
Gayatri Chakravorty Spivak
John Tagg

New Formations is
published three times
a year by
Lawrence & Wishart
99a Wallis Road
London E9 5LN
Tel 0181–533 2506
Fax 0181–533 7369

ADVERTISEMENTS
for enquiries/bookings contact
Sally Davison, Lawrence & Wis

SUBSCRIPTIONS
For 1996, subscription rates to
Wishart are, for 3 issues
UK: Institutions £70, Individuals £35.
Rest of world: Institutions £75; Individuals
£38.
Single copies: £14.99

CONTRIBUTIONS, AND CORRESPONDENCE
should be sent to
The Editor, *New Formations*,
Dept of Politics, University of Bristol,
12 Priory Road, Bristol BS8 1TU

BOOKS FOR REVIEW
Should be sent to
Alasdair Pettinger
Scottish Music Information Centre
1 Bowmont Gardens
Glasgow, Scotland G12 9LR

Prospective writers are encouraged to contact
the editors to discuss their ideas and to obtain
a copy of our style sheet.
Manuscripts should be sent in triplicate. They
will not be returned unless a stamped,
self-addressed envelope is enclosed.
Contributors should note that the editorial
board cannot take responsibility for any
manuscript submitted to *New Formations*.

The collection as a whole © Lawrence &
Wishart 1996
Individual articles © the authors 1996

No article may be reproduced or transmitted
in any form or by any means, electronic or
mechanical, including photocopying, recording, or any information storage and retrieval
system without the permission in writing of
the publisher, editor or author.

ISSN 0 950-2378
ISBN 0 85315 813 4

Text design by Jan Brown Designs, London
Photoset in North Wales by
Derek Doyle & Associates, Mold, Clwyd
Printed in Great Britain
at the University Press, Cambridge

CONTENTS
NUMBER 27 WINTER 1995–1996

Performance Matters

NOTES ON CONTRIBUTORS

Simon Frith co-directs the John Logie Baird Centre at the Universities of Strathclyde and Glasgow. He edited a special 1995 issue of *Critical Quarterly* on 'The Voice', and is the author of *Performing Rites. The Aesthetics of Popular Music*, which will be published in 1996.

Lydia Goehr teaches Philosophy at Columbia Unviersity. She is author of *The Imaginary Museum of Musical Works* (1992) and is currently preparing a book entitled *The Great Refusal: Philosophical Essays on the Censorship, Silence and Secrets of Classical Music*.

Nicholas Cook is Professor of Music at the University of Southampton. Recent books include a Cambridge Music Handbook on Beethoven's Ninth Symphony (1993) and *Analysis Through Composition* (1995). He is currently completing *Analysing Musical Multimedia*.

Martin Stokes is a lecturer in Social Anthropology and Ethnomusicology at the Queen's University of Belfast. He is the author of *The Arabesk Debate: Music and Musicians in Modern Turkey* and edited *Ethnicity, Identity and Music: The Musical Construction of Place*.

Sally Banes is Professor of Theatre Research and Dance Studies at the University of Wisconsin-Madison. Her most recent publication is *Writing Dancing in the Age of Postmodernism* (1994) and her book on images of women in dance since the nineteenth century is forthcoming.

John F. Szwed is Musser Professor of Anthropology, African-American Studies, Music and American Studies at Yale University and is also a musician and record producer. His book *Space is the Place: Sun Ra's Life on Earth* is forthcoming.

John Stokes is Reader in English at the University of Warwick. His new book, *Oscar Wilde: Myths, Miracles and Imitations* is forthcoming.

Gill Frith is Lecturer in English at Warwick University. She is the author of *Dreams of Difference: Women and Fantasy* (1991) and is currently completing a book on female friendship and national identity in British women's fiction.

Karen Lury lectures in the Department of Theatre, Film and Television Studies at the University of Glasgow and works in the John Logie Baird Graduate Centre. Her research interests include youth, technology and performance. She has published in the Nordic journal, *Young* and is an editor of *Screen*.

Les Back teaches in the Department of Sociology, Goldsmiths College, University of London. His most recent publication was *Race, Politics and Social Change*, co-authored with John Solomos, and his next book, *New Ethnicities and Urban Culture* is forthcoming.

EDITORIAL

To introduce this issue of *New Formations* I want to say something about popular performance. The question addressed by all our contributors is what is meant by a 'performance', particularly now that 'the performative' is a routinely used term in the critical lexicon. Writing as a pop critic, I am less interested in performance as a means by which a text is presented, 'licensed' or made 'excessive',[1] than in performance as an experience (or set of experiences) of sociability, and I've always thought that postmodern theorists (much concerned with performance issues) have more to learn from a study of popular music than popular music theorists have to learn from postmodernism. Nick Kaye, for example, concludes his systematic survey of the postmodern in dance and theatre by tentatively identifying the term with 'an unstable "event" provoked by a questioning that casts doubt sharply upon even itself', but his relentless attention to the institutionally defined avant-garde means that he doesn't stop to consider to what extent such instability and questioning have always been an aspect of popular performance – something as much to do with the social basis of the event as with the intentions or principles of the performers.[2]

My feeling is that before trying to make sense of performance as a way of working with a text, we should first be sure we understand how performance is different, how it is non-textual. The question is what makes something a performance in the first place? What are its conditions of existence? How does performance-as-acting relate to performance-as-role-playing? What is the difference between performance on stage and performance off stage? Such questions are central to any discussion of performance in popular culture, in which the most interesting phenomenon is, precisely, the shifting boundary between the staged and the everyday.[3] Even performance art describes a social process. Performance requires an audience and an interpretation; it is a form of rhetoric, a rhetoric of gestures in which, in performance art at least, bodily movements and signs (including the use of voice) dominate other forms of communicative sign, such as language and iconography. Such a use of the body depends on the spectator's ability to understand it as both an object (an erotic object, an attractive object, a repulsive object, a social object) and as a subject, as a willed or shaped object, an object with meaning. Rhetorically, performance is a way not of acting but of posing: it takes for granted an audience's ability to refer these bodily movements to others (in this respect, as in others, Madonna is the most self-consciously 'arty' of pop performers, but by no means pop's only performance artist).

The performance artist, like the pop performer, depends on an audience which can interpret her work through its own experience of performance, its own understanding of seduction and pose, gesture and body language; an

1. See Graham F. Thompson: 'Approaches to "Performance" ', *Screen* 26(5), 1985, p81.

2. Nick Kaye, *Postmodernism and Performance*, Macmillan, London 1994, p144.

3. See Thompson, *op.cit.* p88. I'm also obviously indebted in what follows to the work of Erving Goffman.

audience which understands, however 'instinctively' (without theorising), the constant dialogue of inner and outer projected by the body in movement. For performance art to work it needs an audience of performers; it depends on the performance of the everyday.[4]

From a socio-historical perspective it would doubtless be relevant here to point to the increasing significance of performance in everyday life as an effect of urbanisation and the decline of intimacy (more and more of our dealings are with people we don't know), as an effect of industrial capitalism (we no longer derive our identity from productive labour), as an effect of commodity fetishism (our consumption is now a matter of imagination not need).[5] But whatever the material basis for contemporary performance, it is clearly culturally based. Western performers only make sense in terms of western performing conventions – conventions shaped as much in the home and on the street as in the gallery and on the stage.

The body-in-communication holds in tension not simply the subjective and the objective (the art question), but also the private and the public (the everyday question). In our experience (or imagination) of our own bodies there is always a gap between what is meant (the body directed from the inside) and what is read (the body interpreted from the outside); and this gap is a continual source of anxiety, an anxiety not so much that the body itself but its meaning is out of our control. In most public performances the body is, in fact, subject to a kind of external control, the motivation provided by a score or a script or a routinised social situation, which acts as a safety net for performer and audience alike. It is this safety net which the so-called performance artist explicitly abandons, and one can conclude therefore that the essence of performance art is embarrassment, a constant sense of the inappropriate. If, in conventional theatre, one is embarrassed only when someone forgets a line, is suddenly 'out of character', in performance art one is on the edge of embarrassment all the time because the performer is not 'in character' to begin with (and the nervous tension among the audience at a 'performance' as against a 'performance of a play' is palpable).

Performance in this sense has a low cultural history too, and performances in popular places and genres (in the music hall and vaudeville, popular song and comedy) are, I think, much more akin to performance art than to 'legitimate' art or theatre. If performance artists in the 1960s turned to such popular performance forms as stand-up comedy and burlesque, wrestling and the circus, this was not just a postmodern breakdown of high/low cultural barriers; it was also because they had something to learn.[6] For example, one of the recurring pleasures of popular culture is the difficult or spectacular act, the drama of which lies precisely in its immediacy, in the resulting sense of risk, danger, triumph, virtuosity: we need to see things which we know must be live (even if we also know, as in the case of a James Brown show, that for such things to work they must be elaborately planned and rehearsed – they must always work, that is, *in exactly the same way*). What's valued here is not (as in high culture) seeing something unique, but seeing something difficult, something

4. As Erving Goffman famously puts it, 'All the world is not, of course, a stage, but the crucial ways in which it isn't are not easy to specify.' *The Presentation of Self in Everyday Life* [1959]. Penguin, 1971, Harmondsworth, pp77-8.

5. See John F. Kassan, *Rudeness and Civility: Manners in Nineteenth Century Urban America*, Hill and Wang, New York 1990, pp114-5.

6. See Sally Banes, *Greenwich Village 1963: Avant-Garde Performance and the Effervescent Body*, Duke University Press, Durham, NC 1993.

that takes work. Far from wanting the means of production to be concealed, the popular audience wants to see how much has gone into their entertainment. Performance as labour is a necessary part of the popular aesthetic.

A second point to make here concerns framing. Performance may only make sense through the everyday, but 'public performance' also describes something marked off from the everyday, something in which when the everyday does appear it is as a joke, an intruder (which also means, to reverse the argument, that when the everyday turns out to have been a performance, to have been literally framed, by a view-finder, it comes as a shock: 'Smile, please! You're on *Candid Camera!*'). Such framing involves the application of genre rules, rules which determine how both performer and audience should behave (rules which we can see enacted in even the most domestic of home videos).

As the anthropologist Richard Bauman has pointed out, the distinction between the staged and the everyday is not necessarily a matter of setting. What is at issue is how activities are staged *within* the everyday, and a way of speaking can therefore signify a performance (which describes both an action and an event) by putting an 'interpretative frame' around itself, such that listeners no longer treat what is being said as part of normal conversation.[7] The most obvious example of this is probably the joke: joke telling is certainly a performance, even if it occurs within a casual conversation (or within another sort of performance altogether, a lecture, say) – hence people's claims that 'they can't tell jokes'. What does such telling involve?

The point here is that the relationship between the conversational and the performative is complex, involving not just a particular use of language but also a claim to be competent in such use, and an assumption that one's audience is also so competent, or, at least, able to recognise one's talking skills. Unlike ordinary conversation, that is, a performance can be good or bad, it is evaluated. It follows some sort of formal rule, and the anthropologist's question becomes how is such a performance 'keyed'? How do we know that it is a performance? That it has begun? That it is over? Bauman notes that in anthropological terms a performance may range from the completely novel (spontaneous invention) to the completely fixed (a traditional religious rite). In practice, nearly all popular performances lie somewhere between these two extremes and, as Bauman suggests, this is what enables an audience to judge them: by measuring what is original, personal to this performance, against the conventions of the performance form in general. (This is one of the problems, of course, for performance art: no-one knows if it's any good or not. No-one knows how to tell. And this isn't just a problem for the audience. The success of a performance for a performer can, in the end, only be measured by the audience response – this is what makes it a performance, a kind of oratory. A joke that gets no laughs, a song that gets no response, an act that bores its audience is a bad performance by definition.)

On the one hand, then, a performance is 'an emergent structure', it comes into being only as it is being performed; on the other hand, it is an

7. See Richard Bauman, 'Verbal Art as Performance', *American Anthropologist* 77, 1975.

'enhancement', it involves, in Bauman's words, a heightened 'intensity' of communication: it makes the communicative process itself, the use of language and gesture, the focus of attention. And if for the performer this means prestige (for a good performance, for their skill), for the judging audience too it means an increased sense of control over the usual flow of communication: performance is, in this context, a way of standing back from content and considering form. It is in such self-conscious playfulness that the popular exemplifies what is now described as the postmodern. Whereas in both high and folk cultures, performing rules tend to be naturalised (so that everybody carefully avoids noting what very peculiar events a classical concert or a folk festival are), in popular performance, the rules (and the comic or shocking possibility of breaking them) are always on the surface of performance itself. Peter Bailey thus argues brilliantly that the central performing trope in late nineteenth-century music hall was a kind of knowingness, a *collusion* between performer and (implied) audience, between audience and (implied) performer, which was both inclusive and exclusive, worrying and reassuring.[8]

8. Peter Bailey, 'Conspiracies of Meaning: Music Hall and the Knowingness of Popular Culture', *Past and Present* 144, 1994.

More generally we could say that the 'act' of, say, singing is always contextualised by the 'act' of performing; and if the latter, like any other stage role, is put together behind the scenes, the former takes place in public: we see and hear the movement in and out of character; we watch this aspect of the performance as a performance. The way singers adopt differing roles 'the next song is a slower number' – works differently in different genres, but all methods (irony, earnestness, virtuosity, craft pride, humour) draw attention to the singer's knowledge of what is going on, to their knowledge of our knowledge of what is happening. It's as if the 'as if' of the song performance is foregrounded in order to naturalise the 'as if' of the musical performance.

It follows that pop singers are unlike play actors (though similar to film stars) in two respects. First, they are involved in a process of double enactment: they enact both a star personality (their image) and a song personality, the role that each lyric requires: the pop star's art is to keep both acts in play at once. This is most obvious in the plainest narrative forms, such as music hall or country music, where performers employ a variety of techniques (more obvious on stage than in the recording studio, though used there too) to move in and out of character. Interruption, for example, is a basic vocal device: the performer's skill is to objectify an expressive gesture at the very moment of its expression, to put quotation marks around it. A singer like Elvis Presley performs as his own audience: is it really *me* singing that? (In country music, with its excessively self-conscious equation of realism and formalism, a central place in this process is occupied by songs about the past: the singer in her present persona responds to the naivety or ambition of her past self, as expressed in the song; the performer is thus the singer and not-the-singer simultaneously, just as – and this is essential to country ideology – the past is both the present and not the present.)

Second, in enacting a pop star, the pop singer becomes a site of desire – as a body and as a person. In performance, in the playing of their various song parts, instead of forgetting who they are, singers are continuously registering their presence. (This is, perhaps, most obvious for performers who are most remote – Whitney Houston, for example). Singing, as an organisation of vocal gestures, means enacting the protagonist in the song (the right emotions for this part), enacting the part of the star (the moves in keeping with the image), and giving some intimation of a real material being – a physical body producing a physical sound, sweat produced by work not order, a physicality that *overflows* the formal constraints of the performance.

This is to raise questions about the sexuality or erotics of performance. In particular, what does it mean to make a spectacle of oneself? To perform for an audience as a woman obviously means something different than to perform for an audience as a man – different in terms of both the social connotations of what it means for a woman to show her body publicly, to pose; and in terms of the power play of sexual desire. (Even in the most 'respectable' of the performing arts – classical theatre, the ballet – female performers, like artists' models, were taken in the nineteenth century to be akin to prostitutes, while one could argue that an important strand of performance in the low arts, such as vaudeville and music hall, blues and jazz, has been the continuing, deliberate, emphasis on the performer's off-stage propriety.) As Susan McClary puts it, a woman's problem is how to keep control of herself in a space, the stage, patrolled by an objectifying sexual gaze conventionalized by hundreds of years of patriarchal command. The female performer is inevitably much more self-conscious than a male performer in that she has to keep redefining both her performing setting and her performing narrative if she is to take charge of her situation.[9]

McClary's heroine in this respect is Laurie Anderson; most recent feminist discussion of the issue has focused on Madonna.[10] But women performers in all musical genres have explored what it means to be spectacularly female. As a country singer, Dolly Parton, for example, doesn't only play on a male notion of femininity, but in performing the signs of vulnerability – the little girl voice, the giggle, the nervous flounce – makes their meaning problematic. Parton's remarkable vocal range – in terms of volume/power rather than pitch as such – draws attention to her art as a singer as much as to her life as a woman. As is typical in country music, her voice (as against her body), though a clearly physical sound, becomes the sign, trademark even, of her stardom, the meaning around which all her other signs (the hair, the breasts, the gowns) are organised. The song of dependence (common in her repertoire and often self-written) is therefore so obviously crafted, so clearly designed to display vocal skill rather than an emotional state, that at the very least Parton's audience has to consider her lyrical sentiments as ironic. (It is not surprising that she has built up a strong camp following.)[11]

By contrast, the English music hall star, Gracie Fields, an ungainly, 'homely' woman by showbiz standards, took on character roles much more specifically than Parton and, like other music hall stars, mixed sentimental ballads with comic story songs. By spoofing her voice (rather than her looks), by displaying

9. See Susan McClary, *Feminine Endings: Music, Gender and Sexuality*, University of Minnesota Press, Minneapolis 1991, chapter 6.

10. The most entertaining collection of Madonna essays is Lisa Frank and Paul Smith (eds), *Madonnarama: Essays on Sex and Popular Culture*, Cleis Press, Pittsburgh, PA 1993.

11. Listen to Dolly Parton, *Best of Dolly Parton*, RCA LP 1970.

her vocal range (in terms of style as well as pitch) as a bit of a joke, Fields became endearing – beloved – 'Our Gracie' – as a kind of favourite aunt or big sister. (This meant, among other things, that in her films Fields, unlike Parton, always, only, played herself.)[12]

By contrast again (although less of a contrast than one might imagine), Millie Jackson uses the different conventions of soul feeling and the insult ritual to set up another sort of collusive relationship with her audience – or at least with its female part, speaking for it, drawing on innuendo and the unsaid to unfold a conversation that could be taking place in the launderette and then moving dramatically back to the reality of her presence, on stage, with a band, microphone, lights. Like Fields, Jackson's movement from comic routine to ballad implies that, in the end, the comedy is the assumed role, the ballad the real feeling. The message, for all the ideological aggression, is orthodox: all men are shits (laughs) but we love them anyway (sighs). Her strutting public performance acts out a private resignation.[13]

Two issues are significant here, I think. First (as I've already suggested), *embarrassment*. Performing involves gestures that are both false (they are only being put on for this occasion) and true (they are appropriate to the emotions being described, expressed or invoked). Even the most stylised performer, the one with the most obviously formal and artificial gestures, is expressing the self, displaying in public sounds and movements usually thought of as intimate; what the audience wants to see, as Roland Barthes puts it, is a 'convinced body, rather than a true passion.'[14] In judging a performer we are, as an audience, measuring her gestures against our sense of what she's really like, off stage (what her voice and body really do, in this sort of situation), and even if, from the singer's point of view, this makes it even more important to maintain a clear separation or distance between self and personality, nevertheless, what's on offer is a kind of vulnerability: we might not like her (and in most pop genres performance is, specifically, about being liked).[15]

The performer's problem here is that however carefully crafted the star persona, in performance a real body is involved. Singing is not necessarily or even desirably pretty: singers sweat, they strain, they open their mouths wide and clench their throats. To make the necessary musical sounds, singers have to do things (or simulate doing things) which may not 'fit' the star body, the star persona. As Wayne Koestenbaum says of opera singers:

> Singers look like freaks unless they control themselves, and this possibility of looking grotesque is appealing if you choose (as I am choosing) to embrace rather than to reject a stereotypical freakishness.[16]

On the other hand, we also know from everyday life that the way to deflate embarrassment is through self-mockery – we hastily pretend that the gesture was a joke, was meant ironically. As audiences too we often decide (with delight or disdain) that a performer has gone 'over the top'. This is, in part, the effect of the music in making expressed feelings more intense: a stage performer gets

12. Listen to Gracie Fields, *Stage and Screen*, EMI/World Record Club, no date, which includes a live recording of her show at the Holborn Empire, October 11, 1933.

13. Listen to Millie Jackson, *Live and Uncensored*, Spring/Polydor, 1979.

14. Roland Barthes, *Roland Barthes by Roland Barthes* [1975], Farrar, Straus and Giroux, New York 1977, pp177-8.

15. And as J.O. Urmson points out, in paying to see a performance we also expect that the star (Madonna, say) will, in good faith, continue to *be herself* (whatever the new theme or costume). 'The Ethics of Musical Performance', in Michael Krausz (ed), *The Interpretation of Music*, Clarendon Press, Oxford 1992.

16. Wayne Koestenbaum, *The Queen's Throat: Opera, Homosexuality and the Mystery of Desire*, Gay Men's Press, London, 1993, p168.

the same sort of emotional charge from her soundtrack as a screen performer gets from his. And music's enveloping effect applies to the audience too: the world can only now be perceived in this emotional state, and the narcissism of the singer, exploring her own feelings, becomes our own. We forget ourselves in the music as part of a condition of collective self-indulgence; we are alienated, as Sartre would put it, in the collective ego. (To be excluded from this excitement – the rock critic's common condition – is, oddly, to be embarrassed not for oneself but for everyone else. The point here is that intense or abandoned listening is a loss of physical control – think of the ugliness of the audience in concert photos – and it is this which embarrasses: to be the only person to clap at the end of the first movement, the only person to leap to one's feet screaming. It is not embarrassing – well, I was never embarrassed – to be the only person taking notes.)

But, further, over-the-top artists deliberately set gestures free from their appropriate setting. The great pop performers (whether Judy Garland or Shirley Bassey, Mick Jagger or Prince) don't so much enact emotional roles as hold their enactments up before us in fragments, so we can admire the shape of the gesture itself. It is no accident that such performenrs are camp idols, are beloved (following Susan Sontag) in terms 'of artifice, of stylization'. Such performers seem to have grasped the camp point that the truth of a feeling is an aesthetic not a moral truth: it can only be judged formally, as a matter of gestural grace. 'Sincerity', in short, cannot be measured by searching for what lies *behind* the performance; if we are moved by a performer we are moved by what we *immediately* hear and see.[17]

This brings me to the second issue I want to pick up here, seduction. Guy Scarpetta suggests that a singer is in the same trade as a prostitute, publicly offering a bliss that can only be experienced privately.[18] We realise that the singer is making us an offer ('Know me!') that is essentially false, yet is true to our fantasy of what the offer might be, that it might be just for us ('To know me is to love me.'). The listening fantasy, to put this another way, is that we control the music (the sexual exchange) when, in fact, the performer does. The seductive voice mediates between nature (the real person about whom we fantasise) and culture (the performing person we get); it draws attention both to the social construction of our desire, to its artificiality, and to our obdurately subjective reading of it. The presence of even a recorded sound is the presence of the implied performer – *the performer called forth by the listener* – and this is clearly a sensual/sexual presence, not just a meeting of minds.

A theatrical performance is framed by a suspension of fellow feeling or, perhaps, by a kind of enactment of it: we know the performer is acting anger, so we act our fearful response. In popular performance, though, as in performance art, the boundaries of 'the act' are blurred and an element of our fear is therefore real – maybe she, Millie Jackson, is going to come to my table and ask my partner about my own sexual performance (and there will be further embarrassment when I reveal my fear of humiliation just as she reveals that this was only an act, after all). Or, alternatively, perhaps she, Judy Garland,

17. See Susan Sontag, 'Notes on "Camp" ' [1964], in her *Against Interpretation*, Delta, New York 1966, p277.

18. Guy Scarpetta, *L'Impureté*, Bernard Grasset, Paris 1985, pp207-8.

is not just acting grief but is really crying, which is to embarrass us in a different way, on her behalf. This is a particularly complex issue given that in performance body language is necessarily a combination of direct and conventional expression, referring to both *what* is being done and *why* it is. To read body movements, to interpret them, is always to put them in a story. The same physical acts may be described as writing or doodling, as caressing or harassing; we refer here not to what we see but what to what we infer (because of the situation, the characters, the plot).

The performing text, that is to say, is always the performing context. And that, in the end, is what all the essays in *Performance Matters* are about. Whether the arguments are philosophical (Lydia Goehr), musicological (Nicholas Cook) or political (Martin Stokes); whether the issue is class (John Stokes), race (Sally Banes and John Szwed) or gender (Gill Frith), the argument is the same: the essential *instability* of the performative (the postmodernists' point) is always in practice, momentarily, necessarily, *fixed* – ideologically, by agreement, as a matter of social concern. And my point (taken from a study of popular music[19]) like Karen Lury's (taken from a study of television) is that while it may be all but impossible to capture this interpretative moment academically – to hold it still for analysis – in everyday life we make such meanings all the time.

Simon Frith
May 1995

19. See my forthcoming *Performing Rites: The Aesthetics of Popular Music*, Harvard University Press, Cambridge, MA, chapter 10.

THE PERFECT PERFORMANCE OF MUSIC AND THE PERFECT MUSICAL PERFORMANCE

Lydia Goehr

INTRODUCTION

In 1965 Glenn Gould predicted that 'the public concert as we know it today would no longer exist a century hence [because] its functions would have been entirely taken over by electronic media'.[1] As is well known, Gould stopped giving public concerts himself – in part to underwrite his prediction – and moved his musical life almost exclusively into the recording studio. Gould's prediction startled the establishment and this reaction startled Gould: 'It had not occurred to me,' he wrote,

1. 'The Prospects of Recording', *The Glenn Gould Reader*, Tim Page (ed), Alfred A. Knopf, New York 1985, p331.

> that [it] represented a particularly radical announcement. Indeed, I regarded it almost as self-evident truth and ... as defining only one of the peripheral effects occasioned by developments in the electronic age. But never has a statement of mine been so widely quoted – or so hotly disputed.[2]

2. *Ibid.*

Gould was right: his prediction wasn't radical. Certainly its gadflyish character challenged the comfort of the musical establishment, but its aesthetic and moral substance was thoroughly conservative. Corresponding to a traditional romantic (and later high-modernist) conception of music's transcendental mission, the prediction simply took this conception to its extreme. Summarily put, Gould argued that the conditions of production and reception associated with musical recordings achieve a more honest standing than the comparable conditions associated with live performances. This being so, the 'ministrations of radio and phonograph' are more successful in their mission to convey divine works to contemplating listeners via interpretations that performers strive to make as perfect as possible.

To what, now, did Gould's critics react – surely neither to his aim to produce perfect or 'ideal' interpretations nor to his mere use of recording technology? What really troubled them, it turns out, was the conception of musical performance they thought would dominate the musical world if Gould's prediction proved true. Gould asked musicians to conceive of a perfect performance as one that would be experienced by listeners in its recorded form without the detrimental distractions of the performer's presence. Performers would effectively become invisible; their actions – the actual mechanics of the performance – would never again be seen. Gould's critics, by contrast, insisted that performances could still be successful even if they were events in which visually present performers figure in the listener's musical experiences. Perfect performances, they maintained, should sometimes at least be individually unique, social and humanly-staged musical occasions taking place in concert halls, for only there is the traditional purpose of human communication between performers and audiences dramatically and sublimely fulfilled.

That one may characterise the quarrel between Gould and his critics by differentiating two performance conceptions or ideals according to the presence or absence of visibly acting performers, or according, more abstractly, to the degree of humanness involved, might seem far-fetched. But the history of musical aesthetics and associated history of performance reveals a divergence drawn in these terms, and this divergence shows itself again in the Gould conflict in the modern form of a quarrel over recordings vs live performance. Consider this response from Gould:

> There are those who counsel that only in the theatre, only with the direct communication of artist to listener, can we experience the high drama of human communication. The answer to this ... is that art on its loftiest mission is scarcely human at all.[3]

3. 'Let's Ban Applause', *The Glenn Gould Reader*, p247. Cf. Harold C. Schonberg's remark: 'In a future, fully automated age, it may be that ... all performing musicians will be obsolete. But until that unfortunate day is here, let us be thankful that there still remain interpretive musicians to synthesize the product of the composer'. Harold C. Schonberg, *The Great Conductors*, W.W. Norton, New York 1967, pp23-4.

For most of this paper, I shall move away from Gould and his critics and the particular problems raised by technology to enquire more generally into the tension existing in the world of classical music given the presence of what I take to be two conflicting conceptions of performance. I shall refer to them respectively as *the perfect performance of music* and *the perfect musical performance*. Briefly for now, the former stresses the vehicular and structured, 'Apollonian' ideal of a performance *qua* performance-of-a-work; the latter the open, social and spontaneous, 'Dionysian' ideal of musicianship involved in the performance event. As we shall see, the former has been more explicitly theorised than the latter, probably because it has occupied an élite space, but the latter has gained its strength from claiming a popular and intuitive appeal. We shall also see that though each conception corresponds to a roughly unified picture of musical performance, each in fact is a cluster of more or less coherent parts. Finally, we shall see that though the conceptions genuinely conflict, their successful functioning has not been, because it could not be, contingent upon the conceptions being mutually excluding.

My overall interest in investigating these two conceptions is motivated by a desire to understand classical music as what I shall call *an imperfect practice*. Towards this end I shall argue that it has been the imperfect character of the practice of classical music which has allowed that practice to sustain at least these two genuinely conflicting conceptions of perfection. Lying behind this argument is the thought that practices are imperfect insofar as they are truly critical, critical in the sense that practices survive their self-deceptive but necessary assertions of perfection and of autonomy by allowing strategies of conflict, criticism, or resistance constantly to keep them in check. The critical dimension arises, in other words, from the presence in a given practice of competing conceptions which halt the pretences of any single conception. Musical practice, I believe, demonstrates this metaphysical thesis as successfully in its local and seemingly most mundane details as in its most complex aesthetic foundation.

My other interest is in highlighting the tendency in our dominant aesthetic to neglect the role of human action, a neglect stemming from the age-old preference in western thought for knowing over doing. As Boethius summed up the thought: 'How much more admirable ... is the science of music in apprehending by reason than in accomplishing by work and deed!'[4] To be sure, many theorists have asserted that music has no meaningful existence other than through its sounding out in performance, yet the role of performance, and even more that of the performer, remains under theorised.[5] This undertheorisation is connected to the denial of 'the human' and 'the social' embodied in classical music's modern assertion of autonomy and perfection.

TOWARDS TWO MODES OF EVALUATION

'*Temporibus nostris super omnes homines fatui sunt cantores* – in our time the silliest of all men are the singers.' So observed Guido d'Arezzo in the eleventh century and so begins Paul Hindemith in his chapter entitled 'Performers' nine hundred years later.[6] Hindemith's purpose, though it was not Guido's,[7] is to remind his readers of the unending history of derision and abuse to which performers, be they singers or instrumentalists, have been subject. Who has criticised performers so strongly? Everyone: composers and listeners, theorists and teachers, concert impresarios and opera producers.

Hindemith identifies several historical criticisms: performers lack skill, but are overly confident nonetheless; they are often ignorant, manifest unappealing personality traits, and tend to maintain dubious social connections. Sometimes the criticisms are charitably explained, other times not. Compare the sober observation that performers are so devoted to the means of performance that they are 'unable to participate in any profound knowledge of music',[8] with the exasperated criticism that

> [t]here are singers who have neither talent nor knowledge, but only vanity. This makes them audacious ... singing more loudly and more brutally than the jackass, producing the most terrible cacophonies, and with their false phrasing they turn music into barbarism.[9]

Of course, Hindemith tells us, accompanying this history of degradation has also been a history of praise extolling perfomers to the highest degree. Quoting Coclico, Hindemith refers us to those sixteenth-century singers who surpass their contemporaries because they 'know the rules of art, which they learned from composers'. The quotation continues:

> We may even count them among the composers, in that they improvise free counterpoints over given chorale melodies. The knowledge of all musical

4. O. Strunk (ed), *Source Readings in Music History: From Classical Antiquity through the Romantic Era*, W.W. Norton, New York 1950, p85.

5. In 1970 Hilde Hein commented similarly in her 'Performance as an Aesthetic Category', *Journal of Aesthetic and Art Criticism*, xxvii, 1970, pp381-6; and Paul Thom has done so most recently in *For an Audience: A Philosophy of the Performing Arts*, Temple University Press, Philadelphia 1993.

6. Paul Hindemith, *A Composer's World: Horizons and Limitations*, P. Smith, Gloucester, MA 1969, p149.

7. Guido explains his judgement from his *Prologus antiphonarii sui* (ca. 1025) as follows: 'For in any art those things which we know of ourselves are much more numerous than those which we learn from a master' (Strunk, *Source Readings*, p117). Guido duly invented a musical notation for singers in part to reduce their dependency on their master.

8. Hindemith, *op.cit.*, p150. Hindemith is summarising Boethius's view here that performers 'are separated from the intellect of musical science, since they are servants ... nor do they bear anything of reason, being wholly destitute of speculation', (Strunk, *Source Readings*, p86).

9. *Ibid*. Hindemith is quoting Arnulf of San Gilleno of the fourteenth century.

10. *Ibid.*, p152.

means of expression and possibilities of effects enables them to delight and enrapture men with their well-sounding, sweet, and solemn execution.[10]

11. *Ibid.*

12. *Ibid.*, p168.

13. *Ibid.*, p154.

Hindemith draws the obvious conclusion. There are two extremes: 'For some critics [the performer] is nothing but the low grade medium of transmitting music, a contrivance to produce tones... For others he is the almost superhuman being who, with the wings of his divine talent, carries us into heavenly regions.'[11] Hindemith employs this history to highlight what he calls the 'essential tragedy in the performer's existence.'[12] Yet his attempt to redeem the standing of perfomers is reluctant: '[o]nce we accept the performer as an inevitable necessity in spite of his basic dubiousness, we may as well try to determine what properties make him estimable.'[13] My purpose here is not further to investigate Hindemith's particular attitude towards performers (though he does recommend for his *Kammermusik*, number 1, opus 24/1 that

14. I am grateful to Stephen Hinton for providing me with this example and for telling me also of the provocative nature of Hindemith's instruction given that his piece was designed '*épater le bourgeois*'.

'*die Vortragenden dem Publikum unsichtbar zu placieren*'[14]). My immediate purpose, rather, is to provide more nuance to what he correctly identifies as a double-sided assessment of performers and their art.

As Hindemith recognises, performer assessment has varied over time as musicians' ranks and their functions in a whole array of religious, pedagogical, and social rituals have changed. However, no change in assessment was more decisive than that which occurred at the end of the eighteenth century. Elsewhere I have described the major transformations that took place in our understanding of music at that time, transformations which affected every dimension of the musical world.[15] But there I did not attend sufficiently to the

15. See my *The Imaginary Museum of Musical Works*, Clarendon Press, Oxford 1992.

way these transformations generated new modes of performance assessment corresponding to a new romantic conception of performance.

The conception first crystallised into its modern form against the background of an aesthetic informed by idealist and formalist strains which claimed that the musical art should exist for its own sake. It depended upon the development of a specifically musical conception of music to replace the former functional, 'extra-musical' one. As I have shown before, this replacement involved music's freeing itself from its former ties to the poetic and dramatic word, defining itself as a purely instrumental art of sound. Two aesthetic claims helped define the new borders of 'the musical': the 'transcendental move' which moved musical meaning away from the representation of concrete particulars towards the direct expression of universals, and the 'formalist move' which drew music's meaning from its out-side into its in-side by identifying music's content with its form. Changes in practice matched those in aesthetic theory. Severed from former dependencies on church and court, for example, the concert hall emerged to serve as the predominant and purely musical site for musical performance.

The romantic conception depended, furthermore, upon re-configuring the borders of the very category of performance. The fluid, continuous relation between compositional and performance activities was conceptually trans-formed into a solid distinction between them. This transformation was part and parcel of the development of the work-concept as distinct from that of performance. This entire development had a direct impact on performer assessment.

Traditionally, one of the principal modes of evaluation concentrated on the knowing-doing distinction: were performers mere practitioners, or composers and theorists in addition? Did they merely have skill, or understanding as well? Evaluation took place in a practice where performers either merely embellished on the basis of a pre-given figured bass or, through conventions both of embellishment and improvisation, also composed as they performed.[16] Mere embellishers tended to be lowly regarded as doers who understand not what they did; genuine improvisers were regarded more highly as both knowers and doers. Especially striking was the concern that performers endeavour to be musicians in the fullest and most traditional sense: knowledgeable in high matters philosophical and in low matters technical. Such a concern fitted a practice which permitted continuity rather than rigid separation between its theoretical and practical, and its creative and reproductive, roles – thus, the common use of the general term 'musician' to cover persons who theorised, composed, and/or performed.

Continuity between roles was possible in part because pre-modern performance practice was conditioned by the expectation that musicians would bring to fruition a fully-shaped composition through performance. Walter Wiora chooses to call this practice Aus*führungspraxis* to distinguish it from the modern category of Auf*führungspraxis*. '*Die Ausführungen*,' he writes,

> do not correspond to the composition itself the way copies of a picture correspond to its original. The difference is particularly telling when – as was done in earlier times – one not only followed the prescription of the score but also followed another meaning of the term '*ausfüren*' by trying to give shape to the composition. This included the realization of the *basso continuo* and the embellishment of unadorned melodies.[17]

Auf*führungspraxis*, by contrast, is conditioned by the expectation that compositions be fully composed prior to performance, an expectation which releases performers from the obligation – indeed it forbids them – either to embellish or improvise, i.e. to creatively compose the music in performance. In this practice, performers are obliged to comply as perfectly as they can with the composers' fully-notated scores and to interpret faithfully the works they perform.

Like performer function, then, performer evaluation shifted from being contingent upon composer-performer continuity to being contingent upon their separation. Of course, there would continue to be performers who composed and composers who performed, but evaluatively as conceptually, composers would be held responsible for creating music, performers for its sounding out. Franz Liszt was widely canonised or mythified, despite his also being a composer, as the first *modern* performer.[18]

16. Recall Hindemith's quotation of Coclico.

17. *Das Musikalische Kunstwerk*, H. Schneider, Tutzing 1983, p40.

18. Liszt was also a transcriber of pre-existing works. For more on Liszt as a 'modern' performer and composer, see my *The Imaginary Museum of Musical Works, op.cit.*, 222f, and p239.

With their responsibilities so defined, composers and performers were each released, moreover, from the responsibilities of pure or mere theorists – philosophers, analysts, and critics. Future references to musicianship, and the knowledge associated therewith, would henceforth be constrained by a new degree of awareness of tasks appropriate to each musician type. Judgements sensitive to the new categories naturally helped to legitimate them. But nothing prevented judgements also being made of a comparative sort by and against those who now just 'did', now just 'created', or now just 'thought' and 'criticised'.

How did performers fare in this new arena of evaluation? Since around 1800, performer evaluation has been organised around two interacting modes. In one mode, performers are judged as necessary evils and/or as the great interpreters of musical masterpieces; in the other mode, they are judged as 'circus performers' or as 'servants of the devil', or more positively as inspired enchanters working their magic with the transcendental musical language. In neither mode, though for different reasons, does the one judgement automatically preclude the other. What rationale lies behind these two familiar modes of evaluation? To answer this question I must describe the two conceptions of the perfect performance that together have sustained the performance of classical music as a separate category of modern musical conduct. The first is 'the perfect performance of music', the second 'the perfect musical performance'.

THE PERFECT PERFORMANCE OF MUSIC

The performance conception referred to by the phrase 'the perfect performance of music' is most closely bound up with the solemn, sacred, serious, and sublime aesthetic[19] of the concert hall and with the *Werktreue* ideal central to the development of music as a fine art. It functions most clearly within the élite and autonomous aesthetic governing the symphonic tradition inaugurated by Beethoven, and mythified thereafter by 'the Beethoven cult'. The conception functions in its purest form, both despite and because of Wagner's immense contribution to opera, within concerts of purely instrumental music.

Indeed, the first step in comprehending the perfect performance of music is to regard music as a purely sonorous art. 'The sonorous element in music', wrote Robert Zimmermann in 1865, is 'the ultimate consideration'. Unlike poetry, he explained, in which the sonorous element 'has only a validity subordinate to thought', in music the same element claims 'independent validity'.[20] Musical concerts are correspondingly conceived in their essence as purely sonorous events – 'pure' not in the sense that all essential qualities have literally to be sounded out, but in the sense that all such qualities have to either constitute or derive from the sonorous material.

The perfect performance of music takes the 'of' seriously. The perfect performance of music is the perfect performance of a work. Under a neutral

19. An alliterative description taken from the 1910 *Technical Manifesto of Futurist Painting*, quoted in R. Goldberg's 'Performance: A Hidden History', in G. Battcock and R. Nickas (eds), *The Art of Performance: A Critical Anthology*, E.P. Dutton, New York 1984, p29.

20. Robert Zimmermann, *Allgemeine Aesthetick als Formwissenschaft* [1865], excerpted in Bojan Bujic (ed), *Music In European Thought 1851-1912*, Cambridge University Press, Cambridge 1988, p46.

ontological description, works and performances are co-dependent. Works are made accessible to audiences via mediating performances; performances are necessarily performances of works. Under the romantic aesthetic, this neutrality is overwhelmed. At one extreme, performances are regarded as subservient in purpose to the work, subordinate in value to the work, and derivative in nature of the work. At the other extreme, performers are judged the great interpreters of works which are created just to give the opportunity to these performers to show their interpretative skills.[21] Historically, however, the tilting towards each extreme has been neither equal nor balanced. First, the tilt has mostly favoured works; second, when the tilt has favoured performances or performers, the result has not in fact been simply to favour performances over works, but to try to meet both extremes simultaneously. I shall describe each situation in turn.

IN FAVOUR OF WORKS

One prominent conclusion drawn from the transcendental and formalist claims of the romantic aesthetic determines that most if not all value should be placed in the permanently existing musical works and not in their transitory and fleeting performances. 'The secret of perfection', wrote Stravinsky, 'lies above all in [the performer's] consciousness of the law imposed upon him by the work he is performing.'[22] That value is placed more in what lasts than in ephemeral phenomena is not an unfamiliar claim in the history of music, but in the romantic aesthetic it takes on an unreservedly Platonic profile.

Accordingly, performances *qua* copies of works are regarded as necessarily imperfect; for performances to be perfect they would have to reach the condition of the work itself. But this is ontologically impossible: works last, performances don't and even if they did – say, in recordings – they would still only ever be perspectival representations of the perfect work. Thus, speaking about the perfect performance of music is oxymoronic unless one intends to capture an ideal of the practice that performers strive, but of necessity fail, to meet.

This necessary failure captures what Hindemith called the performer's 'essential tragedy', and what Stravinsky referred to as 'the great principle of submission'.[23] For, from the recognition of a performance's necessary imperfection emerges a demand – for Stravinsky it was a 'moral responsibility' – that the best performance be one that most successfully negates its own presence. The demand here is for performance *transparency*: performances should be like windows through which audiences directly perceive works. Sometimes the demand is also for performer *invisibility*. 'The visual effect of the performance,' wrote Zimmermann, 'does not belong to the work's essence... It is for this reason that orchestral musicians rightly appear in the simplest clothes; it would be best if they were not visible at all.'[24]

The ideal of invisibility embodies two demands, the second more severe than the first. The first asks that, given music's purely sonorous nature, the visual

21. This idea is mentioned and then rejected by Schoenberg in his 'Today's Manner of Performing Classical Music', *Style and Idea: Selected Writings of Arnold Schoenberg*, L. Stein (ed), tr. L. Black, University of California Press, Berkeley, Cali, 1975, p321.

22. I. Stravinsky, *The Poetics of Music in the Form of Six Lessons*, Harvard University, Press New Haven MA 1942, p127.

23. Cf. Robert Hill's comments on 'the bliss of denial', in his 'Overcoming Romanticism: On the Modernization of Twentieth Century Performance Practice', in Bryan Gilliam (ed), *Music and Performance During the Weimar Republic*, Cambridge University Press, Cambridge, 1994, p44.

24. Zimmerman, *op.cit.*, p49. Zimmermann explicitly follows Goethe here; see the quotation from Goethe below.

dimensions of a performance be disregarded by the audience as inessential or as necessary evils. Performers and audiences should separate or abstract out of the total performance event the essential 'aural image' of the work. What is musical about a performance consists entirely in what is heard. The second reminds us that what is actually heard in the concrete soundings out of the work is much less valuable than the transcendent meaning of the works the soundings are supposed to convey. Performers should attempt, therefore, to create the illusion that the work is being conveyed immediately to the audience by undermining their own presence as necessarily flawed mediators.[25]

A useful, though polemical, way to describe the aesthetics of sonorous transcendence is now forthcoming: divine composers should be neither seen nor heard – to underscore the mystery both of absence and of genius; performers should be heard but not seen – but 'heard' only as imperfect pointers towards the transcendent; audiences should be seen but not heard – but 'seen' only in the sense of each listener being present to grasp the work in the privacy of his or her own contemplative experience. A traditional impetus lies behind these aesthetic strictures: the more civilized the event, the 'higher' or 'finer' the condition, the less the appearance should be of ordinary, everyday behaviour.

Such abstract strictures are fully evident in the critical and institutional history of the concert hall. Recall E.T.A. Hoffmann's oft-quoted decree that, in producing *Werktreue* performances, performers should 'not make their personalities count in any way',[26] or Busoni's observation that since 'the "performance" of music, its *emotional interpretation*, derives from those free heights whence descended the Art itself', then '[w]here the art is threatened by earthliness, it is the part of interpretation to raise it and re-endow it with its primordial essence.'[27] Consider also Hindemith's recommendation that performers should never try to express their own feelings, as well as his instruction, inspired by his awareness of the possibilities of technology, for the '*Unsichtbarkeit*' (invisibility) of performers. Recall, as well, other twentieth-century composers who have used computers or other compositional techniques to eliminate, as far as possible, the mediation of human performers if not the performance altogether. 'It is now possible for composers to make music directly', announced John Cage in 1937, 'without the assistance of intermediary performers.'[28]

For institutional examples, note the standardisation of bland, formal dress for orchestral players in modern concert halls. But, more intriguingly, consider the design of concert and opera halls themselves, in which screens were built on the stage or sunken pits were constructed to render the performers or the orchestra as a whole if not utterly invisible then significantly out of the way. The Small Auditorium of the Copenhagen Concert Palais of 1904 has a screen built on stage, the Bayreuth Festival Theatre a fully concealed orchestra. Carl Dahlhaus connects the two examples:

The prevailing doctrine of nineteenth-century music aesthetics – the idea of

25. Cf. Hein: 'It would follow from this [*Werktreue*] view that the ideal performer should be a transparent medium. He imparts information while conveying a minimum of noise; yet, where necessary he alters the original content just sufficiently to make it comprehensible to its audience without deviating from its essential character. He is the bridge between artist and public or, better, a system of locks, designed to transmit the vessel of art from one level to another'. *op.cit.*, p383.

26. E.T.A. Hoffmann, 'Beethovens Instrumentalmusik', in *Musikalische Novellen und Aufsätze*, E. Istel (ed), Grenier und Pfeiffer, Regensburg 1919, p69.

27. Busoni, 'Sketch of a New Aesthetic of Music' in *Three Classics in the Aesthetic of Music*, Dover, New York 1962, p84.

28. 'The Future of Music: Credo', *Silence*, John Cage, Wesleyan University Press, Conn. 1939, p4.

'absolute' music, divorced from purposes and cares … gave rise again and again … to the demand for an 'invisible orchestra' concealing the mundane origins of transcendental music. What Wagner was able to institute in Bayreuth was also, around 1900, attempted in the concert hall.[29]

In fact no musician contributed more than Wagner to showing how the transcendental strictures of the romantic musical aesthetic could be embodied institutionally. In examining the Bayreuth Festival Theatre, biographer Geoffrey Skelton sketched three tenets fundamental to its genesis: it would demonstrate how sacredness is invested in dramatic performance; its function would be to elevate and ennoble the human spirit; and it would symbolise romantic, revolutionary ideals.[30] To achieve these interconnected ends, Wagner required not only the acoustic and dramatic purity of the event, but also, as he himself explained, the illusion of transcendence. Wagner made sense of this illusion by developing the architectural and commercial conditions of an almost Walt Disney-like theatre of effects. But to achieve the specific transformation of the traditional prosaic theatre into a sacred dramatic site, he utilised several architectural and experiential notions of distancing and invisibility. By far the most fundamental notion was that of the invisible orchestra. 'To explain the plan of the festival theatre now in course of erection', he wrote,

> … I cannot do better than to begin with the need I felt the first, that of rendering invisible the mechanical source of its music, to wit the orchestra; for this one requirement led step by step to a total transformation of the auditorium of our neo-European theatre.[31]

Though cognisant of partially concealed and lowered orchestra pits in other auditoriums (in Riga, for example), Wagner believed that the idea of rendering the orchestra completely invisible came to him in 1840 after arriving late at a rehearsal in Paris for a Beethoven Symphony. As Skelton tells the story:

> [Wagner] was put in a room divided from the main concert hall by a partition stopping short of the ceiling. As he recalled … the sound of the orchestra reaching over the partition amazed him: the music, freed of all mechanical side-effects, came to the ear in a compact and ethereal sort of unity'.[32]

Only by concealing the orchestra could one create the illusion that the music was mysteriously emerging out of the silence from nowhere – or from everywhere.[33]

Wagner's idea was not original. Compare Goethe's thought (expressed in *Wilhelm Meister's Apprenticeship*) attributed to Natalie's uncle, his words being recalled by Natalie as she walks with Wilhelm around the 'Hall of the Past':

29. Carl Dahlhaus, *Nineteenth-Century Music,* University of California Press, Berkeley, Cali, 1989, p394. Note that, generally speaking, concert orchestras emerged out of opera orchestras in matters of structure, administration, and personnel, and, so similarly, concert halls out of opera halls. For more, see Adam Carse, *The Orchestra from Beethoven to Berlioz,* Dover, New York 1949.

30. Geoffrey Skelton, 'The Idea of Bayreuth', in P. Burbidge and R. Sutton (eds), *The Wagner Companion,* Cambridge University Press, Cambridge 1979, p389-411.

31. *Wagner on Music and Drama,* A. Goldman and E. Sprinchorn (eds), tr. H. Ashton Ellis, Da Capo Press, New York 1964, p365.

32. Skelton, *op.cit.,* p390.

33. Goldman and Sprinchorn (eds), *op.cit.,* p358. Frederic Spotts also makes this point in *Bayreuth: A History of the Wagner Festival,* Yale University Press, New Haven 1984, p8.

34. *Wilhelm Meister's Apprenticeship*, ed and tr. Eric A. Blackall, Suhrkamp Publications, New York 1989, pp332-3. Cf. Daniel J. Koury's summary of precursors in his *Orchestral Performance Practices in the Nineteenth Century: Size, Proportions, and Seating*, UMI Research Press, Michigan 1986, p270.

35. Goldman and Sprinchorn (eds), *op.cit.*, p365. I have changed the translation of 'Bild' from picture to stage-picture.

36. Eduard Hanslick, 'Richard Wagner's Stage Festival in Bayreuth', *Music Criticisms 1846-99*, tr. H. Pleasants, Penguin, Harmondsworth 1950, p138.

37. See Goldman and Sprinchorn (eds), *op.cit.*, p366. Wagner later developed the idea also of an 'invisible theatre' which would hide the mechanics of the stage production. The idea was taken to a minimalist extreme by Weiland Wagner who hid not only the mechanics, but also reduced the visual image to the bare essentials. See Skelton, *op.cit.*, p409, and Spotts, *op.cit.*, pp78 and 216.

38. I have borrowed these examples from Spotts, *op.cit.*, pp71-3. But cf. Shaw's 'Bayreuth', *Shaw on Music*, Doubleday, New York 1955, pp116-127.

We have been spoilt too much by theatres, where music only serves the eye, accompanying movements, not feelings. In oratorios and concerts the physical presence of the singer is disturbing... A lovely voice is the most universal thing ... and if the limited individual producing it is visible, this disturbs the effect of universality... [W]hen someone is singing he should be invisible, his appearance should not prejudice me.

Natalie continues on her uncle's behalf: '[My uncle] also wanted players in an orchestra concealed as much as possible, because one is only distracted and disturbed by the labourings and necessary strange gestures of musicians.'[34]

The question of originality aside, couldn't Wagner have made the demand for an invisible orchestra more metaphorical than literal, more experiential than architectural? He once thought this possible: 'In my article on Beethoven,' he wrote, 'I explained how fine performances of ideal works of music may make this evil [i.e. the technical apparatus of musical production] imperceptible at last, through our eyesight being neutralized, as it were, by the rapt subversion of the whole sensorium.' For opera, however, the demand for invisibility could not rely solely on experiential capacities. 'With a dramatic representation,' Wagner explained, 'it is a matter of focusing the eye itself upon the stage-picture; and that can be done only by leading it away from any sight of bodies lying in between.'[35]

An invisible orchestra, then, would hide the mechanics of the sound production and give the audience direct visual contact with the stage. It would also help meet Wagner's demand that the audience experience the performance in darkness. With no light emanating from the orchestra pit, with the auditorium lights turned off, and with no distracting 'cheap adornments' on the ceiling or walls, the audience would do what they had rarely ever done before – focus exclusively on the performance. No allowance would even be made for reading programme notes: the audience, Wagner hoped, would already know the work. 'One sees the proceedings on the stage without obstruction – and nothing else' – thus remarked audience member Eduard Hanslick.[36]

Wagner further expected the audience to sit in silence – no interrupting applause as occurs in other theatres. He intended also that his theatre be built sufficiently far from a city so that audiences would better be able to leave their daily cares behind. All such conditions, Wagner maintained, would accentuate the required psychological and aesthetic distancing – the 'mystic gulf' – of the 'imaginary stage world' from the ordinary, real world.[37]

Audience members responded variously to Bayreuth's invisible orchestra. For many it did nothing to undermine their conviction that the orchestra had been given 'an unprecedented role' in Wagner's operas: '[t]he orchestra is all,' declared Edward Grieg after attending a performance of the *Ring*. For critics like George Bernard Shaw, who liked to listen and not look, concealing the orchestra was surely a bonus.[38] No one commented more directly or in more detail, however, than Hanslick: 'Most noteworthy of all,' he wrote, is the invisible orchestra... The orchestra is set so deep that one is reminded of the engine room of a steamship. It is, moreover, almost entirely hidden by a kind of tin roof. The musicians haven't the slightest view of the stage or of the public... Wagner's inspired idea of sparing us the disturbing spectacle of the musicians' fiddling and puffing ... is something to which I gave my blessing long ago and for which ... I have even campaigned. The lowering of the orchestra is one of the most reasonable and enduring of Wagner's reforms; it has already taken hold in the legitimate theatres... And yet, it seems to me that Wagner has gone too far, or ... too deep; for in ... *Das Rheingold* I missed, if not the precision, at least the brilliance of the orchestra... This is ... a boon for the singers, but at some cost to the role of the instruments, to which, especially in this work, is assigned much of the most significant and the most beautiful.[39]

39. Hanslick, *op.cit.*, pp138-9.

Practical problems aside (and there were many), no critic would ever challenge the assessment that Wagner's Bayreuth changed performance in both the concert and opera hall forever. His innovations posed a crucial question: in experiential terms, does the visual absence of performers intensify or sabotage audible presence? Of course, for those interested in 'the works themselves', this problem could be relegated to the status of an irritating side issue. For those interested in performance, however, literal invisibility or even metaphorical transparency was likely to make even *Werktreue*-committed performers feel, as one Bayreuth orchestra player put it, more like machines than musicians.[40]

40. Spotts, *op.cit.*, p12.

IN FAVOUR OF PERFORMANCES

Indeed, performers would be unlikely to survive as an enthusiastic group of participants in the musical world if concurring with the demand for transparency, invisibility, or personality negation ever fully eliminated their individual or collective sense of self. Performers, however accepting of their mediating role between composer and audience, usually aspire to be regarded as more than means; they aspire also to be regarded as ends. Rose Rosengard Subotnik correctly observes that the post-Kantian politics of individualism clashed with the attempt to embody the ideal of *Werktreue* by turning performers into automatons.[41] But how have performers tried to reconcile their desire to be both means and ends?

41. Rose Rosengard Subotnik, 'Individualism in Western Art Music and its Cultural Costs,' *Developing Variations: Style and Ideology in Western Music*, University of Minnesota Press, Minn 1991, p256.

One way has been for performers constantly to remind composers and critics that their activity of interpreting music indispensably mediates the activities of composition and reception. Composers and critics have always agreed. 'Interpretation,' wrote Schoenberg, 'is necessary, to bridge the gap between the author's idea and the contemporary ear.'[42] A piece of music is 'strictly speaking, nothing but a recipe', wrote Paul Valèry; 'the cook who executes it plays an essential role.'[43] Such endorsements of the performers' claim have not resulted, however, in granting them complete freedom, but have underscored instead the complexity of their interpretative activity within the confines of the

42. Schoenberg, *op.cit.*, p528.

43. Paul Valèry, 'A Discourse on the Declamation of Verse', *Selected Writings of Paul Valèry*, New Directions, New York 1950, p155.

THE PERFECT PERFORMANCE OF MUSIC AND THE PERFECT MUSICAL PERFORMANCE   11

44. *Ibid.*, p122.
Stravinsky wrote
accordingly: 'The idea
of interpretation
implies the limitations
imposed upon the
performer or those
which the performer
imposes upon himself
in his proper function
... to transmit music to
the listener. The idea
of execution implies
the strict putting into
effect of an explicit
will that contains
nothing beyond what
it specifically
commands. It is the
conflict between these
two [ideas] ... that is at
the root of all errors,
all the sins, all the
misunderstandings
that interpose
themselves between
the musical work and
the listener.'

45. Erwin Stein, *Form
and Performance*,
Limelight Editions,
New York 1962, p20.

46. From Robert
Jacobson's
*Reverberations:
Interviews with the
World's Leading
Musicians*, Morrow and
Co., New York 1974,
p17.

47. *Ibid.*

Werktreue ideal. The resulting position for performers has been strained as they have striven to reconcile their belief that the perfect performance of music is the product both of a *free* interpretation and of an *unfree* rendition in full compliance with the composer's commands.[44]

In his book *Form and Performance*, Schoenberg's student Erwin Stein showed, however, how close the interaction between rendition and interpretation must in fact be if the performer is to perform the work faithfully. Stein believed that expression and interpretation, like rendition, flow directly out of an understanding of a work's form or structure. 'Many performers', he wrote, 'would have the necessary musicality and skill if they understood the implications of musical structure.'[45] Stein took seriously the etymology of the term 'per/form/ance': a performance is the stylistic completion or accomplishment of the work in due form.

Despite Stein's formalist commitment, his basic understanding of performance is widely shared. Musicality in performance emerges from a thorough understanding of the work. Where, however, performers have tended to depart from Stein is in the greater show of emphasis they have wanted to give to their conviction that their performance requires something more. Certainly, correct rendition and faithful interpretation depend upon knowledge of the work, but performance is more than a demonstration of this knowledge; it is also an *act* of musicianship. As one singer has said: 'The moment of truth is the doing'. In doing, performers say, the intellectual work comes to an end and the instinct takes over. 'Fidelity ... is elemental,' comments Daniel Barenboim accordingly, 'but you cannot stop there.'[46] In the appeal to musical instinct, performers begin to find their redemption within the confines of the *Werktreue* ideal.

This appeal is found most often in performers' discussions of 'technique and style'. Constrained as both technique and style are by a composer's commands, their understanding is closely linked to matters of interpretation and rendition. In this regard, they tell us something about the relationship of performance to work. But they also tell us something about performance itself.

Technique and style are not simply related to one another by an 'and' clause; they are related more closely, as two sides of a coin. Thus, performers say, there is no adequate employment of style without a mastery of technique and no adequate use of technique without a feeling for style. But where does technique end and style begin? How does one confine the other or help secure its satisfactory expression? Barenboim, again, offers a typical answer:

You cannot divide technique and making music. It doesn't work like that...
If I play a passage loudly or softly, it is both a technical *and* a musical
problem. When you have musical demands made in the music, then your
technique comes into use to carry it out. For most people, a great technique
means fast fingers – but a good technique means to do what you must do
musically in terms of dynamics, touch and so on – musicianship, in a word.[47]

But what is musicianship? Philosopher Francis Sparshott thinks the question cannot be fully answered. 'The question,' he writes,

> has scarcely been asked, though few terms play more important roles in our critical chitchat... The ancient contrast between learned and practical music is one thing that has distracted attention from the concept. One can at least say that a performer shows musicianship by displaying a grasp of musical meanings, both structural and affective, rather than just following the score from point to point... [But can] one specify further? Presumably not [because] one is speaking rather of the *level* of understanding shown than of any specifiable matter to be understood.[48]

Sparshott's awareness of our having reached the limits of description has a strong precedent, for whereas technique has traditionally been described in the language of rules and form, style has not received so systematic a description. Nor could it, for, as Berlioz noticed, style captures that part of music that is 'sentiment' not 'science'.[49] Other musicians have expressed the same point differently: learning rules or teaching technique, they have said, is straightforward, but learning how to be an intelligent musician or teaching a performer to play with style requires something more. But, again, what is this elusive 'more'? To be sure, it requires instinct and inspiration, but, with further specificity, it also requires an understanding of how technique and style together fill what one might usefully call the 'performance space' that remains once the work has been left behind.

One way performers have captured the elusive 'more' of their musicianship is by appeal to the illusion that they are actually creating the music. 'The greatest thing for us [performers]', commented Janet Baker, 'is to make a phrase sound like you never heard it before.'[50] '[W]hen you are on stage playing', remarked Gary Graffman, 'you should sound as if you are composing the music.' Of course, the illusion of creativity has to be just that, an illusion, for *Werktreue* performers do not strictly speaking create: 'It is crucial,' Graffman rightly continued, 'for any performer to begin with the music first.'[51]

But performers have then moved on to describe their performance space as an occasion for the theatrical expression of spontaneity, immediacy, and freedom, of feeling and breathing, of conviction and commitment. It is the space, they have said, in which they bring the works out of the abstract and dead museum and infuse them with dramatic vitality. It is a space, also, in which the sameness of the work and the difference of the particular performance compete in an exciting tension. It is a space in which tradition and culture inform the act of performance, and a space, finally, in which a unique acoustical environment is created. With assertions like these, performers have then felt confident about drawing this conclusion also, that their full visible presence, in all its dramatic intensity and glory, is indisputably required. 'It [is] not enough to hear music', once declared Stravinsky, 'it must also be seen.'[52]

Despite the plethora of these sorts of assertions, however, the performer's

48. Francis Sparshott, 'Aesthetics of Music: Limits and Grounds,' in P. Alperson (ed), *What is Music? An Introduction to the Philosophy of Music*, Haven Publications, New York 1987, p84.

49. H. Berlioz, *A travers chants*, Paris 1862, excerpted in P. Weiss and R. Taruskin (eds), *Music in the Western World: A History in Documents*, Schirmer Books, New York, 1984, p349.

50. Jacobson, *op.cit.*, p11.

51. *Ibid.*, pp76-7.

52. Stravinsky, *op.cit.*, p128.

space has been more suggested than systematically investigated within the romantic aesthetic bound to the *Werktreue* ideal. But the suggestiveness has not been employed arbitrarily, for lurking in the background has been another conception of performance altogether. It is a conception, I shall now show, that is less well theorised but which claims enormous intuitive appeal. It is the conception of the perfect musical performance.

THE PERFECT MUSICAL PERFORMANCE

The perfect musical performance is conceptually broader than the perfect performance of music. It attends to the general, though elusive, dimension of musicianship inherent in a performance whether or not the performance is a performance of a work. Moreover, it challenges the pervasive tendency of romanticism to engage, as T.E. Hulme put it, in metaphors of flight that transport music into the spheres of 'circumambient gas'. In contrast to Humboldt's widely shared dictum that the arts move us from the world of reality to the world of ideas, the perfect musical performance celebrates the 'lower' world of the human, the ephemeral, and the active.[53]

53. My thinking about the perfect musical performance has been much helped by reading Battcock and Nickas's *The Art of Performance*, and M. Issacharoff and R.F. Jones's *Performing Texts*, University of Pennsylvania Press, Philadelphia 1988.

To emphasize the human is to resist treating performers as 'automatons' or 'transformer stations'. But this resistance must be tempered, for in the 'gassiest' claims of the romantic aesthetic there is also a deep commitment to humanity. However, such a commitment takes acts of aesthetic creation and contemplation, i.e. acts of the mind, to be the finest acts of humanity and scorns acts of actual or bodily performance. To account for this difference one can follow the lead of theorists who contrast Art with art and distinguish the Human from the human. Then one can meaningfully say that, whereas the perfect performance of music stresses the *H*uman, the perfect musical performance stresses the *h*uman.

The human emphasis must be tempered for another reason. The perfect musical performance does not bring the meaning and function of performance completely down to earth. As with the perfect performance of music, the perfect musical performance uses operations of transformation, transfiguration, abstraction, and transcendence. In both cases, these operations derive from the same ground, a ground constituted by romantic aesthetic theory emerging partially out of pre-modern secular and sacred traditions of theatre, drama, ritual, and spectacle, and adapted to modern musical concerns. Despite the common ground, however, the operations sustain conflicting conceptions of performance.

Like the perfect performance of music, the perfect musical performance suitably adapts an age-old purpose of secular and sacred drama, namely, to transform and transport the audience through transfiguration, or, in other alliterative terms, to elevate and educate through entertainment. Both adapt from these traditions, in other words, the idea of theatrical transfiguration in which meanings are stripped of their habitual or 'taken-for-granted' associations and invested by performers with traits of the symbolic, metaphorical, and mystical.[54] But the perfect musical performance departs from the perfect performance of music when it carries over from these traditions the essentially non-elite, social and participatory dimensions of performance.

Coleridge once defined theatre as an 'amusement thro' the ear or eye in which men assemble in order to be amused by some entertainment presented to all at the same time.'[55] The 'all at the same time' principle is subverted in concert halls when the aesthetic principle dictates a silent and lonely contemplation in a darkened hall. But it is stressed within an aesthetic that regards the total event of performance as a 'socialized activity' to use Richard Leppert's recent phrase;[56] or as 'a musical occasion' that, as Edward Said has also recently claimed, is 'always located in a uniquely endowed site ... what occurs then and there is part of the cultural life of modern society.'[57] The stress given here to the social and cultural dimensions of performance accentuates the extent to which communicative circuits are generated between composers, performers, and listeners in their active and collective engagement with the music.[58]

The perfect musical performance places its emphasis more upon the actions involved in the total context of the performance than upon the mediating language conceived in isolation of this context. Transfiguration or revelation is thus rooted in the participatory act of interpreting the message or 'the work itself' in one's capacity either as performer or listener. Transferring a notion from the great teacher of the theatre Stanislawsky, the condition to be achieved by both performer and listener is a 'creative state of mind', a condition that is achieved through the training of mental attitude and, in the performer's case, of bodily gesture and gait, breathing and muscular movement. In the perfect musical performance, value resides in the creative acts of individuals who give meaning to music in the very moment of each act of performing.

But the 'creative state' implicit within the perfect musical performance does not involve acting as one would take on a role in a play. The uncoupling of performing and acting is as much historical as conceptual – it enabled the perfect musical performance to serve as a specifically musical conception despite its broader roots in theatre. The uncoupling occurred through a process of abstraction or negation. Just as the musical language shed itself of its occasional and representational content, so the act of performance underwent a process of abstraction and developed into something like an empty play – a play without content. Performers played out movements on the stage recalling those of traditional theatre, but the meaning of those movements became purely formal or gestural. Stravinsky captured part of the idea when he described the instrumentalist as 'an orator who speaks an unarticulated language.'[59] But it is the performance, too, that becomes an unarticulated or dematerialised act. As John Cage demonstrated, though for a different purpose, a musical performance is an act of pure or formal theatricality.

To so describe the perfect musical performance is intended to give stress to its specifically modern, musical character, but it is not intended thereby to

54. For more on this transfigurative process, see *By Means of Performance: Intercultural Studies of Theatre and Ritual*, R. Schechner and W. Appel (eds), Cambridge University Press, Cambridge 1990.

55. Quoted by Keir Elan in 'Much Ado About Doing Things with Words (and other means): Some Problems in the Pragmatics of Theatre and Drama', in Issacharoff and Jones, *op.cit.*, p55.

56. 'When people hear a musical performance, they see it as an embodied activity ... the musical event is perceived as a socialized activity', *Ibid.*, pxxii.

57. Edward Said, *Musical Elaborations*, Columbia University Press, New York 1991, pxv.

58. The idea of a circuit is employed also by J.L. Styan, 'The Mystery of the Play Experience: Quince's Questions', Issacharoff and Jones, *op.cit.*, p25.

59. Stravinsky, *op.cit.*, p128.

exclude the emphasis that this conception also gives to dramatic spectacle. Nor could it, because during the nineteenth century the perfect musical performance became identified more with popular forms of performance than elite ones. So connected, it resisted the demands of the *Werktreue* ideal, and catered to the 'lesser' or 'less aesthetic' demands of a more socially-minded audience.[60]

The two traditions embodying the conception of the perfect musical performance in an exemplary way were those of the instrumental soloist or virtuoso and opera. The virtuoso tradition serves, however, as the better example. Complicating the example of opera is the genre's division into elite (German) and popular (French and Italian) forms, and relatedly, the genre's having become entangled in a debate as to its very status as music. Opera was a musical form, but was it purely or only that, or was it a hybrid combination of the different arts? The virtuoso tradition avoided this particular debate: if virtuoso performance was an art, then it was indisputably a musical art. Virtuoso performance also shares enough with opera to justify my using it as the lone example. 'The virtuoso introduced a new element into instrumental performance,' writes Henry Raynor accordingly. 'He won a new audience through his mastery of showmanship, transferring to the concert hall from the opera house the element of danger and physical excitement.'[61]

Within the virtuoso tradition, performers such as Liszt and Paganini were regarded as incarnations of either God or the Devil, as inspired performers or as circus actors. Debussy straddles the contrasts:

> The attraction of the virtuoso for the public is very like that of the circus for the crowd. There is always a hope that something dangerous may happen: Mr X may play the violin with Mr Y on his shoulders; or Mr Z may conclude his piece by lifting the piano with his teeth. [But when] X plays Bach's violin concerto ... he has that freedom of expression, that unaffected beauty of tone, which are essential for its interpretation.[62]

Three questions typically shaped the assessment of the virtuoso: did the open display of romantic inspiration through physical pyrotechnics enamour or horrify the audience? did the virtuoso's physical spectacle on the stage undermine his or her integrity as a musician? and did such an overt physical act signify a good or an evil human nature?

Implicit within this evaluation was the evaluator's overt recognition of the virtuoso's dependence upon *live* performance. For accentuated, first, in the performance was the one-off, non-repeatable unfolding of time, a condition that sustained in the performance qualities of immediacy, spontaneity, and uniqueness, and in the attending audience qualities of fear, expectation, and excitement. Adorno once employed Beckett's notion of *'je vais continuer'* to capture the sense in which music is 'as irreversible as time itself', bound as it is to the 'fact of succession'. 'By starting', Adorno wrote, the musical performance 'commits itself to carrying on, to becoming something new, to developing.'[63]

60. Eric Gans makes a comparable point. 'The high/low cultural distinction ... is not founded on the sociological opposition between mass and élite, but on that between individuality and participation.' 'Art and Entertainment', in John Rahn (ed), *Perspectives on Musical Aesthetics*, W.W. Norton, New York 1994, pp51-2.

61. Henry Raynor, *Music and Society since 1815*, Tuplinger Publishing Co., London 1976, p66.

62. C. Debussy, *Three Classics in the Aesthetic of Music*, Dover, New York 1962, p22.

63. T. Adorno, 'Stravinsky', in *Quasi una Fantasia: Essays on Modern Music*, tr. R. Livingston, Verso, London, 1992, pp150-1.

In its development through musical time, in its transitory and fleeting expression, Adorno continued, music achieves its transcendence and in so doing asserts its freedom. Early romantics comparably and positively understood temporality to ground the possibility of music's creative and free spontaneity and transcendental immediacy. Unlike the *Werktreue* ideal, the virtuoso ideal (linked as it increasingly became to improvisatory ideals of music-making, i.e. the endless melody pointing to the infinite) gave value to the idea that it was the fleeting performance itself, rather than the work, which carries musical meaning. The temporal performance embodied the transcendental musical drama: it set into play the ritual of transformation through which performers communicated the musical message to their audiences. 'The demon began to flex his muscles', Schumann wrote to Liszt in 1840:

> He first played along with [the members of the audience], as if to feel them out, and then gave them a taste of something more substantial until, with his magic, he had ensnared each and every one and could move them this way or that as he chose. It is unlikely that any artist, excepting only Paganini, has the power to lift, carry and deposit an audience in such high degree.[64]

But the virtuoso's drama would not have made sense to its audience if temporality alone had constituted its essence; if, in other words, the emphasis on temporality had led to the performers' visibility or presence being either literally or metaphorically denied. Liszt's performance 'simply has to be heard – and seen,' thus continued Schumann. 'If Liszt were to play behind the scenes, a considerable portion of poetry would be lost.'[65] 'We have now heard [Liszt],' another critic wrote,

> the strange wonder, whom the superstition of past ages, possessed by the delusion that such things could never be done without the help of the Evil One, would undoubtedly have condemned ... to the stake – we have ... seen him too, which, of course, makes a part of the affair.[66]

One more critic, reviewing a Paganini concert for the London *Tatler*, chose to record his momentary dismay when a 'packed audience' threatened to hide Paganini from view, leaving the critic merely to 'hear' him. Fortunately, 'a lucky interval between a gentleman's head and a lady's bonnet' favoured his endeavour to see 'the long, pale face of the musical marvel.' (Was it the prevalence of these sorts of comments that led Paganini himself to complain that 'no one ever asks if you have heard Paganini, but if you have seen him'?)[67]

Stravinsky elaborated further on the argument for visibility: 'Those who maintain that they only enjoy music to the full with their eyes shut,' he wrote, 'do not hear better than when they have them open.' Closing one's eyes is just an excuse to attend to one's feelings while giving the appearance that one is listening to the music. Stravinsky also had a less cynical reason: the details an

64. *Schumann on Music: A Selection from his Writings*, tr. H. Pleasants, Dover, New York 1965, p157.

65. *Ibid.*, p158.

66. Weiss and Taruskin, *op.cit.*, p363.

67. *Ibid.*, p342.

audience sees actually shape their understanding of performance. 'The sight of the gestures and movements of the various parts of the bodies producing the music is fundamentally necessary if [music] is to be grasped in its fullness. All music created ... demands some exteriorization for the perception of the listener.'[68] In his *Poetics of Music*, he gave the argument more details:

68. Igor Stravinsky, *An Autobiography*, W.W. Norton, New York 1936, pp72-3.

> [W]hat shall we say of the ill-breeding of those grimacers who too often take it upon themselves to deliver the 'inner meaning' of music by disfiguring it with their affected airs? For, I repeat, one sees music. An experienced eye follows and judges, sometimes unconsciously, the performer's least gesture. From this point of view one might conceive the process of performance as the creation of new values that call for the solution of problems similar to those which arise in the realm of choreography. In both cases we give special attention to the control of gestures... For music does not move in the abstract [i.e. independently of performance]. Its translation into plastic [or performance] terms requires exactitude and beauty.[69]

69. Stravinsky, *op.cit.*, p128.

The net result of taking performer visibility into account is the inevitable amplification of the concept of musical performance itself. Performance becomes something more than the abstracted sonorous event. Even if the sonorous event remains central, the perfect musical performance, unlike the perfect performance of music, regards that event as inseparable from the actual performers who produce the sounds, from the formal, visual choreography of their musical movements, and from the real spaces or environments, acoustic and cultural, which shape it. But this amplification must be further nuanced. For the design of the perfect musical performance is not so much to extend the borders of the category of music itself – music remains essentially the audible art of sound; its design, rather, is to recognise, as the perfect performance of music wants to deny, that the situatedness of the performance of this art in the real world is not to the latter's failing but to its genuine aesthetic merit. Whereas a perfect performance of music, therefore, ideally achieves its transcendent and enduring meaning by negating itself to better illuminate the work it performs, a perfect musical performance ideally achieves its transcendent and equally as enduring meaning precisely by asserting its uniqueness as a temporal event that is fully socially and visibly situated.

What happens, now, to a practice which tries to move in two different directions at once? What, more precisely, is the nature of the conflict which emerges when two competing conceptions or ideals of perfection vie with one another for the dominant role in the practice? The interesting quality of the conflict, I want to show in my conclusion, derives less from what differentiates the two conceptions *per se*, than from what differentiates them given what they share.

CONCLUSION

When Glenn Gould wrote that 'for better or worse, recording will forever alter our notions about what is appropriate to the performance of music',[70] he offered an argument comparable to that regarding photography's impact on painting. In both cases, the technology of recording or reproduction would make possible a new degree of fidelity, representational or interpretative, formerly unrealisable. Unless the paintbrush could approximate to the condition of the camera, or the concert hall to that of the recording studio, painting and live performance would both have to reevaluate their traditional aesthetic (and for Gould their moral) purposes and possibilities.

70. Gould, *op.cit.*, p336.

Concert halls have long tried to accommodate technological advancement as they have striven for acoustic perfection. Gould acknowledged this fact, though he was critical of it. Regardless, he had overriding arguments. In a recording studio, performers could produce their most truthful interpretation of a work in solitude – a prerequisite for genuine creativity, he said. They would also be released from the pressure of performing the work in one sitting; they would have the 'take-two' opportunity and, then, the opportunity to edit and splice. Performers could avoid, furthermore, engaging in the 'wooing' showmanship demanded by live audiences; one would find performances being judged more than performers. 'One should not voyeuristically watch one's fellow human beings,' Gould wrote, 'in testing situations that do not pragmatically need to be tested.'[71] Performers could also avoid anti-democratically imposing upon their listeners their particular interpretations. Gould was thinking here about the critical distance granted to listeners who, in the privacy of home, could listen to recordings in their own time and as individuals without their judgement or experience of the works being influenced by the authoratively-dressed performers or by 'the herd' judgement of status-conscious audiences. Of course, as Gould well recognised, lurking now would be the danger that listeners would not listen at all, but adopt a 'casual attitude' by turning music into comfortable, wallpaper muzak.[72]

71. 'Glenn Gould in conversation with Tim Page', Page, *op.cit.*, p452.

72. I have collected these objections together from numerous essays by Gould mentioned by title in earlier notes.

Gould had other arguments, but it suffices to repeat their shared conclusion: the technology offered by the recording studio could bring musical performance closer to meeting the moral and aesthetic aspirations of the conception of the perfect performance of music than concert halls had ever yet done or ever would be likely to do.

What about Gould's critics? Clearly Gould's moral demands did not outweigh their aesthetic demands, for they simply retaliated by reminding him of all that would be lost in musical performance were the conception of the perfect musical performance – with its emphasis on human presence, visibility, drama, and the immediacy of communication – to be rejected altogether in favour of the perfect performance of music. But they did not then recommend the exclusive functioning of one conception instead of another, but rather seemed content to allow the continuing functioning of both.[73]

That critics seemed content in this way suggests they would also accept my

73. See especially Gould's conversation with Arthur Rubenstein, *The Gould Reader*, p283ff.

first conclusion, that striving to embody one conception of perfection sustained by a performance tradition sometimes cannot and should not demand that that tradition be homogeneous or singular in such a conception; different conceptions of perfection can, and sometimes have to, co-exist within a single tradition. But this conclusion acknowledges only the mere phenomenon of co-existence; it does not yet address in any detail the situation in which conceptions co-exist but conflict.

There are different ways to understand the conflicts that emerge within traditions or practices, or more specifically, between the conceptions, ideals, or values they support. For my purposes, however, it suffices to describe only the kind of conflict that arises when a shared ground – perhaps a world-view, a theory, or a basic set of values – finds itself expressed by, or realised in, genuinely conflicting conceptions or ideals.

Thus, expressions of a shared ground may differ from one another if the shared ground is essentially incomplete or underdetermined, and hence imperfect. In this view, expressions are attempts to make determinate or to perfect an imperfect ground. The relation between the shared ground and its expressions is akin to the relation that holds at a local level between a prescriptive theory and its correlative determinate actions, a stage direction and its enactments by actors, or an architectural drawing and the particular buildings which are its realisations. That which is prescribed is made precise in each action or realisation, but the latter may permissibly assume different forms. Returning to the general level, genuine conflict between expressions of a shared ground arises when these expressions (conceptions, ideals, or values) are incommensurable, incommensurable because they cannot be ranked so as to give one priority over the other, or when no clear trade off or easy synthesis between them is forthcoming.

Confronting genuine conflict one may respond in more or less radical ways. Adopting a radical attitude one might regard it most expedient to endorse one expression or conception anyway, and in so doing reject any rival conception out of hand. Often this endorsement will be accompanied by a claim that the conflict no longer exists because it has been resolved. Perhaps one will employ previously unforeseen criteria to show how the rival conceptions can now be ranked. The non-radical attitude, by contrast, suggests tolerance: if one acknowledges that alternative expressions of a shared ground are possible, one may well allow the alternatives to co-exist. Indeed, one may well see that being tolerant has clear advantages regardless of the continuation of conflict.

Recall now our two conceptions of the perfect performance. Both realise or track a shared ground, and to one another they stand in a position of genuine conflict. How should one characterise the historical expressions and responses to this conflict and the consequences emerging therefrom?

We already know that their conflict came to be expressed through a division between the elite and popular forms of classical music practice, most clearly between the practice's orchestral or community-based symphonic tradition that nonetheless stressed the individualistic nature of aesthetic experience, and the individualist, soloistic or virtuoso tradition which nonetheless stressed the social nature of musical experience. But we also know that this division never became so sharp as to allow either conception ever to become wholly or exclusively identified with either tradition. Rather, both conceptions were present in both traditions even though the balance of power between them varied. Thus, we must once more emphasise the historical interaction and overlap that has existed between the performance traditions, conceptions, and thus also the modes of evaluation that together, and not in separation, have constituted the modern practice of classical music.

But this 'interaction and overlap'. I now want to insist, neither emerged out of, nor resulted in, relations of unification or consolidation, but, rather out of, and in, critical antagonisms. This is demonstrated best by the isolated moments and historical tendencies when, and in which, the conflict received various combinations of radical and non-radical articulations and similar combinations of responses.

Recall, first, how the Gould conflict presented a moment of threatened radical conflict. For Gould, perhaps, the result of the conflict was unsatisfactory. But out of the conflict performers learned something more and something new about what it means to perform. They became conscious of their striving to be both ends and means, to be both heard and heard through, and when seen, seen and seen through. From Gould's case we learn at least this: that when a challenge is posed in the extreme it is not required, for the challenge to be successful, that it be met with a radical response.

Consider, next, the broader tendency towards radical conflict which arose insofar as the perfect performance of music emerged as the conception most closely identified with the high bourgeois culture of the German symphonic tradition and the elite aesthetic theory associated therewith. As such, and in the name of purity and fineness, it found itself increasingly articulated independently of its rival conception as if it could do all the work in the practice on its own. This tendency towards the radical denial of its rival, its declaration, in other words, of dehumanised autonomy in the name of a perfected Humanity, proved self-deceptive in practice however. For the perfect performance of music never, and never could have, succeeded in regulating even the *Werktreue* tradition on its own. As I have tried to show, this conception always required, to function successfully and to sustain its very assertion of transcendence, the conceptual, aesthetic, as well as the commercial co-presence or shadow of the non-elite conception. Indeed, one might explain this relation of dependency by saying that the self-deceptive claim on behalf of the conception of the perfect performance of music was sustained by, as in turn it forced, a critical position of antagonistic tolerance.

To expand this last point, consider those performers who upheld the virtuoso tradition and brought to the public's attention the merits of the perfect musical performance. Should they be regarded as having responded radically to the extreme demands of the ideal of the perfect performance of music? I do not think so. In fact, these performers tried to carve out a complex position in which they accepted the principle of the *Werktreue* ideal but resisted the most stringent demands of the performance conception to which that ideal had become most closely associated. Many performers thus aimed to be both great virtuoso and great *Werktreue* performers at the same time, and they did this by aspiring to produce a perfect performance of music as they aspired also to produce a perfect musical performance. Their resulting position demonstrated not only that a single performance is a complex event insofar as the performers may simultaneously strive to meet conflicting ideals, but also that the non-elite conception of virtuoso performance striving towards the ideal of the perfect musical performance had a legitimate, though antagonistic, role to play in a practice increasingly seeing itself in elite terms. Thus again, the non-elite conception served to sustain the existence of the elite conception, although, by constantly asserting itself as different, it kept the elite conception in check.

What conclusion, finally, should a meta-theorist draw when confronted with a practice that has historically been regulated by conflicting conceptions? The meta-theorist, like any given performer, may respond in various ways, though the issues involved in meta-theoretical responses differ from those facing actual performers. Consider one viable position extrapolated from familiar strains of critical theory. On finding that the conceptions regulating a practice are self-deceptive, incomplete, or dependent, one might recommend, in the name of truth or emancipation, that those conceptions and the associated practice be clarified. The critical procedure takes what is truthful from any given conception with the purpose of transforming the practice into one which no longer depends upon, or is maintained by, any self-deceptive or antagonistic elements or oppositional conflicts. The procedure does not hope, then, to 'leave everything as it is', but intends for its outcome to have a transformative effect on the practice. In other words, for the critical theorist, the meta-theoretical outcome – one might say, the philosophical positioning – comes to play a crucial and complex role within the practice itself.

This critical procedure is, as I said, viable, but it undermines its purpose when it strives to do away with plurality and conflict and seeks instead a unifying consensus for the practice based on conflict-free ideals. For, by seeking such a consensus, it tends to ignore the potentially transformative or creative consequences that emerge from the presence in a practice of more than one conception, any one of which might have some element of self-deception, and any one of which might conflict with another. I believe, as I have tried to show, that creative products – new problems and solutions, new activities and greater learning – may emerge precisely from the constructive recognition by a practice's participants of the precise points of difference between its conflicting conceptions. I prefer, therefore, to allow the modern practice of classical music to remain imperfect both in its ground and in its expressions of that ground, precisely because that antagonistic imperfection has served, and is likely to continue to serve, as an indispensable condition for the practice's critical and healthy functioning.[74]

74. Many thanks to my colleagues at Wesleyan University and to Steven Gerrard, Patricia Herzog, Stephen Hinton, Gregg Horowitz, Thomas Huhn, Richard Taruskin, Leo Treitler, and Kendall Walton for their very helpful comments and advice. Special thanks to Donald Moon whose book *Constructing Community: Moral Pluralism and Tragic Conflicts*, Princeton University Press, New Jersey 1993 proved indispensable.

MUSIC MINUS ONE: ROCK, THEORY, AND PERFORMANCE[1]

Nicholas Cook

Performance ... lies so much in dexterity and habit that I scarce think it a subject proper for discourse. Upon the whole, performers in great perfection shall be dunces in [theoretical] skill.

Roger North[2]

1. My thanks to José Bowen, Dai Griffiths, and Robynn Stilwell for their suggestions based on a draft version of this article.

2. Mary Chan and Jamie Kassler (eds), *Roger North's Cursory Notes of Musicke*, School of English, University of New South Wales, Kensington, NSW 1986, p157.

Musical canons are always retrospective; it was nearly the middle of the nineteenth century before the classical repertory as we know it solidified. (If an exact date is to be given, it might be 1841, exactly fifty years after Mozart's death, when a review of Beethoven's Ninth Symphony described it as 'the keystone of a truly remarkable artistic period, exalted by J. Haydn, Mozart, and Beethoven'.[3]) So it seemed like the end of an era when, in the late 1980s, the record companies started reissuing a selection of the previous quarter of a century's recordings in boxed sets of CDs, thereby confirming the emergence of the rock canon. And it was at just this time that music theorists first began to grapple with rock. Of course the academic study of popular music was a relatively well-established field by then; but the initiative had been taken by sociologists and culture theorists, and later by sociologically-inclined musicologists. The result was a climate of opinion in which close musical readings of the type familiar in the study of the western art tradition were looked upon with suspicion, if not downright hostility, on the grounds that they represented at best an illegitimate transference of approaches derived from another repertory, and at worst a deliberate attempt at academic mystification. Music theorists, however, had an equally compelling argument: why, they asked, should the *music* of rock not be accorded the same detailed scrutiny as any other widely valued repertory?

3. From an 1841 review of Beethoven's Ninth Symphony in the *Allgemeine musikalische Zeitung*, quoted in David Levy, 'Early Performances of Beethoven's Ninth Symphony: a Documentary Study of Five Cities', Ph.D. diss., Eastman School of Music, University of Rochester, 1979, p391.

Rock theory might be said to have come of age in November 1990, when a session on rock was included at the Annual Meeting of the Society for Music Theory at Oakland, California; papers were given by Graeme Boone, Matthew Brown, John Covach, Walter Everett, and Dave Headlam. And recent publications by the last two of these authors highlight in a particularly tangible form some of the issues involved in, and difficulties attendant on, the theorising of rock. My intention in this article is to focus these difficulties around what I see as two related issues: the concept of authority that is built into music-theoretical discourse, and the theorising of musical performance. I shall argue that, in both these respects, approaches developed for the analysis of the art music repertory have been transferred too directly and uncritically to the analysis of rock; my aim is to identify some of the unhelpful conceptual baggage these approaches bring with them. Rethinking such approaches is a precondition for a more adequate theory of rock. But this article is not so much about theorising rock as about what rock can tell us about theorising music in general. In short, I shall suggest that until we know how to theorise musical performance we cannot reasonably claim to have an adequate theoretical approach to rock, or to the art tradition either.

I

4. Dave Headlam, 'Does the Song Remain the Same? Questions of Authority and Identification in the Music of Led Zeppelin', in Elizabeth West Marvin and Richard Hermann (eds), *Concert Music, Rock, and Jazz since 1945*, University of Rochester Press, Rochester, NY 1995, (hereafter *Concert Music*) pp313-63, from which all the references in this piece to Headlam's work came. The first part of the present article is a much expanded version of an argument sketched in the concluding chapter which I contributed to this collection (see footnote 7 below).

Dave Headlam's 'Does the Song Remain the Same? Questions of Authority and Identification in the Music of Led Zeppelin'[4] is about the relationship between Led Zeppelin's songs and the blues or other sources on which they were frequently based. Headlam's central question is 'in what, if any, context may Led Zeppelin be considered the originator of its own most distinctive songs?' and he seeks to answer this in what he provocatively refers to as 'purely musical' terms. His argument turns on the distinction between the mere fact of deriving one piece of music from another, and its incorporation within a significantly new aesthetic whole. Headlam maintains that songs like 'You Shook Me' and 'I Can't Quit You Baby', both of which were derived from originals by the Chicago bluesman Willie Dixon, fall into the first category; both, he says, are 'virtual transcriptions of the originals transplanted to a rock ensemble'. (Of course, this already means that they inhabit a quite different sound world from the original.) But 'Whole Lotta Love', which is based on Dixon's 'You Need Love', evidences a much more thoroughgoing transformation; for example, Headlam points out, the anacrusis motive of Dixon's song is stripped down into a repeated riff, while the song as a whole is expanded into a large-scale sectional form through the addition of what he describes as an improvisatory, psychedelic middle section. And he adds: 'The power and effect of "Whole Lotta Love" … derives in large part from the formal contrast and combination of the two seemingly disparate elements – driving, rhythmic blues-riffs and free-form psychedelic effects – into a coherent whole'.

The last two words represent the heart of the matter. 'Whole Lotta Love', Headlam is saying, is an artistic entity in its own right because it has its own characteristics and because these cohere to form an aesthetic unity. Moreover, he claims, these characteristics are representative of Led Zeppelin in general; songs like 'Whole Lotta Love' 'share musical elements with the original versions, but are transformed formally, timbrally, rhythmically, motivically, and harmonically into the defining features of the Led Zeppelin sound'. The songs, then, are not merely unified in themselves. They cohere within the *oeuvre* of Led Zeppelin as a whole, by virtue of what Headlam calls 'the unifying force of the band as "authors"' – in much the same way as each of (say) Beethoven's compositions acquires an added resonance through being related to the others. But of course, Headlam is much too sophisticated to identify 'authors' in this sense with the flesh-and-blood individuals who make up the band. Rather, he is availing himself of the structuralist and post-structuralist conception of the author as an interpretive construct; referring specifically to Foucault, he writes that 'in this view, the "author" constitutes a principle of unity among a class of works, somewhat akin to a theory, under which disparate works can be grouped together by their shared characteristics stemming from that authorship'. By demonstrating coherence, then, by showing how even apparently diversified musical configurations embody an underlying unity – in short, by operating in its most familiar manner – musical analysis provides an essential criterion of both authorship and the identity of the musical work that authorship underwrites.

This approach has the obvious advantage of making theory matter. In other ways, however, it might seem a perverse approach to the rock repertory. Given that the adaptation and re-adaptation of existing material is a commonplace of most popular music traditions, why should it *matter* whether or not Led Zeppelin are regarded as authors? Wouldn't it be more sensible to recognise that the practices of popular music undermine the idea of authorship as constructed within the western art music tradition? As Headlam explains, however, there is a historical context to these issues, and specifically to the distinction (which he adopts from Arnold Shaw) between the genuinely creative 'reworking', such as 'Whole Lotta Love', and the merely derivative 'cover' (for instance, 'You Shook Me'). 'Genuinely' creative, 'merely' derivative: there is nothing fortuitous about the ethical overtones of these terms. The negative connotations of the 'cover' date back to the mid-1950s, when North American record producers habitually took songs by black artists and re-recorded them (in a suitably toned-down form) for white audiences, using white musicians; it was notorious that the original artists generally made no money out of the songs' subsequent success, though the record and publishing companies did. And Led Zeppelin became tarred with the same brush as a result of their own failure to credit the artists from whom they adapted their songs. Several court cases resulted, among them Willie Dixon's successful action in respect of 'Whole Lotta Love'. (Despite this, the current CD release of the song – *Led Zeppelin II*, on Atlantic 19127-2 – still credits it solely to the four members of the band.)

There have recently been signs of a convergence of interest between music theorists and copyright lawyers;[5] had Dixon's action been taken in the 1990s, it is almost possible to imagine the kind of analytical demonstration which Headlam offers in relation to 'Whole Lotta Love' being invoked as evidence for the defence. Forensic musical analysis, if it may be called that, concatenates aesthetic value and intellectual property rights; the one is seen as endorsing the other. But what is revealing is that, at the same time as he argues in favour of Led Zeppelin's status as authors, Headlam also relates their derivative practices to Jimmy Page's and John Paul Jones' previous experience as studio musicians. As he puts it, in such a context 'originality was not valued as much as the replication or recreation of the appropriate style', and accordingly 'stylistic and quotational compilation was a natural outgrowth of the band members' previous studio experiences'. There are suggestions here of another possible

5. A conspicuous example is the special session on musical plagiarism at the 1994 Annual Meeting of the College Music Society in Minneapolis.

line for the defence ('m'lud, my clients didn't know what they were doing'). But that isn't what Headlam is primarily aiming at. What he is really doing is drawing a line between the two roles that Led Zeppelin and other rock musicians play in relation to their music: the role of 'genuine' composers (as in 'Whole Lotta Love'), and the role of 'mere' performers (as in 'You Shook Me' and 'I Can't Quit You Baby'). And his whole argument is constructed on the assumption that it is the first of these that is crucial in establishing aesthetic legitimacy.

In this way, Headlam recognises but does not theorise the derivative practices of rock music; his distinction between the rock musician as composer and the rock musician as author renders some of these practices amenable to interpretation along established music-theoretical lines, while eliminating others as viable objects of study. Again, he recognises the collectivity of the production and dissemination of popular music, but the whole thrust of his argument is to enable traditional style-analytical approaches to be applied to collectively-produced music without giving any further attention to its collectivity. The very title of Headlam's chapter betrays its underlying motivation; after all, 'authority' and 'identification' only emerge as 'questions' in the music of Led Zeppelin by virtue of their anomalous relationship to the art musical tradition, and in particular to the ideology of the autonomous work of art on which music theory, as we know it, is predicated.

II

On the last page of his chapter, Headlam writes that, in the genuinely creative reworking, 'the transformation must be so complete that the reworking and the original can stand side by side and both be accepted completely on their own terms, with an appreciation of the elements that bind and separate the two'. I would like to draw attention to two aspects of Headlam's language here: his prescriptive use of the word 'must', and the always revealing term 'appreciation', which sets up the idea of a critical observer (who else is likely to set the two versions of the music 'side by side' so as to assess the elements that 'bind and separate' them?), while neatly combining the connotations of education and evaluation. And the link between analysis, education, and evaluation – in short, the impulse towards canonisation – becomes even more evident in Walter Everett's significantly-named 'The Beatles as Composers: The Genesis of *Abbey Road*, Side Two'.[6]

6. In *Concert Music*, pp172-228. Side 2 of *Abbey Road* corresponds to tracks 7-17 of the CD release.

Everett relies principally on Schenkerian analysis to demonstrate the compositional properties (unity, coherence, and so forth) of the Beatles' music, and not only at the level of individual songs; he reads the whole of Side 2 of *Abbey Road* as a single 3-2-1 structure in C major, with a strong secondary emphasis on A major. Many critics, of course, are opposed in principle to the application to popular music of an analytical method designed for the elucidation of the Austro-German masterworks. But it might be pointed out in

Everett's defence that Schenkerian analysis has been fruitfully applied to many repertories for which it was not intended, ranging from medieval polyphony to *koto* music. And if it is objected that Schenkerian analysis ignores things like timbre and texture – which are often essential in popular music (and classical music too, for that matter) – then the viability of the Beatles' songs in a host of vocal and instrumental transcriptions demonstrates the central role that pitch structure plays in them. Finally, if the idea of analyzing the whole of Side 2 of *Abbey Road* as a single musical structure seems excessively ambitious or abstract – is Everett *really* claiming that listeners hear a prolongation of 3 right up to the beginning of 'The End'? – then exactly the same can be said of attempts to analyse entire song sets or operas in terms of tonal structure. The problem, if there is one, does not relate specifically to popular music.

What I want to emphasise, however, is not the technical aspects of Everett's demonstration of structural coherence, but its motivation. A less inclusively-minded analyst might present a Schenkerian reading of Side 2 and leave it at that. But Everett wants to go further; in his own words, he 'searches for an overarching theme in this group of songs that were chosen and joined in a very conscious manner'. He points out that the secondary tonal centre, A, is associated with lyrics that deal with selfishness and self-gratification, whereas the lyrics that emphasise generosity cluster round C. The interlocking tonal centres, then, have a symbolical as well as a purely musical significance. And seen in this light, 'The End' takes on the attributes of a moral as well as a musical resolution; 'McCartney', writes Everett, 'comes to the earth-shaking realisation that there is only as much self-gratifying love ("the love you take"), that of A major, as there is of the generous kind ("the love you make"), that of C major... [I]t seems rewarding to hear this uplifting message as a very personal final gift from McCartney to his mates, as well as from the Beatles to the world'. As I have written elsewhere, 'Such a reading is "rewarding" because it draws out from the music its potential for moral improvement. In this way Everett's essay shows how the music of the Beatles displays the ethical qualities that have since the Romantic period been seen as the hallmark of great art. It is in effect an exercise in aesthetic legitimation, an argument for the inclusion of the Beatles along with Bach and Beethoven in the basic curriculum of a liberal arts education.'[7]

Writing in the music appreciation tradition characteristically passes from the analysis of structural unity to the assertion of expressive and ethical value without it ever being quite clear exactly what the connection between these things might be. And this applies to Everett's essay, as I shall try to demonstrate through a close reading of his commentary on a passage from 'Here Comes the Sun' (which was credited to George Harrison). The passage in question is the six times repeated refrain 'Sun, sun, sun, here it comes', which is followed by four bars that build up an E^7 (V^7) arpeggio. Everett provides a Schenkerian analysis of the song, and on the basis of this he says as follows:

The voice leading of this middle section (mm. 31-32) consists of a series of

7. 'Music Theory and the Postmodern Muse: An Afterword', in *Concert Music*, pp422-39. To be fair, it is also a plea for the academic musical establishment to interest itself in the kind of music most inhabitants of the world actually listen to, a plea which recognises the linkage between canonic values and academic viability.

upper-neighbour chords ... that fall in fourths, from C to G to D to A, with a structural gentleness that enhances the suggestion of a meditative state. Harrison's meditation becomes truly transcendental when the dominant harmony of measure 33 reveals that the root of the A major chord of measure 32, heard six times as a point of tonal arrival, truly functions as an upper neighbour to the third of V harmony.... The composer's enlightenment is seemingly celebrated in measures 33-36 by the retransition's radiant unfolding of V^7 harmony, culminating on the exuberant seventh, D6.

We can pick out the sequence of words that conveys Everett's message in this passage: gentleness, meditative, transcendental, enlightenment, radiance. These richly suggestive terms tell a spiritual story by themselves, a story that Everett links plausibly enough with Harrison's contemporaneous interest in transcendental meditation. But they need to be tied in with the musical text if they are to be persuasive as a summation of the music's expressive trajectory.

And this is what Everett sets out to achieve. He explains the meditative quality of 'Sun, sun, sun, here it comes' (bars 31-2) in terms of the series of neighbour-note chords whose 'structural gentleness' is seen as arising, I take it, from their linear rather than harmonic derivation. But it is analytically just as easy, and arguably a good deal more straightforward, to reduce this passage to a series of parallel tenths (B-A-G# over G natural-F#-E), with only the C major at the first 'Sun' (bar 31) appearing as a neighbour-note chord. Seen this way, Everett's series of upper neighbours disappears, while the series of fourths becomes purely harmonic. Yet the impression of gentleness of which he speaks remains; I would ascribe it to the triple-metre interpolation and the very fact of multiple repetition, as well as to the measured sharpwards unwinding of the music from C to E; the effect is reminiscent of what Gerald Abraham called Chopin's harmonic 'daydreams'. Another consequence of the parallel-tenths reading is to underline the way in which the A chord at 'comes' (bar 32) is what Schenker would call a mere 'illusion of the foreground'; seen this way, it isn't necessary to argue, as Everett does, that its root 'truly functions as an upper neighbour to the third of V harmony' (and when I listen to the music I don't hear the A moving to G#). But again the overall impression remains as Everett describes it: a chord that locally sounds like a point of tonal arrival turns out to be an approach to a more structural harmony, giving rise to an opposition between adjacent hierarchical levels. Once again, though, we need to factor in those aspects of the music that are not captured in a Schenkerian analysis; if the final dominant creates a 'transcendental', 'radiant' effect, this is surely in large measure because of the way in which the tessitura and timbre of 'Sun, sun, sun, here it comes' brighten during the last three repetitions of the phrase. The effect is like the sweep of a band-pass filter and, for me at any rate, irresistibly suggests the build-up of light as the sun emerges from behind a cloud. Whether to speak of 'the composer's enlightenment' at this point amounts to more than a simple metaphorical transference I cannot say.

I am trying to make two points. The first is that the connection between the technical and the expressive stories that Everett tells really isn't that strong; you can change the analysis, but leave the expressive interpretation as strong or as a weak as it was in the first place. To this extent the argument from technical analysis to expressive interpretation might be seen as sleight of hand; indeed I would say it isn't really an argument at all, but a coupling of two quite distinct assertions. The other point arises from the multiplicity of viable analytical interpretations available even within the Schenkerian approach (for of course it is not my intention to suggest that Everett's reduction is *wrong*). If there is more than one way to read the passage, then there is something decidedly problematic about his repeated use of the word 'truly'; it amounts to no more than an exhortation in disguise. And this is by no means the only occasion on which Everett avails himself of such vocabulary, which embodies a rhetoric of authority that is deeply embedded in the music appreciation tradition and in music theory in general.[8] What I am drawing attention to is not the judgmental quality of Everett's language, for example when he speaks of McCartney's 'elegant polyphony' or the 'inspired composition' of *Abbey Road* as a whole; individual readers will have their own views regarding the assimilation of the Beatles into the masterwork tradition that is conveyed by such terms.[9] It is rather the way in which Everett deemphasises his own role as interpreter; he gives the impression that he is simply explaining the music as it is. His writing projects what Ellie Hisama has called the 'disembodied voice of authority'.[10]

III

I would like to set this rhetoric of authority into its historical context. And as good a way to approach it as any is via the idea of the 'authoritative edition' or *Urtext*, which has been the focus of so much musicological endeavour since the second half of the nineteenth century.

The aim of the *Urtext* is to remove the accretions of a work's reception (which may range from misprints that have acquired the force of law to the retouchings or bowdlerisings of later editors), and so to arrive back at the score as the composer intended it. As is the case with historically 'authentic' performances, then, the authority of the *Urtext* is a reflected one; its source is seen as lying in the composer's intentions, and both musicologists and performing musicians use the language of intentionality with what must strike any literary theorist as gay abandon. Music theory, however, replaces this language with one that curiously combines nineteenth-century metaphysics with post-structuralism. Writing near the beginning of the present century, Heinrich Schenker (from whom so much of present-day music theory emanates) specifically attacked the notion of composers' intentions, not so much on the grounds that they can never be established, but rather that they are irrelevant. The context of his remarks is what he sees as the 'false theory' of the church modes; even Beethoven, he says, in the quartet Op. 132, tried to

8. For instance, on p196 he refers to 'the true nature' of a particular chord in 'Because', when again the salient point would appear to be its ambiguity.

9. This assimilation goes back at least as far as Wilfrid Mellers's *The Music of the Beatles: Twilight of the Gods*, Faber, London 1973.

10. 'The Question of Climax in Ruth Crawford's String Quartet, Mvt. 3', in *Concert Music*, pp285-312, p285, footnote 2.

11. Heinrich Schenker quoted in *Harmony*, Oswald Jonas (ed), tr. Elisabeth Mann Borgese, University of Chicago Press, Chicago 1954, pp60-61.

12. Roland Barthes, tr. Stephen Heath, *Image, Music, Text*, Fontana, London, 1977, p148: 'the birth of the reader must be at the cost of the death of the Author.'

13. Heinrich Schenker, tr. and ed. John Rothgeb, *Beethoven's Ninth Symphony: A Portrayal of Its Musical Content, with Running Commentary on Performance and Literature As Well*, Yale University Press, New Haven 1992, p20.

14. Heinrich Schenker, tr. and ed. Ernst Oster, *Free Composition*, Longman, New York 1979, p128.

15. See Maynard Solomon, 'On Beethoven's creative process: a two-part invention', *Beethoven Essays*, Harvard University Press, Cambridge Mass 1988, pp126-38.

16. See Sylvan Kalib, 'Thirteen Essays from the Three Yearbooks "Das Meisterwerk in der Musik" by Heinrich Schenker: An Annotated Translation', Ph.D. diss., Northwestern University, 1973, pp160-62, 316.

compose according to this theory. But a great artist like Beethoven 'could not get himself to utter an artistic untruth, even though his conscious efforts were guided in that direction'.[11] Schenker conjures up a memorable image of the genius-composer who speaks with a voice that is not his own:

> In order to banish F major once and for all from our perception, [Beethoven] carefully avoided any B-flat, which would have led the composition into the sphere of F major. He had no idea that behind his back there stood that higher force of Nature and led his pen, forcing his composition into F major while he himself was sure he was composing in the Lydian mode, merely because that was his conscious will and intention.

In the final resort it is not, then, Beethoven who wields the pen; like Barthes, Schenker proclaims the death of the author.[12] However it is not the reader but the 'ultimate necessities of the masterworks' to which birth is thereby given.[13] Schenker's analytical method is devoted to explicating the intrinsically musical laws according to which the masterworks are shaped, and for him the possibility of explication in such terms represented the one demonstrably authoritative criterion of musical value. In his definitive theoretical work, *Der freie Satz*, Schenker enthusiastically cited Mozart's account of how he 'saw' his compositions in the form of a beautiful picture, with every detail of the music imagined 'not all in succession ... but somehow all at once'.[14] As is nowadays well known, this account is a nineteenth-century fabrication from the pen of Friedrich Rochlitz.[15] But that in no way lessens its significance for what might be called the ideological underpinning of music theory. The synoptic vision of a musical work that Rochlitz described, however fictitiously, embodies all the qualities that analysts have traditionally looked for in music: unity, identity, and authorial value. For Schenker, such a synoptic vision was the province of the creative genius alone; through analysis, however, it was possible to gain at least an intellectual apprehension of the genius's intuition.[16] In this way, unlike the *Urtext* of historical musicology, the *Urlinie* of Schenkerian analysis possesses an intrinsic authority: it recaptures what might be called the moment of truth in which a masterwork is revealed, so providing what Schenker (who did not favour the term *Urtext*) saw as the only adequate basis for a truly authoritative edition.[17] And in speaking of revelation, I mean to imply that, for Schenker, there is ultimately but one source of authority, one Author: true coherence, he wrote, is found only in 'God and ... the geniuses through whom he works.'[18]

Seen in this perhaps incongruous light, the agenda of Headlam's essay on Led Zeppelin may become more intelligible, and with it the remarkable accommodations he has had to make in order to assimilate rock into the interpretive paradigm of established music theory. Faced with the plurality of complementary versions that is normal in popular music, Headlam's first imperative is to establish an authoritative text for analysis, a rock equivalent of the *Urtext*. He becomes a little defensive as he explains his procedure:

One objection to my analytical treatment of the songs might be that Led Zeppelin continually changed and evolved in their concert versions of these songs... Despite these improvisations, however, each song has a fixed studio version that has become definitive, and formed at least the basis for improvisations on stage. I consider the studio versions justification for my analysis.

It might, of course, be pointed out that Headlam's use of the term 'improvisations' to describe Led Zeppelin's concert performances prejudges the issue; it is only by virtue of comparison with a fixed text that the concert performances can be described as improvisatory, and in this way the aural/oral aspects of rock performance are implicitly subordinated to a text-based theory.

Headlam's second imperative is, as we have seen, to construct a stable authorial persona in place of the contingencies of group composition; like Schenker, Headlam is concerned with what the music does, and not with the intentions of individual band members. When he speaks of 'Led Zeppelin', then, Headlam is referring to an authorial construct and not to a group of musicians – although his uncertainty as to whether 'Led Zeppelin' should take a singular or a plural verb betrays a certain lack of ease with this strategem. (Everett appears to be equally uncomfortable about this. At one moment he quotes George Martin's recollection that 'it was more a question of being a good team than of isolating individuals as being producer, arranger, or songwriter'; the next moment he is saying that 'Harrison's meditation becomes truly transcendental', or referring to 'the composer's enlightenment'.) And this brings to light the strange inversion that takes place in Headlam's adoption of the post-structuralist concept of the author. For Barthes, the death of the author represented a decentring of authority. But for Headlam it represents quite the opposite. By dint of replacing the flesh-and-blood author (or rather authors) with a theoretical construct, he achieves the extension to a new domain of a concept of authority that is unambiguously rooted in nineteenth-century value systems. Here is the source of the 'disembodied voice of authority' to which Hisama refers.

IV

It is the conflation of authorship and authority – a conflation equally characteristic of Romanticism and modernism – that explains the remarkable difficulty we seem to have in theorising, rather than swerving away from, multiple authorship in music; Schenker's ultimately theological (which is to say monotheistic) conception of authorship is only one instance of a quite general antipathy towards the idea of art being a communal production. What makes this difficulty remarkable is that multiple authorship is such a common phenomenon. It is by no means restricted to the group composition of rock and other forms of popular music;[19] notorious examples from the art music tradition include the Mozart/Süssmayr Requiem and Mussorgsky/Rimsky-

17. See Nicholas Cook, 'The Editor and the Virtuoso, or Schenker versus Bülow', *Journal of the Royal Musical Association*, Volume 116, pp78-95; and 'Heinrich Schenker and the Authority of the Urtext', in Tokumaru Yoshiko *et al* (eds), *Tradition and its Future in Music*, Mita Press, Osaka 1991, pp27-33.

18. Schenker, *op.cit.*, p160.

19. John Covach broaches this issue in 'Popular Music, Unpopular Musicology', in Nicholas Cook and Mark Everist (eds), *Rethinking Music*, forthcoming.

20. A contemporary instance is what might be called the 'compositions by committee' from the People's Republic of China, the best known of which is the *Butterfly Lovers' Concerto* (by Chen Gang and others).

Korsakov's *Boris Gudonov*.[20] The notoriety in each of these cases is a relatively recent phenomenon, and derives from the realisation that a highly valued text does not represent the unadulterated vision of its named composer. And it is not so long since another form of multiple authorship was the norm; Beethoven's symphonies were performed as reorchestrated by Wagner (or Bülow, or Weingartner, or Mahler), while period keyboard music was performed in Liszt's or Bülow's or Busoni's editions. The idea of the *Urtext*, like that of historical performance practice, goes back to the days of Brahms, but its acceptance as the norm of informed performance dates back hardly further than the 1960s. It is as if the tenets of modernism became established in performance only at the dawn of postmodernism.

In referring to reorchestrations and editions as instances of 'multiple authorship' I am, of course, broadening the term, and I propose to broaden it still further. Once again rock shows the way. Like most popular music, it involves collaboration and negotiation between songwriters, composers, band members or solo stars, producers, engineers, and record company personnel; the result is, to use Lisa Lewis's term, a highly segmented process of creation.[21] And a glance at the credits on recent CDs will show that this segmentation is increasingly recognised by the music industry; lyrics, music, production, even bass lines or samples may be individually credited. But as Lewis says,

21. Lisa A. Lewis, *Gender Politics and MTV: Voicing the Difference*, Temple University Press, Philadelphia 1990. p63. Of course an individual musician may, on occasion, undertake two or more of these roles.

> This system of assigning credit represents only a small modification in the model of individual authorship in that it maintains the focus on the individual rather than the collective. Because no consensus for collective authorship has emerged to counter the historical focus on the individual author (despite the collectivity of modern production), authorship discourse has become increasingly conflicted and contradictory under industrial capitalism.[22]

22. Lewis, *op.cit.*, pp64-5. A few bands credit their songs collectively to the band (for example, U2 General Public), or credit them to all individual band members (for example, early Genesis albums). I owe this observation to Robynn Stilwell.

Such segmentation is equally a feature of the art music tradition. The repertory as we know it today is the result of collaboration and negotiation between composers, performers, patrons and other sponsors, impresarios, editors and publishers. To be sure, the production process in classical music is less collective than that of popular music; it is easier to distinguish the different roles, if only because they are largely sequential (whereas in popular music production they are largely simultaneous). And whereas authorship in popular music is bewilderingly fragmented, with almost as many patterns of collaboration as there are songs, classical music is dominated by one massively important variety of segmentation: the division of labour between composer and performer. Nevertheless, if authorship discourse has become conflicted and contradictory in relation to popular music, the same applies to the art music tradition.

Lewis observes of popular music that 'Unaware of how segmented music production really is, the public will often assume that the performer is also the composer of the music.' And she adds that even when performers 'have no involvement in composition ... it is still possible to make a song one's own through the act of performance'.[23] For instance, Madonna's 'Material Girl' remains Madonna's 'Material Girl' regardless of the fact that Peter Brown and Robert Rans wrote the song, and Mary Lambert directed the video; in fact one of the aims of the video seems to have been to contribute to the construction of Madonna as a genuine author rather than an industry puppet (to borrow Lewis's terms again[24]). Now this argument will not transfer directly to the art music tradition; few listeners, surely, think that Nigel Kennedy wrote Brahms's Violin Concerto, and even Rubinstein did not appropriate Chopin's nocturnes to the extent that audiences thought he wrote them. (Indeed the case of Kreisler points to the reverse phenomenon: to gain credibility for your compositions, you have to ascribe them to someone else, preferably dead.) At the same time, people buy Kennedy's video of Brahms' Violin Concerto because it is Kennedy's and not because it is Brahms'; reissues of historic recordings are bought by music-lovers who want to hear Rubinstein, not to acquire yet another recording of the Chopin nocturnes. The segmentation of musical consumption – the fact that audiences are interested in performances and not just (in some contexts, not primarily) in compositions – is such an obvious fact of life that it almost seems redundant to mention it, and this is amply borne out by the advertising pages of any news-stand CD magazine. To identify authorship with the production of scores, or even with the kind of compositional manipulations Headlam discusses in 'Whole Lotta Love', is to narrow the concept to the point that it does not adequately reflect the ways in which music is either produced or consumed.

In the case of classical music, then, the contradiction in authorship discourse is essentially between how music is experienced and how it is written about. According to the publisher's blurb, the *New Oxford Companion to Music* (hereafter *NOCM*) is 'indispensable ... to a wide and diverse readership in search of information and enlightenment on anything to do with music'. Except, that is, for its performance! The *NOCM* finds a place in its two capacious volumes for composers known only to the musically erudite (Certon, Harding, and Horovitz, for example). But names like Furtwängler, Toscanini, Horowitz, and Michelangeli are simply not there; there is the 'music minus one' of my title. And as I see it, the explanation for this extraordinary state of affairs (imagine an encyclopedia of sport that did not mention any sportsmen or women!) lies in the way we use language in relation to music. We do not talk about music as if it were social experience; we talk about it as if it consisted of capital assets. We categorise the music of the past in terms of *works*, which essentially means authoritative texts coupled with an established (or at least accepted) provenance. Our vernacular for music is as irremediably platonist as our technical vocabulary for it; we talk about performance as performance *of* works, deriving a situated experience of music from an ideal, timeless entity. Language, in short, leads to the marginalisation of performance. Perhaps the best indication of this is the way in which, as I said, we establish the aesthetic legitimacy of performers by demonstrating that they aren't just performers but, in some sense, composers.[25]

23. *Ibid.*, pp65, 66.

24. *Ibid.*, p63; on Madonna, see p108. In brief, my argument regarding the video is that its multiplication of contradictory Madonnas (the singer-Madonna and the actress-Madonna) constructs, by implication, an over-arching persona: the author-Madonna (see Nicholas Cook, *Analysing Musical Multimedia*, forthcoming). This approach is, of course, very much along the Foucaldian lines that Headlam advocates.

25. A particularly revealing example of this strategy is Matthew Brown's ' "Little Wing": A Study in Musical Cognition', in John Covach and Graeme Boone (eds), *Analysing Rock Music*, forthcoming.

V

How should we think of the relationship between work and performance? Obviously this is much too big a question to answer comprehensively in an article like this (and anyhow I am not sure I know what a comprehensive answer would look like[26]). But all I am aiming for here is to suggest how issues of musical performance and multiple authorship intersect with one another, and for this purpose it will suffice to set out three models of musical performance: two impossible ones, and one possible one.

The first model arises from taking seriously the platonist language we use to talk about music; I shall call this the *NOCM* model. According to it, music consists of sonatas and symphonies in the same sense that literature consists of novels and poems, and the job of making these works perceptible is simply a technical one; performers, in other words, serve the same kind of function as printers – they have to be there, but we don't have to talk about them. Arnold Schoenberg spelt out the implications of this model quite explicitly when he told Dika Newlin that

> Music need not be performed any more than books need to be read aloud, for its logic is perfectly represented on the printed page; and the performer, for all his intolerable arrogance, is totally unnecessary except as his interpretations make the music understandable to an audience unfortunate enough not to be able to read it in print.[27]

Presumably Schoenberg said this on the rebound from some negative performing experience, or maybe he was being mischievous; at any rate, it is very hard to take the *NOCM* model seriously, because it is so massively out of kilter with how music is used in everyday life (though not, to be sure, with how it is used in the theory classroom, where one recording tends to be as good as another, and no recording is better still). And what is revealing is that when we *are* faced with an instance of performance that can be accommodated by the *NOCM* model, we tend to be unhappy about calling it a 'performance' at all. Suppose that you compile the score of Schoenberg's *Klavierstück* Op. 33a into a MIDI file, and output it through a Yamaha Disklavier grand piano: is this a performance, rather than a realisation? Is it a performance when a tape composition is played back in public (and do you clap, unless the composer is in the auditorium)? I don't think the issue is simply whether or not you can have a performance without performers. It is whether or not there is any scope for the performance to be other than what it is a performance *of*. In other words, I am suggesting that the idea of performance embodies a principle of *difference*, and this is something I shall come back to later.

The second, and equally impossible, model of performance is just the opposite; I shall call it the 'free improvisation' model. As I said with reference to Led Zeppelin, improvisation is generally understood as a relational term: one improvises against an existing text, or at any rate in relation to a specific

26. I do, however, know where to start: Lydia Goehr's *The Imaginary Museum of Musical Works: An Essay in the Philosophy of Music*, Clarendon Press, Oxford 1992.

27. Dika Newlin, *Schoenberg Remembered: Diaries and Recollections (1936-76)*, Pendragon, New York 1980, p164.

convergence of stylistic conventions. That is why the term 'free improvisation' has had to be coined, in order to denote a performance in which not only fixed texts but even predetermined stylistic conventions are abjured. The problem, of course, is that it is impossible to abjure stylistic conventions. To take a specific example, the recordings of Karlheinz Stockhausen's *Aus den sieben Tagen* draw on an easily recognisable musical style, that of the Darmstadt avant-garde; indeed they reflect the stylistic idiosyncracies of the individual musicians who played in them, and above all the personal style of Stockhausen himself. *Aus den sieben Tagen* is also interesting as an accommodation of the impossible project of free improvisation within the institutional and promotional structures of the 'work' tradition. Stockhausen's brief poetic texts, which were composed during a period of meditative retreat, evoke a desired effect and occasionally add a more or less inscrutable direction; they are so non-specific with respect to acoustic outcome that it is not obvious how you could determine whether a given performance was a performance 'of' one of the texts or not. (In other words, I have no idea how a case of plagiarism in relation to *Aus den sieben Tagen* could be advanced or defended, unless of course it had to do with copying the words.) The texts and the sounds are incommensurable; the relationship between the work and the performance consists of nothing but difference. And under these conditions the appropriateness of the term 'work' seems as questionable as the term 'performance' did in the case of the *NOCM* model. The texts published under the title *Aus den sieben Tagen* are probably most sensibly seen as documentation of the free improvisations which Stockhausen and his musicians recorded and marketed under the same name, rather than as in any useful sense a 'work' in their own right – even if they do appear in the Universal Edition catalogue.

Both the impossible *NOCM* model and the equally impossible 'free improvisation' model resist the division of authorship between composer and performer. The one possible relationship between work and performance – possible in the sense that it does not tend towards the denial of either the one or the other – builds on the idea of collaboration. Musical works (or compositions, or pieces, or events) are represented very differently in different cultures, whether by means of a notation that specifies sound qualities, or a tablature, or an aural/oral tradition, or a combination of these. But in every case the specification is significantly incomplete. For instance, western staff notation specifies pitch and rhythm comprehensively but is intrinsically vague about timbre and articulation; the increasing density of composers' markings since the middle of the last century only serves to highlight the limitations of the notation in these respects. Chinese *ch'in* tablature, on the other hand, specifies pitch, timbre and articulation in detail but is almost indeterminate as regards rhythm; it's as if there were a general principle that a high level of specificity in one domain has to be compensated by a corresponding lack of specificity in another. The consequence is that there is in each case an irreducible difference between the music as it is represented and the performance. And what I want to argue is that this difference constitutes an arena for meaningful collaboration and negotiation between composer and performer, or (to put it more abstractly but also more accurately) between the musical representation and its interpreter.

The most obvious way in which a musical representation can invite collaboration is what I suggested above: it is incomplete and requires further determination on the performer's part.[28] Beethoven's Ninth Symphony is a typical enough example. We have a more or less fixed text; at present there is a surprisingly large number of doubtful readings,[29] but their extent should not be exaggerated and will in any case diminish as editions based on a more careful and comprehensive examination of the sources become available. The text and a relatively continuous performance tradition, then, constrain the bounds of viable interpretation. All the same, from Mengelberg to Hogwood, from Toscanini to Harnoncourt, there is an astonishing range of difference between performances, which is also to say between text and performance. And then there is Furtwängler, who created great waves of tempo change in tandem with the prolongational spans of the music, inserting his own interpretation into the interstices of Beethoven's score.[30] Furtwängler spoke of the performer's need to 'laboriously reconstruct' the composer's 'overriding vision' of the work, but the result of his prolonged engagement with the symphony was a highly personal way of performing it;[31] Furtwängler's Ninth sounds (and was no doubt intended to sound) nothing like Mengelberg's or Toscanini's. And yet, of course, when we speak of Furtwängler's Ninth we do not mean to deny that it is also Beethoven's Ninth, or to suggest that Furtwängler's Ninth is something other than Beethoven's. The term 'Beethoven's Ninth' has the idea of collaboration already built into it.

In this way Beethoven's Ninth Symphony is, in a significant sense, indeterminate; if we don't easily recognise its indeterminacy – if we think of the Ninth Symphony as something fixed – then that may be largely the result of our platonic language for music. And if the Ninth Symphony is in a significant sense indeterminate, then this is all the more true of earlier music in which performers were expected to realise continuo parts, clothe slow movements in elaborate ornamentation, and so forth; as I said, composers of the last century and a half have moved towards ever more detailed specification of the intended performance. But this movement is not what it might seem. Paradoxically, it results in a second way in which musical representation can invite collaboration. At first sight Stockhausen's *Klavierstücke*, for instance, look like the last word in compositional specification, especially as regards time; complex rhythmic patterns are subsumed under irrational tempo proportions like 7:3, which are sometimes themselves subsumed under further irrational proportions. And the physical demands of performance – for instance enormous leaps without enough time to make them – sometimes approach or even exceed the bounds of possibility. But then that is just the point. Both in physical and conceptual terms. Stockhausen's *Klavierstücke* lie substantially beyond the limits of literal performance, and so demand a manner of performance that is other than the literal. They instigate a process of personal

28. For a general discussion see Michael Krausz, 'Rightness and Reasons in Musical Interpretation', in Michael Krausz (ed), *The Interpretation of Music: Philosophical Essays*, Clarendon Press, Oxford 1993, pp75-87. Krausz remarks that 'This incompleteness is a feature of the presently entrenched genre of musical interpretation' (p75).

29. See Jonathan Del Mar, 'Appendix 2: The Text of the Ninth Symphony', in Nicholas Cook (ed), *Beethoven: Symphony No. 9*, Cambridge University Press, Cambridge 1993, pp110-17.

30. Nicholas Cook, 'The Conductor and the Theorist: Furtwängler, Schenker, and the First Movement of Beethoven's Ninth Symphony', in John Rink (ed), *The Practice of Performance: Studies in Musical Interpretation*, Campbridge University Press, Cambridge, 1995.

31. Wilhelm Furtwängler (ed Ronald Taylor), *Furtwängler on Music*, Scolar Press, Aldershot 1991, p12.

interpretation; each performer has to decide what effect is intended and develop his or her own strategies for achieving it, resulting in a performance that is significantly different from what is specified in the score.

And I would maintain that this is not simply an idiosyncratic foible on Stockhausen's part, or the result of compositional systematisation running riot, but a significant (and largely unrecognised) characteristic of the avant-garde tradition. To take just one more example, Luciano Berio's *Gesti* for alto recorder achieves very much the same result, though by quite different means. Berio's notation, invented specially for this piece, separates the two principal sites of activity in playing the recorder: the mouth and the fingers. Each of these has its own stave, almost in the manner of a duet. At the beginning of the piece, Berio asks the performer repeatedly to finger one or two bars (any one or two bars) from a specified Telemann sonata movement; the mouth part, by contrast, consists of a dense series of highly specific notations for degrees of lip tension, fluttertongue, singing through the instrument, and inhaling. 'Because of the frequent "contradictions" between the tension of the lips and the finger positions,' writes Berio, 'and because of the speed of changing patterns, the resulting sound is unpredictable… Sometimes the instrument will produce no sound at all.'[32] In this way, Berio withdraws the specification of intended sound, the core aspect around which the other elements of recorder performance – finger movement, breath control, and the rest – are normally coordinated and integrated. He deconstructs the act of performance; he compels the performer to reinvent his or her technique, resulting again in a personal interpretation that cannot but be significantly different from any other performer's.

By means of an apparently high level of compositional specification, then, both Stockhausen and Berio force the performer to assume what can only be called a compositional role in relation to the audible outcome; the relationship between composer and performer, between the text and its interpreter, becomes one of collaboration, just as in the case of Furtwängler and the Ninth Symphony. In saying this I do not mean to suggest that these instances are exceptional, that performers fulfil a compositional role only in the paradoxical works of the avant-garde or when they are artists of Furtwängler's stature. On the contrary, I am arguing that *all* performance is in some sense compositional, or to put it more straightforwardly, that musical authorship is always divided. And what is telling in this regard is the passion with which musicians defend multiple authorship and the compositional indeterminacy that underlies it (though, to be sure, they do not put it this way). A good example is the crusade which Schenker initiated against nineteenth-century interpretive editors who buried the masterworks of the past under a mass of performance directions; Schenker's object was not simply that the editors' directions were wrong, but that to constrain performance in this way represented a miscomprehension of its essential nature.[33] This has become one of the basic principles of the historical performance movement.

But perhaps the most striking example is a negative one, like Sherlock

32. Luciano Berio, *Gesti* for Alto Recorder, Universal Edition, Vienna, UE 15627, p3.

33. As William Rothstein points out, this is why Schenker did not, and would not, publish 'performing' editions of his own. William Rothstein, 'Heinrich Schenker as an Interpreter of Beethoven's Piano Sonatas', *19th-Century Music* Volume 8, p24.

Holmes' dog that did not bark in the night. Until the intervention of modern technology, musical sound was evanescent; it was possible to hear how composer-performers played their own music only sporadically during their lifetimes, and not at all after their death. Nowadays, of course, everything has changed. We *know* how such composers as Bartok, Rachmaninov, and Britten played their music; realising the composer's intentions, as performers say, is something that we can now *do*. And yet, in practice, we don't. A pianist preparing a piece by one of these composers may well listen to the composer's recording, just as she or he may well listen to other pianists' recordings. And obviously she or he will hear the composer's recording as possessing a certain kind of authority that the others don't, just because it is the composer's. But few pianists will feel constrained to earnestly reproduce the wayward rhythms of Debussy's playing, any more than conductors are likely to lovingly replicate Elgar's portamenti; that just isn't what performance is about. Performers sometimes justify this by arguing that composers rarely play their own music well, and that we shouldn't too readily identify their recordings with their *real* musical intentions. But the truth is much simpler than this convoluted argument would suggest. Classical performers are just the same as pop stars: to borrow Lisa Lewis's terms again, they see themselves (and are seen by the audiences) as authors, and not as puppets.

VI

34. Lawrence Rosenwald, 'Theory, Text-setting, and Performance', *Journal of Musicology*, Volume 11, p61-2.

Lawrence Rosenwald has praised Richard Taruskin's seminal study of the Ninth Symphony in performance on the grounds that Taruskin 'moves precisely from a consideration of various actual performances back to a fresh analysis of the piece – not the piece itself, whatever that phrase might mean, but the piece considered as something existing in the relation between its notation and the field of its performances'.[34] Insofar as music theory is defined as the study of music in terms of 'the piece itself', rather than the contexts of its production and reception, 'that phrase' has generally been assumed to mean the score. This isn't to say that theorists don't care about anything except scores; of course they care about how music is created, how it is performed, how it is experienced. But theory is focused around scores, and this is justifiable not only on methodological grounds (because you have to start *somewhere* when studying any complex phenomenon) but also because Western art music has always signified as writing and not just as sound. By this I mean that composers' choices and historical influences are tied up with how things look, or make sense, on the page; they can't be understood purely in terms of how the music sounds. Indeed the sometimes incommensurable relationship between what is seen and what is heard is an integral part of the collaboration between composer and performer, the negotiation between text and interpreter, that I have already described.

But obviously the score-based approach will not work with rock or with any other primarily aurally/orally-transmitted music, at least without major adaptation. If the only difference between art music and rock were that one relies heavily on scores and the other doesn't, then the strategy adopted by Headlam and Everett might work well enough: as I said, they treat acoustic texts (that is to say recordings) as if they were a kind of score, indeed as if they were kind of *Urtext*. The trouble is that no rock text functions like an *Urtext*. What we might call the *Urtext* model consists of a hierarchy with a dominant text (say a Beethoven symphony) at its apex, and a variety of subordinate and derivative texts at the lower levels (bowdlerised editions, adaptations for school orchestra, arrangements for chamber groups or keyboard, and so forth). But rock does not offer this; instead, it offers a multiplicity of texts, the sum total of which defines a rock song as a cultural entity. This is not to say that no version of a song is ever privileged over others; groups like Rush, who explicitly aim for an accurate reproduction of their recordings in live performance, are in effect treating these recordings as a kind of *Urtext*, and the same might be said of the 'look-alike' bands modelled on the canonic groups of the past. But such privileging of a single text is by no means the norm in rock; much more representative is the multiplicity of concert versions to which Headlam refers, all too briefly, in his analysis of Led Zeppelin's music.

The *Urtext* model, to which Headlam and Everett seeks to assimilate rock music, works from the top down; there is a kind of 'trickle-down' effect – as Conservative politicians say – from the authoritative text to successively lower, and less authoritative, layers of the hierarchy (such as Led Zeppelin's 'improvisations on stage', to repeat Headlam's phrase). But an approach predicated on multiple texts and multiple authorship – the model I want to advocate for theorising rock – equally has to work the other way round, that is to say from the bottom up. What does this mean? For one thing, it means trying to understand performances in their own terms, rather than immediately referring them to whatever they are supposed to be performances *of*; a perhaps useful way to express this is that we need to attend to the illocutionary force of rock texts, to what they *do* rather than what they represent.[35] (Examples include the embodied meanings that Robert Walser has discussed in relation to heavy metal, and Allan Moore's 'sound-box' model of production; but the field of performance also includes the extensive networks of stylistic and intertextual references on which rock performers play, quite independently of the particular songs they are performing.[36]) For another thing, it means taking advantage of the full range of available rock texts, by which I mean not only original releases, single remixes, concert recordings, and remakes, but also demos, studio tapes, and covers; to use Rosenwald's word, it is the field of these texts, the network of differences between them, that must be the primary object of study if rock is to be understood as a performing art. One problem here, as John Covach has pointed out, is that much of the necessary spade-work has still to be done.[37] It is easy for theorists to forget how far their apparently effortless readings depend on the kind of so-called 'positivistic' source studies that have barely begun in popular music.

But I said that music theory means the study of musical *pieces*, and I am not

35. On illocutionary force see J.L. Austin, *How to Do Things with Words*, Harvard University Press, Cambridge, Mass 1962; see also my chapter 'Analysing Performance, and Performing Analysis' in Nicholas Cook and Mark Everist (eds), *Rethinking Music*, Volume 1, *op.cit.*, Oxford.

36. On embodied meanings in heavy metal, see Robert Walser, 'The Body in the Music: Epistemology and Musical Semiotics', *College Music Symposium*, Volume 31, pp117-26; on the 'sound-box', see Allan Moore, *Rock: The Primary Text: Developing a Musicology of Rock*, Oxford University Press, Buckingham, 1992, pp106-110; on stylistic and intertextual references, see Philip Tagg, 'Analysing Popular Music: Theory, Method, and Practice', *Popular Music*, Volume 2, pp37-67.

37. John Covach, *op.cit.*

suggesting that, in order to theorise music as performance, we should somehow forget about theorising it as composition. What I am suggesting is that there is no clear line between composition and performance, and that we therefore have an opportunity to transfer much of what we have learnt about music as composition to music as performance. For instance, insights into compositional choice and strategy, the extent to which a given choice entails others, the defining and solving of problems, the contribution of conventional schemata towards such definition – all these approaches are as applicable to performance as they are to composition (and between them they account for a great deal of what is done under the name of musical analysis).[38] And I am also suggesting that, just as we traditionally understand performances in terms of the works they are performances of, so we need to understand works in terms of the performances they emerge from. In other words, we need an analytical approach that doesn't presuppose the identity of a song as a meaningful whole, but lets it emerge in answer to the question 'by virtue of what are these texts received as representations of the same abstract entity, such that what is heard derives meaning from being heard in this context?' As I see it, Headlam's article on Led Zeppelin is important to the extent that it problematises the issue of identity in rock music. But I also see it as importantly misguided in that it offers a premature solution, a quick fix whose source lies in nineteenth-century conceptions of authorship and authority, and not in detailed scrutiny of the available texts.

Why have theorists concentrated on rock, and particularly progressive rock, while virtually ignoring other genres of popular music? The answer is perhaps obvious: because of the coincidence of the Romantic values underlying music theory and the Romantic values underlying rock. Borrowing Lisa Lewis's terms for the last time, we could say that rock musicians, and in particular progressive rock musicians, see pop musicians as industry puppets but themselves as genuine authors. And for this reason the top-down, masterpiece-oriented rhetoric of traditional music theory fits rock all too well; it builds upon the existing ideology of rock instead of subjecting it to critical examination. I am suggesting, then, that a bottom-up approach (pursued in conjunction with the top-down one) is a precondition for a more critical engagement of theory with rock, and for any engagement with pop. But I don't want to stop there. We have become used to theorising western art music in almost exclusively top-down terms, subordinating the music of all periods to a Romantic ideology, and so ending up with a picture that is not so much incorrect as incomplete and unbalanced. The most obvious manifestation of this is the lack of any serious theoretical engagement with performance, and by this I mean not only the finished performance but the process of negotiation with a text, of collaboration with its composer, that takes place in rehearsal. To hear an interpretation evolving as musicians rehearse is to hear multiple authorship in action. Rehearsal is one of the principal sites for the making of musical pieces, and yet it seems to be unknown to theory.

If we were to stick to western art music, with its tradition of authoritative

38. Matthew Brown's ' "Little Wing": A Study in Musical Cognition' *op.cit.*, is a rare example of the application of a problem-solving approach to performance.

scores and its adulation of composers at the expense of performers, then we might just about be able to avoid rethinking the top-down approach that is built into music theory as we know it today. Popular music, where multiple texts and multiple authorship are the norm, makes such rethinking *almost* inevitable – but not quite, as Headlam's and Everett's articles show. At the risk of being prescriptive, I would like to suggest that instead of somehow forcing popular music into the framework of current theory, we would do better to use popular music as a catalyst for opening theory up to new perspectives, to the benefit of our understanding of all music.

'Alaturka Fantasies': Deceit, the Voice and the Arabesk Stage in Turkey

Martin Stokes

Critics of a form of popular culture known in Turkey as Arabesk point with great frequency to its lack of concern with 'reality'. Indeed, it is not difficult for the unsympathetic observer to criticise Arabesk for its failure to deal with the real world. The texts of the songs and the films portray a world of doomed lovers, manipulated by unscrupulous employers, deceived by the objects of their obsessive love. Betrayal leads to humiliation and self-destruction. A focus on the texts can lead one inexorably to the conclusion that Arabesk invites people to blame fate (*kader*) and the 'lying world' (*yalan dünya*) for their problems, to give up their dreams of social improvement, and to abandon themselves to the ephemeral and solitary pleasures of drink and smoke. This conclusion is precisely that of a generation of social commentators whose condemnation of Arabesk brings together republican disquiet with the 'degenerate' orientalism of the genre, and the pessimism of mass-cultural theory.[1] It somewhat wilfully ignores a world which is, in many ways, diametrically opposed: the exuberant and intensely social domain of Arabesk performance, in clubs (*gazino*), public concerts and wedding-salons (*düğünevleri*) across the country, where, to quote Nilufer Göle's memorable phrase, 'men and women belly dance to a *piyanist-santör* under disco lights in order to work out their urbanite fantasies and Alaturka proclivities ...'[2] This 'fantastic' urbanism and orientalism is highly significant to the audiences and fans of Arabesk, a genre which is sometimes referred to as *fantezi*. In this article, I discuss fantasy in Arabesk texts in relation to a distinct aesthetic (one which simultaneously reflects and constitutes social reality) of veiled and ambiguous truths, truths concealed by ornament and artifice, which can only be found through a search and a leap of faith. This aesthetic shapes Arabesk fanship, and explains much of its utopian appeal to the marginalised and peripheralised in contemporary Turkey. In using the 'textualising' theoretical apparatus of mass cultural theory and cultural studies, I will argue that critics and sympathetic observers alike have missed a vital point which can only be grasped through performance.[3] The more general direction of this article is towards replacing a tendency to think of events in terms of texts by a consideration of texts as events.

1. See Ertan Ergibel, *Niçin Arabesk Degil?*, Sureç, Istanbul 1984 and *Türk Müzigi*, Edebiyat Fakültesi Basimevi, Istanbul 1993; Nazife Güngör, *Arabesk: Sosyokulturel Açidan Arabesk Müzigi*, Bilgi, Ankara 1990; for a more general view, see Georg Stauth 'Local Communities and Mass Culture', Georg Stauth and Sami Zubeida (eds), *Mass Culture, Popular Culture and Social Life in the Middle East*, Frankfurt 1987.

2. Nilüfer Göle, 'Istanbul'un Intikami' in *Istanbul* 3, 1992, pp36-9.

3. I draw heavily from Michael Gilsenan's much cited discussion of lying in Lebanon 'Lying, Honour and Contradiction', Bruce Kapferer (ed), *Transaction and Meaning*, Institute for the Study of Human Issues, Philadelphia 1976.

LOCATING PERFORMANCE

Whilst Arabesk is ever present in its mass-reproduced form, Arabesk performance is curiously difficult to locate in contemporary Turkish urban life. The best known Arabesk singers, in particular Müslüm Gürses, Ibrahim Tatlıses, Orhan Gencebay and Ferdi Tayfur, rarely perform in public for the majority of their fans. Some, such as Orhan Gencebay, have virtually quit the Arabesk stage in Turkey, having established the prestige and material means to concentrate on producing films, cassettes and performing at a small number of lucrative live events, mainly abroad. Others, such as Müslüm Gürses, play to wealthy audiences in Istanbul's more expensive *gazino* clubs. Less well established singers tend to view the world of the 'market' (*piyasa*), with its round of appearances at weddings, circumcision festivities, downmarket *gazinos* and provincial fairs, and its exorbitant demands on their time, energy and health, with resigned dismay. Cassette piracy and the ongoing deregularisation of the Turkish media airwaves has meant in recent years that cassettes do not ensure a singer's livelihood unless they can produce and distribute them themselves, and achieve sales rivalling those of Orhan Gencebay and Ibrahim Tatlıses.[4] For those who cannot, and are obliged to accept deals with the cassette companies, cassettes are seen as advertisements for more lucrative live performances, a means of keeping oneself in the public eye, and not a means of earning a living. It follows that as soon as singers are able to rely on large enough cassette sales, and establish some control over the means of cassette production, or, indeed, branch out into other enterprises, they perform less and less frequently. There are, in other words, factors rooted in the entrepreneurial tendencies of musicians in Turkey and the cassette industry which make singers more or less likely to perform in public, and explain why the biggest stars are so rarely to be seen.

4. Tatlıses' 1988 cassette, *Allah Allah* has sold over 2 million copies in Turkey.

The largest and most conspicuous of these occasional live performances are called 'People's Concerts' (*Halk Konserleri*) run in large cities by the municipality as part of civic celebrations, such as fairs and festivals. One of the most notable of these in Istanbul are the concerts given in Gülhane Park. The situation of the park is significant: it is near the Sirkeci train station and the Eminonu ferry terminal and hence relatively easy to reach by train and boat from the suburbs and squatter towns of this sprawling city. This contrasts with the large concerts of Turkish art music and highbrow 'Turkish pop' held in Rumelihisar, by the Bosphorous, which can be reached easily by car, but only with difficulty by public transport, and even then at some expense. I attended a whole series of Gülhane Park concerts in the summer of 1990, joining thousands of fans in long waits for performers who were seldom advertised far in advance (for fear of attracting what are often considered to be 'unruly' crowds). When eventually they did appear, the performances were often brief. Some 70,000 people had come to hear Müslüm Gürses on 25 August 1990. Not only was his performance brief, but his heavily amplified voice was lost in layers of distortion and reverb. Since this crowd had travelled large distances and had put up with innumerable hardships to hear this celebrated voice, they might have had grounds for complaint, but this was not in evidence. A distinct aesthetic of evasiveness appears to lie at the heart of the event, an aesthetic which has at least one dimension in the amplification of the voice.

Alan Lomax's much discussed cantometric codings[5] have illuminated techniques of vocal raspiness, 'width', 'noise', glottalisation, sobbing and heightened speech, and the 'wordiness' of song styles, and subsequent ethnomusicologists have begun to explore the cultural significance of vocal techniques.[6] In many contemporary contexts in urban, industrial societies outside of Europe and North America, the electronic amplification of vocal sound is a distinct feature of vocal performance, modifying and adapting techniques which were conceived without this form of amplification in mind. Perhaps assuming some kind of technological neutrality, in which the microphone and amplification system merely makes the voice louder, or perhaps interpreting it in terms of the destruction of non-western traditions which they (explicitly or implicitly) seek to preserve, ethnomusicologists have seldom commented on this striking fact. High amplification and distortion can hardly be ignored in the context of Arabesk performance. They have a distinct effect, which can only be intentional, even if it is not the subject of much verbal elaboration. This effect might be summarised as follows: the words and the person uttering them are concealed, or masked, placing the listener in the position of having to search for the voice in a mass of ambiguous and opaque acoustic data. Many Turkish musicians stress the paramount importance of being understood (*anlaşılma*), of revealing meaning (*mana*) and expression (*ifade*). Critics of Arabesk in fact explicitly point to the lack of verbal articulation skills amongst Arabesk singers: their *diksiyon* is poor, and one cannot make out what they are saying. The distortion of the text and the voice introduced by heavy amplification and reverb in live performance therefore constitute something of a puzzle.

This practice might be understood as part of a more generalised aesthetic. These concerts are magical, glittering affairs, monuments to the world of imagination and artifice (*hayal*) which pervades Arabesk films, texts and promotional posters. The warm-up acts which precede the main star are punctuated by magicians and belly-dancers, who construct (in ways which are too often dismissed as proletarian kitsch) their own complex domains of intrigue and sexual artifice. *Hayal* has a double-edged quality to it. On one hand it celebrates a certain belief in the creative powers of fantasy. In their discussion of the pictorial 'performances' of Tiepolo, Alpers and Baxandall discuss a quality of *incantesimo*, 'the shaping power of fantasy',[7] which, in spite of the remoteness of this cultural reference, aptly evokes the fantastic creative powers of the voice that seem to be celebrated on the Arabesk stage. On the other hand, *hayal* has an almost mocking tone, evidenced by the way the term is used most commonly in the Turkish language. *Hayal* describes daydreams, unrealistic fantasies. Someone's *hayal gücü* (capacity to fantasise) is the object of amused contempt. Failure to attain one's desires is described as 'broken *hayal*'

5. Alan Lomax, *Folk Song Style and Culture*, Transaction Books, New Brunswick 1968.

6. See especially Steven Feld, *Sound and Sentiment: Birds, Weeping, Poetics, and Song in Kaluli Expression*, University of Pennsylvania Press, Philadelphia 1982.

7. Svetlana Alpers and Michael Baxandall use performance as a metaphor throughout their recent study of Tiepolo, *Tiepolo and the Pictorial Intelligence*, Yale University Press, New Haven 1994. Tiepolo 'performs' the repertoire of Veronese. Architecture and lighting conditions determine Tiepolo's art in the same way that the acoustics of a building are taken into account in musical performance. The concept of performance is now to be found in unexpected critical quarters.

(*hayal kirikligi*). This negative weighting of the term cannot be far from the experience of large Arabesk concerts. What one had come so far to hear and see, and endured so much for, was hardly visible or audible, vague, immaterial and brief. At the heart of the performance there is then tantalising play upon revealing and concealing, an aesthetic principle which is, of course, central to the art of the belly-dancer and magician, but no less significant for the Arabesk singer. The whole performance may indeed be construed as *hayal*: an elaborate play on appearances, facades and shadows. Whilst few Turks comment upon the event in these terms, my use of the notion of *hayal* may not be entirely inappropriate. The word *hayal* is used to refer not only to imagination and fancy, but also to the shadow plays (*hayal oyunlari*) which constituted the staple form of popular urban Turkish visual culture before television and cinema.

The notion of *hayal* suggests that Arabesk performance organises a certain set of relations between 'the real' and fantasy. Western popular music provides a point of comparison. On one hand, the 'rock myth' produces authenticity in rock performance, that is to say, moments of direct, 'real' communication between souls which are untrammelled by concerns with technique or technology.[8] The performance stage, with its implied hierarchies, ranks and differences, is ritually crossed by communication and physical movement. In rock myth, a separation is established only to be broken down. Other kinds of rock and pop construct a world of self-conscious artifice; spectacular and fantastic, but distanced and remote. This form of performance is no less concerned with the production of 'the real' than the first, as Baudrillard points out in a much cited discussion of Disneyland and Watergate.[9] Disneyland suggests a world of real, serious adult concerns that lies outside the gates. Watergate suggests a world of real politics which does not involve the systematic and deceitful abuse of power. However, as Baudrillard argues, neither of these propositions are possible any longer. The real world has ceased to exist. Reality itself is a simulation, an affect of power.[10] This radical deconstruction of the notion of fantasy alerts one to the creative efforts that are involved in the production of truth and fantasy on stage, which produce in turn a common sense set of assumptions about what and where a stage is, and what appropriately happens on it.

The practices and traditions of the Arabesk stage are quite different in this respect. The Arabesk star remains isolated and aloof, absorbed in a world of introspective, masochistic emotion. Müslüm Gürses (for many, the performer who pushes the rhetorical and performative tropes of Arabesk to their extreme) did not once verbally address the audience, and looked upwards into the lights for the entirety of a 45 minute set. 'Real life', however, literally wanders across the stage. In most cases these incursions are part of the concert traditions of the Turkish stage. People queue up at the sides in order to walk across each number and present the singer with a kiss, some flowers and a request. Populists, such as Ibrahim Tatlıses, often engage in a bit of brief banter with the presenter if they are particularly cute infants, but this is a

8. Simon Frith, ' "The Magic That Can Set You Free": The Ideology of Folk and the Myth of the Rock Community', Richard Middleton and David Horn (eds), *Popular Music 1*, Cambridge University Press, Cambridge 1981.

9. Jean Baudrillard, *Simulations*, Semiotext(e), New York 1983, p23.

10. *Ibid.*, p42.

highly ritualised exchange (songs for flowers). Often however, these incursions are unexpected and violent. In 1989 Bülent Ersoy, a flamboyant transsexual singer of Turkish art music and Arabesk, was shot on stage by a young man when she refused to sing a nationalist song. This event shocked me, but passed with relatively little comment in the Turkish press, and seemed on the whole to be the subject of little more than amused comment on the part of my Turkish friends. In an equally shocking sequence of events, a female Arabesk star, Bergen, was abducted by her estranged husband (who had previously maimed her by pouring the acid from a car battery over her face) and killed outside a cafe in Adana in 1988. The event could have been lifted directly from any of her films, and the Turkish tabloids were not slow to make the connection. But this event was simply presented as one of scores of 'crimes of honour' (*namus davaları*) which occur in Turkey on a daily basis, and did not attract disproportionate attention. What appeared to me as dramatic and horrifying confrontations of fantasy and reality seemed to pass with little comment in Turkey.

If I am correct, this has much to do with the fact that the world of Arabesk is not as clearly bracketed from (or aligned with) the world 'outside' of Arabesk as the processes of bracketing in other traditions of performance. In the 1980s, Arabesk was constantly evoked in discussions and debates about the state of the nation. In these discursive contexts, Arabesk came to stand for a principle of 'Eastern' disorder, frequently aligned with Kurdish separatism and 'Islamic fundamentalism' (*irtica*), but was also extended to cover a number of changes in the texture of social life that had accompanied the civil government of Turgut Özal's Anavatan Party (ANAP). Arabesk came to stand for everything from kitsch commercialism to the pretensions of *nouveau riche* provincials, from the disasters of schemes designed to alleviate Istanbul's chronic traffic problems to the cynicism and hypocrisy of those in high office. 'Everything is Arabesk', people never tired of telling me. Under these circumstances it was not surprising to Özal's critics that the ANAP governments should have made such concerted efforts to court Arabesk stars, and (successfully) sought to reverse the official media bans that had excluded the genre from official state airwaves.[11] Özal undoubtedly did seek to identify Arabesk as a liberal issue as a part of a wider programme for Islamist *laissez-faire* politics. The extension of the Arabesk stage to cover (or stand for) 'everything' was therefore part of a set of distinct ideological programmes pursued simultaneously by the Islamist right and their critics during the late 1980s. Critics perceived Özal as an 'Arabesk type', of precisely the kind that appeared to be flaunting their newly founded social acceptability in society at large.[12]

It is difficult to resist concluding that Özal did indeed begin to model his political performance on the Arabesk stage. His style of political oratory made use of a heavily Arabised lexicon, clearly interpreted in Turkey as a means of aligning the speaker with Islam and the south-east, and opposing him or her to the secularist, modernist reform tradition of Mustafa Kemal Ataturk and the Turkish left who have now appropriated it. It was not only the words he used,

11. See Martin Stokes, *The Arabesk Debate: Music and Musicians in Modern Turkey*, Clarendon Press, Oxford 1992 and Meral Özbek, *Popüler Kültür ve Orhan Gencebay Arabeski*, Iletisim, Istanbul 1991.

12. See Hasan Cemal, *Özal Hikayesi*, Bilgi, Ankara 1989 (especially pp154-185) for a lengthy left critique of Özal which discusses this very point, amongst other things.

but the way he pronounced them, emphasising continuities rather than differences between Arabic and Turkish, in precisely the same way that the vocal techniques of Arabesk emphasise continuities between Turkish and Arab singers. Finally, crucial political decisions were made in flamboyant and theatrical ways, ways which set a highly personal seal on his politics. In 1990, the ANAP government had decided on a policy of caution in relation to the impending Gulf War. The risk of losing the Iraqi oil pipeline revenues, and a huge transit trade, were such (to the business elite which dominated ANAP decision making) that Turkey's 'traditional' pro-NATO stance became highly problematic. This cautious position was outlined at a briefing for foreign diplomatic correspondents on 8 August, but the event was interrupted by a communication from the Anatolian News Agency: Özal had decided to cut the pipeline, and commit Turkey to the western alliance against a 'traditional ally'. As Robins perceptively suggests, the theatrical nature of this decision had been carefully planned: 'Özal evidently wanted to personalise the decision and deliver it with a flourish ... (the Kemalists) balked at both the style and the substance of Özal's brash partisan action'.[13] The style encapsulated a certain defiant machismo, associated with a stereotype of south-eastern masculinity paraded by many Arabesk stars on stage (notably Ibrahim Tatlıses). One is reminded forcibly of Messick's assertion that 'semen and words are the associated ejaculations of potent male maturity':[14] indeed, vocal performance in Arabesk is often described in terms of ejaculation (*bosaltma*). Seen as a style of performance which encodes the values of what is perceived in Turkey as a distinctly 'south eastern' machismo, Özal's politics did indeed have much in common with Arabesk.

The flow of Arabesk into 'the real world', and vice versa, is therefore of intense political significance. This reflects a more general problem. The question of the relation between what happens on the stage (given the widest possible use of the term) and what happens elsewhere cuts a deep course through cultural analysis. However one defines a certain mode of heightened, stylised human behaviour, in particular through the use of terms such as 'performance' (or indeed 'ritual'), one immediately runs up against the question of how one distinguishes performance from non-performance. The involvement of theories of performance and play with anthropological thinking about ritual, notably in the work of Victor Turner, was accompanied by a move away from substantive definitions of ritual/performance towards the notion of process. In his later work, Turner increasingly thought in terms of ritualising as opposed to ritual, playfulness as opposed to play, stressing the possibilities of the penetration of the everyday by playful, performative, ritual processes. In the hands of his students (notably Richard Schechner) the deconstruction of the categories of ritual, performance and play as separate, bounded forms of activity or consciousness was almost complete, leaving them in a somewhat contradictory position. Can performance be meaningfully separated from non-performance? Schechner negotiates this issue in an interesting way. Whilst on one hand he defines performance as 'twice-behaved

13. Philip Robins, *Turkey and the Middle East*, Pinter, London 1991, pp70-71.

14. Brinkley Messick, *The Calligraphic State: Textual Domination and History in a Muslim Society*, University of California Press, Berkeley 1993, p79.

15. Richard
Schechner, *The Future
of Ritual: Writings on
Culture and
Performance*,
Routledge, London
1992, p1.

16. *Ibid.*, p40.

17. Ernestine Friedl,
*Vasilika: A Village in
Modern Greece*, Holt,
Reinhart and Winston,
New York 1962.

18. Michael Herzfeld,
*The Poetics of Manhood:
Contest and Identity in a
Cretan Mountain
Village*, Princeton
University Press,
Princeton 1985; and
Michael Gilsenan,
'Domination as Social
Practice:
Patrimonialism in
North Lebanon:
Arbitrary Power,
Desecration, and the
Aesthetics of
Violence', *Critique of
Anthropology*, Volume
6, Number 1, 1986,
pp17-37; and 'Word of
Honour', in Ralph
Grillo (ed), *Social
Anthropology and the
Politics of Language*,
Routledge, London
1990.

behaviour'[15] with definable properties involving display, risk and danger, on the other, he is insistent that the frames that indicate performance are not necessarily fixed and consensually marked (as Bateson suggested), but often 'absent, broken, porous and twisted'.[16] He provides a number of telling examples: the change of mood in a sporting performance following serious injury, or performance games (which he calls 'dark play') enacted by his NYU students involving others as participants and spectators without their being aware that a performance is taking place. Here, performance is something that slips in and out of non-performance life, often ambiguously marked.

The most influential discussions of performance and rhetoric in social anthropology have come from the study of Mediterranean societies in which so much social activity is carried out under the scrutiny of village audiences – an aspect of everyday life that led Friedl to define rural Greece as an 'agonistic' society.[17] More recently, Herzfeld and Gilsenan have provided influential arguments stressing the necessity for understanding moral codes in the Mediterranean world, particularly those surrounding notions of machismo and violence, in relation to rhetoric and performance.[18] These writers consider performance in terms of the production of meaning and the play of power in everyday life. Performance often runs along the basic fault lines of power. As Gilsenan points out, in North Lebanon the key performers are the lords and their *agha* henchmen. Their every utterance, gesture and act is imbued with the deepest significance, whilst those that cannot compete in the honour stakes lead lives of insignificance and humiliation. However, as he points out, in performance, nothing can be taken for granted. A performance can be undermined, upstaged, and turned into high comedy, backfiring disastrously on those who have tried to stage manage the event.

These observations, rooted in the ethnographic observation of small town life in the Mediterranean, have not only made a significant impact on social anthropology, but are extremely valuable in the context of a discussion of the more explicitly 'staged' world of musical performance. Here too, nothing can be taken for granted. As we have seen, the performers can suddenly find themselves involved in the Schechnerian 'dark play' of somebody else's performance as in the case of Bülent Ersoy and Bergen. It might also be undermined by the drunken antics of a member of the audience. Since much Arabesk performance takes place in *gazino* clubs selling alcohol, particularly an aniseed spirit known as *rakı*, this kind of event was one I often witnessed. The *rakı* table has many of the characteristics of a stage, around which a highly formalised performance of male solidarity and prestige takes place. Robust shouts of appreciation from the *rakı* table to the stage are an art form in themselves (as elsewhere in the Middle East), eliciting laughter and applause from those seated nearby. When these give way to flamboyantly bestowed gifts of money or flowers, or elaborate improvised dance routines in front of the singer, one is aware not only of the multiplicity of performances going on at any one moment, but the struggle involved in occupying centre stage, and filling it with one's own voice. At the centre of this complex performative politics is the presence of a solo voice, a voice which is applauded, heckled and even killed.

LOCATING THE VOICE

Most Arabesk stage names play on the word for voice – *ses*, as in Tatlıses ('Sweet voice'), Gürses ('Strong voice') or Güzelses ('Beautiful voice'). The voice is central to Arabesk, but it also has a clearly delineated dramatic role in performance. As in most urban Turkish genres, musical functions are divided between the solo vocalist (*Sanatçı*) and backing musicians (*müszisiyen*). Musical specialisation of this kind has a long history in Middle Eastern and Asian musical cultures, and its precise contours are subject to change over time. As far as Arabesk is concerned, it is less in evidence in early Orhan Gencebay recordings (for example, *Bir Teselli Ver* of 1969), which make use of a band which is essentially a small group of soloists grouped around a single microphone. The opposition of soloist to group has emerged later under studio conditions in which there is the possibility of setting soloists in dramatic antiphonal opposition to a large monophonic group of strings. This is given visual emphasis in performance, during which the band remains seated, and the soloist moves around the stage alone. Güngör identifies this practice with Zeki Müren's use of a hand held microphone and a T-shaped stage in the mid 1970s.[19] One figure mediates, sometimes a western-style conductor, and sometimes the lead violinist, who stands behind the singer, often following him or her around the stage, accompanying when he or she is engaging in free rhythm improvisations, and conducting with his gestures when the full band is to play. In this sense, the choreographic impact of live performance elaborates a socio-musical play on the relationship of a single figure (shadowed by solo instruments) to the group. It is striking, given the clarity of this opposition, that the outline of the solo voice is rendered ambiguous by technology and vocal timbre. The remaining part of this article is concerned with how one might understand some of the apparent contradictions in the role of the solo voice.

In cultural terms, the solo (musical) voice has a complex and dramatic role to play. Two accounts of the dramatic role of the voice serve to illustrate two points: one is the way in which the voice reveals unutterable secrets, unutterable largely because of their threat to political stability. The second concerns the separation of the voice from the process of communication. In both accounts the voice undergoes a process of transformation, and attains a separate and autonomous existence, demanding action to be taken on its account. I heard the first when discussing Muslim prohibitions on musical expression with a musicologist in Istanbul, Suleyman Şenel. He had come across a story collected by a local folklorist from his own home province, Kastamonu, on the Black Sea coast. A *vezir*, the story goes, had two servants, one of whom he kills and has thrown down a well. He instructs the other servant not to tell anyone. The servant cannot keep the secret, and in desperation

19. Nazife Güngör, *Arabesk: Sosyokulturel Acidan Arabesk Müzigi*, Bilgi, Ankara 1990.

shouts it down another well. Reeds grow at the bottom of the well, which local musicians use for making musical instruments. As they play these instruments, the reeds reveal their grisly story (*kammazlık yapıyor*), and the corpse is pulled out of the well. Interestingly, the story is given overtly as a reason why music is a sinful activity. Although one can only speculate, the story might be taken as arguing the opposite: that there are unacknowledgable moral imperatives which make music necessary. Two elements stand out in the context of this discussion: one is that the musical voice utters unspeakable and politically disturbing truths, and the other is that the voice is, as it were, detached from its original owner.

A second account is constituted by a film released in Turkey in 1986 called *Ses – The Voice*, starring Tarik Akan. Tarik plays a political prisoner who has been kept in prison during the military regime of 1980-3 and subjected to torture. He returns to his home village in a traumatised state. This village is a small fishing community on the Aegean which has become a resort for wealthy Turkish tourists. One of these tourists is a loud swaggering man, who has turned up with his family for a holiday. Tarik overhears him in a cafe, and the realisation slowly dawns that this is the voice of one of his torturers. He abducts him, blindfolds him without allowing him to see his own face, and takes him to a ruined village. The film ends with the tables turned: Tarik sitting in stony silence in front of his blindfolded and bound persecutor, who implores him to speak and reveal his identity. Here once again the voice reveals a truth which has been concealed in the brutal play of power in the torture chamber. The oppressor is exposed. Here as well the voice is detached from its body. The very disembodiment of the voice is the axis upon which the dramatic machinery turns. Tarik extracts his revenge both by mimicking his own ordeal, but also by doing the precise opposite: leaving the bound and blindfolded man untouched, and denying him the sound of his own voice. These ways of imagining the voice and its powers are widespread in Turkey. Here we see them in two very different narratives relating to specific political issues: the first concerned with the relationship between two competing moralities (a censorious Islam and a notion of political justice) and the second concerned with human rights, revenge and the reconstitution of civil life after the 1980 coup.

These ways of imagining the voice resonate with Arabesk performance in a number of striking ways. Firstly they resonate with themes of diguise, deceit and betrayal which are a pervasive element of Arabesk song texts and films. Secondly, they resonate with the aesthetic of voice in the context of live performance. What is striking about performance is the way in which the physical qualities of the sung voice mask the words, and, paradoxically, interrupt the line of communication between the singer and the audience. Taking these two points in turn, one can begin to put together an aesthetic of the voice and performance in ways which allow for a different set of interpretations of the themes of deceit and betrayal in Arabesk lyrics, and of Arabesk as a more general phenomenon.

THE 'LYING WORLD': DECEIT AND BETRAYAL IN ARABESK TEXTS

The theme of truth and falsehood pervades Arabesk lyrics, and the plot of Arabesk films would be impossible to imagine without it. The lyrics used by certain Arabesk singers make more use of it than others, and within the repertory of each singer, notions of truth and falsehood are inflected differently. The most embittered rhetoric against deceit and deceivers is to be found in the texts of songs sung and popularised by Müslüm Gürses. There is scarcely a single song which does not contain this kind of language, which is deployed in varied ways. 'The lie' is imagined as part of a temporal sequence, in which the singer realises 'now' that everything he had believed to be true was falsehood and betrayal; the physical substance of his past imagined self fades, in the way that the image of a photograph fades over time leaving nothing but paper ('parchment/cloth'). By extension, future dreams are impossible:

Mazideki güzel günler demek yalandı
Bir köseye atilan resmim bez oldu

So the beautiful days of the past were a lie
My picture, thrown into a corner has turned to parchment
('Hüzünlü Günler', Müslüm Gürses)

Aldanman cocuksu mahsun yüzüne
Mutlaka terkedip gidecek bir gün

Don't let your childlike innocent face be deceived
He/she will definitely leave you one day and go
('Gidecek Bir Gun', Müslüm Gürses)

The most common rhetorical posture is to damn everything that occupies his entire life as a lie. The sloganistic intensity of these lines, emphasised by their elliptical grammar (with subjects, objects and persons left undefined or ambiguous) is typical of many of Müslüm Gürses' lyrics. The moral problems implied by this rhetorical posture are colossal in a society which is almost entirely Muslim. Whilst speculative strands of Islamic theology have allowed for the possibility of thinking of creation as a veil of appearances which separates the believer from God until it is removed by death, God and his creation are theoretically indivisible. To describe any aspect of creation as being imperfect, let alone 'a lie', approaches blasphemy. Arabesk singers flirt with poetic ideas adopted from popular Muslim traditions in Turkey. The description of the world (of human affairs) as a lie in opposition to divine truth is one which has many parallels in heterodox beliefs, literatures and practices which are widespread.

Doğruluk misali kendisi olmus
Kulunu yalancı yapmış yaratan

Whilst he (God) has become the apogee of truth
The creator has made his slave a liar
('Kullarına Kul Yapmis', Müslüm Gürses)

Of course, the force of these lyrics cannot be interpreted simply in terms of the 'persistence' of traditional beliefs in the disenchanted urban context of modern Turkey. They dramatically isolate the subject, and point to the injustice of a decidedly contemporary world which promises much but delivers nothing, and elucidate the pathos of the individual forced to conform to an ethos which opposes his or her deepest and truest desires. They also identify the listening subject as the possessor of a secret (*sırr*), that is to say someone who understands the concealed emotional order of the world. These kinds of positions, outlined in the Arabesk of Müslüm Gürses, are recognised by most Arabesk fans to be extreme, and the *Müslümcular* (at least those who attend his live performances) are correspondingly drawn from the most peripheralised and disadvantaged sections of urban Turkish society.

The Arabesk of Ibrahim Tatlises is more varied. This reflects the fact that he came to Arabesk in the late 1970s as a singer of the rural repertoire of south-east Anatolia. This folk song repertory contains almost no reference whatsoever to the themes of deceit and betrayal, which are peculiar to Arabesk. His best known songs, composed for him by well established Arabesk musicians, are, however, full of references to these themes, notably his 1981 cassette *Yalan, The Lie*. The obsessive concern with deceit and betrayal emphasised in this song are peculiar to Arabesk. This can be noticed in a comparison between repertories, which otherwise, even to Turkish listeners, have much in common. Rural folk music songs which are popularised either through television and radio or the commercial music industry make minimal reference to lying and falsehood. Similarly, these themes are hard to find in the art music repertoire, which has also overlapped with Arabesk in the careers of singers such as Zeki Müren, Muazzez Abaci and Derya Caglar. There are more exceptions here, since practitioners of the art music genre write lyrics and compose with the commercial imperatives of an Arabesk dominated market in mind. One should also note that the co-option of Arabesk stars (including Ibrahim Tatlises) by the Özal government is widely perceived to have meant the end of traditional, doom laden, opposition Arabesk. The more recent cassettes of Ibrahim Tatlises (post-*Allah Allah*) have been evaluated by some as the product of a process of *şenlenmesi* ('jollification').[20] This must be seen as a consequence of a celebrated government-led attempt to doctor the masochistic and fatalistic elements of the music and create a so-called 'painless Arabesk' (*Acısız Arabesk*). In Ibrahim Tatlises' more recent hits, the emphasis is indeed on the pleasurable and often successful pursuit of the love-object, and not the obsessive, masochistic introspection of failure.

A similar point might be made in relation to an Arabesk star whose work has long been appropriated by intellectual commentators in Turkey as the acceptable face of Arabesk, Orhan Gencebay. The fascination with Orhan

20. Meral Özbek,
Popüler Kültür ve Orhan Gencebay Arabeski,
Iletism, Istanbul 1991, p120.

Gencebay resides largely in his phenomenal skills as a prolific composer and instrumentalist. Even fans are inclined to find his vocal skills and lyrics of negligible interest. However, if one turns to his lyrics, one notes the way in which he rhetorically interrogates the 'traditional' themes of Arabesk. Notably, a track on his 1987 cassette *Dünya Dönüyor* puts the case against blaming fate and the lying world. The insistent refrain, 'It is not a lie, it is not a lie' (*yalan değil*) might almost have been conceived as a direct rejoinder to Ibrahim Tatlises's 1981 cassette, *Yalan (The Lie)*. He makes the point of his oppositional stance to the traditional pessimism of Arabesk quite clear in an interview accompanying a transcription of the music and its text. Fate, explicitly, is *not* blamed for his separation from his lover.[21] It is also worth noting that a period in which the lovers have been together is implied.

21. See interview, 'Önce Yasamak' in *Müzik Magazin* 7, 1987, p20.

The theme of deceit and betrayal in Arabesk song texts is accompanied by an equally insistent discussion of deceit and betrayal in Arabesk films. In *Bende Özledim*, Ferdi Tayfur plays a villager adrift in Istanbul whilst waiting for a visa to work in Libya. He is injured in an accident by a wealthy man who sets him up in business (as a mechanic) by way of compensation. Whilst working in Istanbul, his father dies and leaves him some money, with which he sets up his own haulage business. A woman who lives in the same apartment seduces him under the illusion that he is rich and Ferdi is pressured into marrying her. She eventually gets bored, gambles away most of Ferdi's hard earned cash, and then begins an affair with Ferdi's patron. Inflamed by jealousy, Ferdi drives after the lovers in his lorry, crashes, and loses his sight. His sight returns whilst he is recovering in the house, but he keeps this from his wife. When his former patron comes to the house to resume his affair with Ferdi's wife, Ferdi catches them in the act, rips off the bandages covering his eyes, shoots both and runs back to his natal village. The police surround the house and he is taken away. The neat dramatic symmetries of Ferdi's betrayal and the means by which he takes his revenge do not need to be laboured. However, it is worth noting that the success and poetic justice of his revenge are short lived. In the end the rich have had their pleasure, and the poor and virtuous man has been humiliated and eventually crushed by the forces of law. He is denied even the release of death. As with the song lyrics, there are many permutations upon this theme in Arabesk films. A few even have happy endings, but these are a distinct minority. What his film does have in common with most others however is the dramatic isolation of the virtuous 'traditional' village man, exploited, exposed and humiliated by the agents and conditions of modern urban life.

Explanations of these pervasive themes of deceit and betrayal by critics of the genre are subsumed by the general outlines of mass cultural critique mentioned earlier. The films and song texts point to the inevitability of failure and humiliation, and invite listeners to blame fate and the 'lying world'. Arabesk, according to these explicitly condemnatory readings, is a recipe for passivity and morbid introspection, which deflects the people's awareness of class and the material conditions which enslave them, and prevents any possible realisation of the practical political steps which they might take. Crude attempts to quantify the damage done by Arabesk have even been produced by social psychologists. In all of these accounts, Arabesk is seen at best as a resourceful way of 'making do', sometimes likened explicitly to the informal transport arrangement of the *dolmuş* (shared taxi) system. As with these riotously dangerous and illegally overcrowded *dolmuş*, one can, indeed, must, admire the resourcefulness of Arabesk, but condemn the final result as no substitute for sound, rational planning.[22]

22. Ertan Egribel, *Nicin Arabesk Degil?*, Süreç, Istanbul 1984.

These readings of Arabesk have been challenged by more recent commentators in Turkey. Meral Özbek's study of Orhan Gencebay is motivated by a recognition of the failure of the Turkish left to come to a politically useful understanding of Arabesk.[23] Drawing heavily on the work of the British New Left, Özbek's book marks the decisive entry of cultural studies into indigenous debates on culture and modernity. Just as the British New Left mobilised themselves around a recognition that mass cultural critique had allowed the right a free hand in appropriating popular culture for its own ends,[24] Özbek is also dismayed by the ease with which rightist political parties have been able to co-opt Arabesk. Özbek's study mounts a counter-offensive, introducing for the first time the notion of *popüler* (popular) as opposed to *kitle* (mass) culture into the Arabesk debate. This makes possible interpretative strategies for perceiving Arabesk in terms other than those of passivity and despair. On one hand, she points to utopian currents in Arabesk imagery, based on feeling and emotion rather verbal political argument. On the other, she notes that the insistent imagery of the true love of the poor man being crushed by the deceitful machinations of the rich man indicates a certain *paylaşımcı rasiyonalite* ('sharing rationality') which opposes the dominant capitalist ethos. She also notes the ways in which Arabesk functions as a kind of Geertzian cognitive map enabling the listening subject to negotiate their way around the more problematic aspects of Turkish modernity. The pervasive imagery of the taxi-driver, car mechanic and lorry-driver in Arabesk films and lyrics lends substantial weight to this theory. The book's method focuses on discussion with Orhan Gencebay and careful analysis of the song texts and films, situated in an extremely detailed historical analysis of the Turkish recording and film industry. The problem is that this material cannot yield the conclusions that Özbek needs. Gencebay's lyrics, as stated above, do present a more complex discussion and problematization of themes of love, fate and betrayal than those of other Arabesk singers, but otherwise they provide very little in the way of explicit political commentary. However, in direct question and answer situations, Gencebay's sympathies for Özal are hard to ignore. The answer to the problem of how to construct more sympathetic interpretative strategies in relation to Arabesk cannot be gained from these channels, as Özbek clearly understands. They can, however, from music, and more specifically, from the voice. As she points out:

23. Meral Özbek, *op.cit.*

24. See Michael Kenny, *The First New Left: British Intellectuals after Stalin*, Lawrence and Wishart, London 1995.

> Those who comment on Orhan Gencebay's Arabesk by looking only at the words and particularly those words which concern 'fate', miss out on the

vocal element which gives meaning to the words and completes the meaning by revealing the emotions.[25]

25. Meral Özbek, *op.cit.*, pp104 (my translation).

At this point, we can return to the role of the voice.

THE SEARCH FOR THE VOICE

Özbek's problem lies not so much in her lack of confidence when dealing with the question of musical structure, but the lack of models within musicology and ethnomusicology for understanding the significance of the voice in a genre such as Arabesk. The important point that she makes seems to me to be wrong in one crucial respect. Özbek's model of the voice in Arabesk suggests a kind of 'topping up' process, whereby the words outline a meaning and the vocal performance fills it up, with nuance and colour. Vocal performance in Arabesk seems to be doing something a little more complicated: it actually obscures the words, or adds something which operates at cross purposes to the words. There are at least two vocal performance traditions in Arabesk which achieve this in different ways. On one hand there is a group of Arabesk singers who have come into the genre as accomplished folk music singers. The techniques known in Turkish as *gırtlak* are significant here, and Ibrahim Tatlises is the most notable exponent. *Gırtlak* involves what western singers would call a 'head voice', with a heavy glottalisation of most phonemes. That is to say, vowels and consonants are formed as far back in the throat as possible, in ways which permit glottal fricatives (somewhat similar to the Arabic *ain* which is absent in spoken Istanbul Turkish) and a range of vocal ornamentations peculiar to this style. A second element of this style involves singing at the top of the tenor register. All of Ibrahim Tatlises' phenomenal vocal skills are concentrated into a range of about an octave. These techniques produce vocal formants which are electrifyingly (and uniformly) loud, and create a stupendous vocal 'presence'. The aesthetic thrill of this singing style, which is a persistent topic of discussion and evaluation on the part of fans, is bound up with these two techniques appropriate to *gırtlak*. However, both techniques systematically obscure the verbal message. Vowel formants disappear at the top of a tenor register, and consonants blend into a mess of glottal fricatives.

The second set of techniques (which are seldom distinguished carefully from the first) relate to the art music tradition. Here the influence of Müzeyyen Sennar, a singer who developed a highly idiosyncratic handling of Turkish art music texts in the 1960s and 1970s is critical. Zeki Müren, Adnan Şenses and Bülent Ersoy, in one way or another, owe much to her style. This might be characterised by the foregrounding of a certain kind of ornamentation which largely obscures the musical and textual structures it is supposed to ornament. The central techniques here are a wide ranging vibrato, covering as much as a tone, and accompanied by a kind of 'mouthing'. The amplitude of the vibrato varies constantly (quite unlike European *bel canto*), almost as if the singer is at random turning a vibrato knob up and down. A second technique involves a varied degree of vocalisation, in which the words are 'sung' to anything from a whisper to a shout. In the latter case, the introduction of a certain tracheal quality to vocal production is in evidence, giving the impression of violent bodily forces squeezing the melody and the words out of shape. This somewhat crude attempt to summarise techniques that are acquired after years of training might be concluded with the brief observation that these vocal techniques fade in and out, modifying every word and melodic fragment upon repetition. Bülent Ersoy's recording of *Geceler* provides a perfect illustration of all of these techniques, in which every repetition of the long drawn out notes on the word *geceler* (nights) is performed in a different way. Zeki Müren's *Kadere Davacıyım* presents a more dramatic scenario. A long closing sequence over a repetition of a phrase from the chorus and the word *davacıyım* ('I protest') has a straight rendition progressively giving way to sobs and shouts. The body consistently, and dramatically, erupts into the verbal text, not only modifying it but obscuring it. As stated at the outset, this masking process is compounded by the use of high amplification and reverb in performance.

In conditions of performance it seems necessary to understand the voice *not* as a vehicle for communication, but a material, physical object which occupies space and is capable of concealing what it is usually held to reveal. One explanation of this is the fact that so much of the what Arabesk is known to 'talk about', in particular Kurdish identity (Ibrahim Tatlises is Kurdish) and homosexuality (as in the case of Zeki Müren and Bülent Ersoy) is literally unsayable. In this sense, Arabesk enables discussion of politically unmentionable but unavoidable issues. Here, what is hinted at is known. In another sense though, what is hinted is not necessarily 'known'. The voice conceals rather than communicates, and *what* it conceals is not really the point. In this sense, the voice is something that one enters and explores. Two analyses of the voice come to mind. John Shepherd's discussion of gender and timbre[26] contrasts the 'pure' sounds of classical musical performance with, drawing on Barthes' much-cited essay on the grain of the voice,[27] the 'jouissance' which is to be experienced in more 'dirty' voices, which involve participation and timbral completion on the part of the listener. This kind of vocal 'grain' is a more conspicuous component of the popular aesthetic. Shepherd develops Barthes' argument by discussing the gendered properties of popular timbre, in particular those 'male' and 'female' voices which shape the socio-musical domain of male and female sub-cultures. The second analysis of voice is part of an intriguing history of opera. Michel Poizat provides a Lacanian reading of Barthes's discussion of *jouissance*. Poizat points to the way in which the operatic voice obscures the text, and the way in which operatic drama might be seen in terms of the presentation of a disembodied, objectified voice. The heroes and heroines approach self-annihilation as a subject in order to offer (themselves) as pure voice.[28] The heroic role of tenors and sopranos is particularly significant. Firstly, as Poizat argues, the production of high notes 'destroys meaningful articulation' and secondly it aligns the objectified voice with persistent cultural notions of the divine qualities of high voices.[29] In operatic

26. John Shepherd, 'Music and Male Hegemony' in Richard Leppert and Susan McClarey (eds), *Music and Society: The Politics of Composition, Performance and Reception*, Cambridge University Press, Cambridge 1987.

27. Roland Barthes, 'The Grain of the Voice' in *Image, Music, Text*, tr. Stephen Heath, Fontana, London 1977.

28. Michel Poizat, *The Angel's Cry: Beyond the Pleasure Principle in Opera*, Cornell University Press, Ithaca NY 1992, p35.

29. *Ibid.*, p130.

drama the voice becomes the object of a quest. The objectification of the voice in opera reflects and mediates a set of drives established in early infancy. The first cry of the infant is a pure, bodily, utterance. The mother hears and responds. At this crucial juncture, the child realises that the cry has achieved something, and the second cry is bound up with, and shaped by the response of the mother and the child's knowledge of that response. The second cry is circumscribed through having been brought into the signifying field of the other. The first cry is thereby 'lost', and becomes the object of a psychic quest for a 'lost phonic materiality'.[30]

30. *Ibid.*, p102.

Those traditionally engaged with the study of 'others' have been inclined to deplore the universalising claims of these kinds of theory (since they perpetuate hegemonic intellectual structures), but in both cases, taken as models which could be adapted to fit different situations rather than theories which can be scientifically applied, they provide a clue to a complex problem of interpretation. Shepherd suggests the potential significance of precisely the kind of 'dirty' sounds of which Arabesk is full, but the gender equation breaks down in Arabesk. Whilst the 'head' voice is foregrounded in *gırtlak* singing, and *gırtlak*, through its demands and assertiveness, is only sung by the most macho singers (such as Tatlises), the more varied singing (which involves but is not restricted to 'chest voice') has no clear gender connotations, and is sung by straight male and female art music singers as well as by transvestites and transsexuals such as Zeki Müren and Bülent Ersoy. Poizat's discussion of objectified voices resonates well with Turkish Arabesk and the varied cultural models through which the voice is understood in Turkey, even though cognitive psychology has a long way to go before his Lacanian explanation could be successfully 'proved'. In the Turkish context, the voice is clearly considered to be something separable and physical. However, it is not so much the object of a quest (as in Poizat's reading of the operatic tradition) but a tactic, a resource which is used in a complex game of concealment and revelation.

Both arguments suggest the possibility that one searches 'in' the voice for something, whether reassuring, politically resonant gender stereotypes or orgasmic memories of the first cry. It is not my intention to argue against either of these propositions, although the first seems more easily demonstrable than the second, in Turkey at least. Arabesk sets up, in addition, a different kind of vocal quest. The performance constructs a listener who is obliged to search in the mass of vocal sound for the melodic line and the text. Both the text and its physical location in vocal performance are shrouded in ambiguity. One is obliged, if one wants to 'understand', to enter into a complex interpretative domain. In this domain the line between what is there and what isn't, the line between truth and fantasy, is kept vague. The listening subject is one who searches for the voice, and, through the search, becomes a member of a community of people who possess the interpretative ability and esoteric power to determine a truth which others simply cannot see. This is a familiar configuration for those who have studied the highly emotive, utopian politics of oppressed, subaltern groups, groups who are denied a voice in formal contexts and whose only realistic strategy is to maintain a sense of esoteric dignity and to wait for their day to come.

Arabesk offers not one, but a variety of such quests. The significance of these highly idiosyncratic voices lies in the differences between them. In reducing Arabesk to a single type of voice organised around the expression of *acı*, pain, critics miss the point of the multiplicity of Arabesk voices, in and through which listeners define themselves and the nature of the community of fans to which they belong. One can sketch out a few possible positions on the basis of this article. In the voices of Bülent Ersoy and Zeki Müren, the listener searches for a text through vocal techniques which articulate mercurial, violent passions. The flow of these techniques across the text (the tradition of what is called 'word painting' in the context of western European art music history is quite absent) dramatises a struggle between control and disorder. The voice of Ibrahim Tatlises constructs a heroic figure pitting his masculine physical resources in an effort to communicate against overwhelming odds. The most interesting figure is Müslüm Gürses, 'Baba' ('Daddy') to his fans. This is a man with few obvious star qualities. He is (even to his fans) extremely ugly. In opposition to the 'thin' (*ince*) voice of Ibrahim, that of Müslüm is 'thick' (*kalin*). His on-stage persona could almost be defined as anti-charismatic. On one long bus journey in which I was seated next to a young Müslümcu, Abdullah, who was a plasterer from Gaziantep on his way to a disco-dancing competition in Istanbul, I jotted down a phrase which he kept repeating: '*dinleyeceksin ... anlayacaksın: dünyanın bir Türk babası varmış*' ('Listen and you will understand: there is just one Turkish *baba* in the world'). The notion of Müslüm as 'Baba' preoccupied me, and at first I missed the significance of the repetition of the phrase '*dinleyeceksin ... anlayacaksın*' ('keep listening ... you will understand'). The grammar of this phrase clearly marks the process of quest on the physical territory marked by the 'thickness' of Müslüm's voice. The idea of Müslüm Gürses as the focus of a popular, utopian politics that flourished in the atmosphere of despair on the peripheries of large Turkish cities in the 1980s is thus neither inappropriate nor implausible. But this only makes sense in relation to the voice in performance. By interpreting Arabesk as text, its critics have missed the point.

From 'Messin' Around' to 'Funky Western Civilization': The Rise and Fall of Dance Instruction Songs

Sally Banes and John F. Szwed

INTRODUCTION

> Listen while I talk to you
> I tell you what we're gonna do
> There's a new thing that's goin' around
> And I'll tell you what they're puttin' down
> Just move your body all around
> And just shake …

'Shake', by Sam Cooke, was recorded at the height of the dance instruction song craze of the 1960s. In this genre – which originated in African American dance and music traditions – choreographic instructions are given or 'called' while the dance is in progress. This article will focus on the dance instruction song wave of the 1960s, tracing its roots and its decline. Along the way we will analyse the rhetoric of the song, both in terms of its lyrics and its music.

In her book *Dance Notation*, Ann Hutchinson Guest calls notation 'the process of recording movement on paper'.[1] The development of written notation for dance since the Renaissance in Europe and America has been a fluctuating process of analysis in which the dance is described in terms of a body of shared dance values. For instance, Baroque dancing masters in Europe wrote down floor patterns and the ornamentation of footwork and turns with the assumption that arm movements, carriage, and other aspects of dance style were common knowledge, while Laban sought ways to describe scientifically information that was not only quantitative (body parts in use, divisions of time and space), but also qualitative (for example, energy use).

The use of notation for theatrical dancing requires a system that is fully descriptive, since the choreographer's patterns are not necessarily shared by others. Social dancing, however, may be encoded in much more abbreviated ways, partly because of its close relationship with its music and partly because its sequences are redundant in several ways.

However, the dance instruction song is a form of dance 'notation' that is part of an oral, rather than written tradition, and is popular, rather than élite.[2] This popular genre of American song, which clearly has African roots, has appeared in mainstream culture in successive waves, beginning just before

1. Ann Hutchinson Guest, *Dance Notation: The Process of Recording Movement on Paper*, Dance Horizons, New York 1984.

2. Alec Wilder, *American Popular Song*, Oxford, New York 1972, uses the term ' "dance instruction" song'. We use his term, but without the quotation marks. Marshall and Jean Stearns, *Jazz Dance: The Story of American Vernacular Dance*, Macmillan, New York 1968, call these 'dance-songs with instructions'.

World War One with songs such as 'Messin' Around' and 'Ballin' the Jack'. It has spread from the United States to become an internationally known phenomenon. Thus in the twentieth century, the broad dissemination of African American social dance instruction to audiences of all ethnicities and classes through the mass media – by means of sheet music, records, radio, television, and cinema – has taken its place alongside the dance manual and the private lesson of the Euro-American elite that dated at least from the Renaissance.

The dance instruction song, spread via these modern mass technologies, has a privileged place for the historian of culture and performance, because it is *about* the mass distribution of dance and bodily knowledge, and thus has served crucial aesthetic, social, and political functions. It has played an important part in the democratisation of social dancing; it has spread African American dance forms and styles throughout Euro-American culture and other, subaltern cultures; and it has helped create a mass market for the work of black artists. In short, the dance instruction song has contributed to the formation of a syncretic dance culture – and bodily culture – in multicultural America.

The dance instruction song in mass culture may be traced at least to the beginning of the twentieth century, although it has longer vernacular roots in the African American community. Even though songs have occasionally been used to teach European dances – the Beer Barrel Polka, or the Lambeth Walk – it is important to note that the dance instruction song primarily comprises African American dances, from Ballin' the Jack and the Black Bottom, to the Twist, the Loco-Motion, the Mashed Potato, and the Funky Broadway, to the Hustle, the Smurf, and the Vogue. The song/dance titles range from the internationally recognisable, like the Charleston, the Shimmy, the Madison, the Boogaloo, the Frug, the Limbo, the Jerk, the Watusi, and the Bump, to the more obscure, like the Georgia Crawl, Stewin' the Rice, the Clam, the 81, the Lurch, the Bounce, and the Boomerang. As well, in the African American dance and song tradition, many of these dance instruction songs make reference to 'animal' dances: the Bird, the Duck, the Funky Chicken, the Horse, the Pony, the Raccoon, the Dog, the Funky Penguin, the Monkey, and so on.

3. 'The Jerk', for example, originally recorded by the Larks in 1964, gave rise to a long line of successors: for instance, Clyde and the Blue Jays' 'The Big Jerk', Bob and Earl's 'Everybody Jerk', and even the Larks' follow-up, 'Mickey's East Coast Jerk'. See Steve Propes, 'The Larks and the Jerk', *Goldmine*, 26 August 1988.

This genre is so powerful that it has not only spawned various series of dances, like the entire Twist, Jerk, or Dog successions;[3] it has also given rise to a metagenre – a group of songs commenting on or parodying the dance instruction song. These songs create instructions for dances that are physically impossible, either because of the limitations of human physiognomy – for instance, Dr Hook's 'Levitate' (1975), which commands the listener, 'I want you to raise your right foot … Awright, now raise your left foot … No no no no no, don't put your right foot back down!' – or because they are far too general and large-scale – for example, Tonio K's 'Funky Western Civilization', which, after cataloguing the evils of western history, instructs its dancers to do all sorts of nasty things to one another: 'You just grab your partner by the hair/Throw her down and leave her there' or 'You just drag your partner through the dirt/Put him in a world of hurt'. And Loudon Wainwright III's 'The Suicide Song' (1975) gives new meaning to the dance of death by mixing instructions for shaking one's hips with those for cutting one's wrists. It seems that the parodic dance instruction song has been around nearly as long as the genre itself. But we also want to suggest that one symptom of the dance instruction song's decline during the disco era – the late 1970s and early 1980s – was a disproportionate increase of parodies compared to the number of 'actual' or 'serious' dance instruction songs.[4]

ROOTS OF THE DANCE INSTRUCTION SONG

Dance instruction songs, in the form of dance rhymes and rhythmic verbal-movement games, were already long-established practices when they were first recorded in African American communities as early as the mid-nineteenth century. One of the fullest and earliest accounts of slave dancing records a portion of a dance song from Virginia: 'She *bin* to the north/she *bin* to the south/she *bin* to the east/she *bin* to the west/she *bin* so far *beyond* the sun/and she is the *gal* for me'.[5] Thomas W. Talley collected a number of what he called 'dance song rhymes' in *Negro Folk Rhymes*, and typical is 'Jonah's Band Party', which he saw developed at various occasions as a child:

> Setch a kickin' up san'! Jonah's Ban'!
> Setch a kickin' up san'! Jonah's Ban'!
> 'Raise yo' right foot, kick it up high,
> Knock dat Mobile Buck in de eye'.

> Setch a kickin' up san'! Jonah's Ban'!
> Setch a kickin' up san'! Jonah's Ban'!
> 'Stan' up, flat foot, Jump dem Bars!
> Karo back'ards lak a train o' kyars'.

(Talley notes that 'Jonah's Ban',' 'Mobile Buck,' 'Jump dem Bars,' and 'Karo' were dance steps.)[6]

The roots of this genre reach back to the instructions and commentary by slave musicians at both slave gatherings and white plantation balls; to the African American folk song, game, and dance tradition; and earlier to the close relationship between West African dancing and the musicians' cues.[7] There is a link here with Euro-American forms such as square dancing, quadrilles, and play party games, but there is also strong evidence that there is a hidden history of these Euro-American forms – that in the United States, they were partly shaped by African American interventions, including black musicians, callers, and prompters at square dances and contra dances, as well as African American games or styles of game-playing.[8]

That the dance instruction songs are related to rhythmic games synthesising Euro-American and African American traditions is nicely illustrated in a song

4. For further comments on dance crazes, see Katrina Hazzard-Gordon, *Jookin': The Rise of Social Dance Formations in African American Culture*, Temple University Press, Philadelphia, PA: 1990; and Stuart Cosgrove, 'The Erotic Pleasures of the Dance-Craze Disc', *Collusion*, February–April, 1983, pp4-6. Also, see Jim Dawson, *The Twist: The Story of the Song and Dance That Changed the World*, Faber and Faber, Boston and London 1995; and the 1993 documentary film *The Twist* by Ron Mann.

5. William B. Smith, 'The Persimmon Tree and the Beer Dance', (1838) reprinted in Bruce Jackson, *The Negro and His Folklore in Nineteenth-Century Periodicals*, University of Texas Press, Austin 1967, pp3-9.

6. Thomas W. Talley, *Negro Folk Rhymes*, Macmillan, New York 1922, pp258-262.

7. Dance instruction songs have also been noted in the carnivals of Haiti and Trinidad, and in Argentinian tango, areas with either a majority of peoples of African descent, or with a history of significant African cultural influence.

8. On African American musicians and callers, see Paul Oliver, *Songsters and Saints: Vocal Traditions on Race Records*, Cambridge University Press, Cambridge 1984, p22.

from the 1960s – Rufus Thomas' 'Little Sally Walker', which is a virtual catalogue of free-floating, recombinative formulaic game and song phrases, mixing an Anglo-American traditional children's chanting game with standard African American vernacular dance calling phrases such as 'Put your hand on your hip/Let your backbone slip', all set to a rhythm-and-blues beat.

> Little Sally Walker
> Sitting in her saucer
> Rise, Sally, rise
> Wipe your weepin' eyes
> Put your hand on your hip
> Let your backbone slip
> (I want you to) Shake it to the east
> Shake it to the west
> Shake it to the very one that you love best ...
> Little Sally Walker
> I see you sitting in your saucer
> Rise and do the jerk
> I love to see you work ...[9]

Roger D. Abrahams recorded girls' jump rope rhymes from Philadelphia in the early 1960s that were parallel to or derivative of dances of the period, such as the Madison and the Baltimore.[10] Since these girls taught their younger brothers and sisters how to play these games, the interaction between dance and games is difficult to unravel.

There is also a connection between these songs and military marching chants – or cadence counting, or 'Jody calls', introduced to the US Army by African Americans – which help co-ordinate the drill movements of large numbers of troops: 'Jody was here when I *left*/You're *right*'.

Sheet music renditions of dance instruction songs were printed before the turn of this century. Nearly twenty years before 'Ballin' the Jack' (1913), which Alec Wilder calls the first dance instruction song, black audiences were dancing to 'La Pas Ma La', introduced by the African American dancer-comedian Ernest Hogan in his Georgia Graduates minstrel show and published in 1895.[11] Less explicit in its choreographic instructions than later songs marketed to whites, 'La Pas Ma La' often simply names or calls other dances to be performed, like the Bombashay and the Turkey Trot. According to Marshall and Jean Stearns, this served as a shorthand for those who knew black dance conventions. But the choreography for the Pas Ma La itself *was* given, if somewhat elliptically, in the chorus:

> Hand upon yo' head, let your mind roll far,
> Back, back, back and look at the stars,
> Stand up rightly, dance it brightly,
> That's the Pas Ma La.[12]

9. Bessie Jones and Bess Lomax Hawes, *Step It Down: Games, Plays, Song, and Stories from the Afro–American Heritage*, Harper and Row, New York 1972, discuss the African–American version of this 'ring play' song.

10. Roger D. Abrahams, 'There's a Brown Girl in the Ring', in Kenneth S. Goldstein and Robert H. Byington (eds), *Two Penny Ballads and Four Dollar Whiskey*, Folklore Associates, Hatboro, PA 1966, pp121-135.

11. See Stearns and Stearns, *op.cit.*, pp100-102, and Oliver, pp33-34.

12. Stearns and Stearns, *op.cit.*, pp100-101, 117; the Stearns spell the name of the first dance invoked the Bumbishay, while Oliver spells it Bombashay.

But if 'La Pas Ma La' was marketed primarily to black audiences, during the first American mass dance craze 'season' of 1912-1914, many other dances and their notation – in the form of music and lyrics published in sheet music, as well as live demonstrations in Broadway revues and musicals – began to find commercial viability among mass white audiences (that is, both consumers at theatrical spectacles and participants at parties and dance halls). In fact, live performances and sheet music (or instructions, with pictures, published in newspapers and magazines) all formed part of a package that provided a network of verbal, aural and visual demonstrations of the dance.

There were occasional early efforts to reach Euro-American audiences with conventional oral instruction – as in 'One Step Instruction' (c.1915), a Columbia record of dance music with an instructor interrupting the music to describe the steps. But these were short-lived failures.[13]

The song 'Ballin' the Jack', written for the Ziegfeld *Follies* of 1913 by two African American musicians, Chris Smith and Jim Burris, describes traditional African American vernacular dance steps, and it is a paradigm of the early dance instruction song. It contains a great deal of information about various aspects of the choreography.

13. 'One Step Instruction' was part of a newspaper promotion give-away. See *Early Syncopated Dance Music*, Folkways Records RBF 37.

> First you put your two knees close up tight
> Then you sway 'em to the left, then you sway 'em to the right
> Step around the floor kind of nice and light
> Then you twis' around and twis' around with all your might
> Stretch your lovin' arms straight out in space
> Then you do the Eagle Rock with style and grace
> Swing your foot way 'round then bring it back
> Now that's what I call 'Ballin' the Jack.'[14]

14. Stearns and Stearns, *op.cit.*, pp98-99.

Here we have choreographic instructions that describe the structure of the step, call a figure (in the form of an already known dance, the Eagle Rock), and also give advice on style and energy use ('nice and light', 'with all your might', 'with style and grace').

Similarly, Perry Bradford's songs 'Bullfrog Hop' (1909) and 'Messin' Around' (1912) provide explicit choreographic instructions, including some similarities to the later, more widely disseminated 'Ballin' the Jack'. In 'Messin' Around', for instance, Bradford explains:

> Now anyone can learn the knack
> Put your hands on your hips and bend your back,
> Stand in one spot, nice and light
> Twist around with all your might
> Messin' round, they call that messin' round.[15]

15. *Ibid.*, pp107.

Bradford's 'Original Black Bottom Dance' (1919) encodes instructions in a catalogue of other figures, including previous dances by the songwriter:

Hop down front and then you Doodle back,
Mooch to your left and then you Mooch to the right
Hands on your hips and do the Mess Around,
Break a Leg until you're near the ground
Now that's the Old Black Bottom Dance.

Now listen folks, open your ears,
This rhythm you will hear –
Charleston was on the afterbeat –
Old Black Bottom'll make you shake your feet,
Believe me it's a wow.
Now learn this dance somehow
Started in Georgia and it went to France
It's got everybody in a trance
It's a wing, that Old Black Bottom Dance.[16]

16. *Ibid.*, pp110-111.

In addition to the description of the steps and the calling of other figures or dances, the dance explains the timing (like the Charleston, it is on the 'afterbeat'), promises positive psychological affect, and makes reference to altered states of consciousness.

Even though these dance instruction songs were published in the form of sheet music, prior to the introduction of recording and broadcast technologies they were part of an oral tradition of instruction through popular performance, at first in minstrel shows and black vaudeville, and then in both black and white revues and musicals. The African American musician Clyde Bernhardt describes a 1917 performance by Ma Rainey and her black minstrel company. In the finale, Bernhardt remembers:

> The whole chorus line come stepping out behind her and she dance along, kicking up her heels. The song had dance instructions in the lyrics, and as she call a step, everybody would do it. Soon the whole cast was out on stage, jugglers, riders, singers, comedians, all dancing wild with Ma Rainey shouting and stomping. She call 'WALK!' and everybody walked together before breaking out fast. She call 'STOP!' and everybody froze. After many calls she finally holler 'SQUAT!' and the whole group squatted down with a roar. Including Ma Rainey.[17]

17. Clyde E.B. Bernhardt, as told to Sheldon Harris, *I Remember: Eighty Years of Black Entertainment, Big Bands, and the Blues*, foreword by John F. Szwed, University of Pennsylvania Press, Philadelphia PA 1986, p26.

Audiences, that is, learned the dance visually and aurally in public performances, rather than by learning to read cryptographic notation or taking private lessons. Accessible to all, this was a democratic form of dance pedagogy. Eventually, as the mass medium of television edged out live popular entertainments like vaudeville and travelling shows, broadcast programmes such as American Bandstand and MTV replaced the live visual demonstrations.

THE RISE OF THE DANCE INSTRUCTION SONG

By the 1920s, Broadway musicals with all-black casts regularly introduced new dance crazes to whites by demonstrating the steps and singing songs exhorting spectators to do the dance, such as the Charleston, danced to the song by James P. Johnson, in *Runnin' Wild* (1923).[18]

The Stearns give an account of the process by which the African American dance rhyme, a folk form, was transformed into the commercial dance instruction song. At first, the structure was 'a *group* dance performed in a circle with a few "experts" in the center'. As these experts improvised, inserted, and invented steps, the chorus on the outside repeatedly executed the steps named in the title of the dance. Often, the dance was simply named, rather than described, and if there was description, it was cursory. Later, however, as the dances reached the commercial market, 'editorializing ... as to its purported origin, nature, or popularity' began to appear as part of the song's format. And the group dance with improvised steps metamorphosed into a couple dance with a fixed choreographic structure and order. 'Although the verse names new steps, and the chorus describes the main step, the aim is simply to sell the dance', they lament.[19]

According to the Stearns, it was the Tin Pan Alley appropriation of these vernacular African American dances, in the form of the dance instruction song, that fostered their surfacing to the mainstream from black folk culture, and indeed, their survival. But oddly enough, although they were writing at the height of a new dance instruction song craze in the 1960s, the Stearns claim that by the end of the 1920s, 'the days of the dance-song with folk material were passing' and 'the demand for dance-songs faded. The practice of including instructions in the lyrics of a song dwindled and gradually hardened into a meaningless formula'. And, they claim, with the advent of the blues, 'dance-songs were forgotten', although the dances themselves persisted.[20]

But it is our contention that, far from being forgotten or hardening into 'a meaningless formula', dance instruction continued in the blues (and beyond). William Moore's 'Old Country Rock' (1928) has shouted instructions sprinkled through the record:

> Young folks rock.
>   Boys rock.
> Girls rock.
>   Drop back, man, and let me rock.
> ....
> Now let's go back to the country again
>   on that old rock.
> Rappahannac, Rappahannac,
>   Cross that river, boys, cross that river.

And boogie-woogie pianists continued to simulate the ambience of live dances

18. See Stearns and Stearns, *op.cit.*, pp140-159, on black musicals in the 1920s. Also, see Allen Woll, *Black Musical Theatre: From Coontown to Dreamgirls*, Louisiana State University Press, Baton Rouge 1989.

19. Stearns and Stearns, *op.cit.*, pp100-101.

20. *Ibid.*, pp113-114.

21. Rod Gruver, 'The Origins of the Blues', *Down Beat Music 71* Maher Publishing Co., Chicago, 1971, pp16-19.

on recordings up until the 1950s.[21] During the course of the twentieth century, the dance instruction song consistently re-emerged in times of heightened racial consciousness or change – times like the 1920s, the 1940s, and the 1960s – as a subtle component of an ongoing cultural struggle between black and white America that includes provisional and partial reconciliations. Even as white America violently resists political and social progress by African Americans, a steady, subterranean Africanization of American culture continues, and emerging generations of white youth eagerly learn the bodily and cultural codes of black America by practising its dances. And even where whites sang songs that presented black dances derisively or stereotypically – as in the case of rockabilly Carl Mann's 'Ubangi Stomp' or Johnny Sharpe and the Yellow Jackets' 'Bombie', both of which apply the 'n-word' to Africans – the description and instructional elements were there nonetheless.[22]

22. But see also African American songs which describe animals dancing in Africa, such as The Ideals' 'Mo' Gorilla'.

While European Americans had danced to music performed by African Americans for generations, they did not as a group perform black moves or dance to exactly the same music enjoyed in the black community. When whites did so, it was either in an exaggerated, stereotyped way, in the context of the blackface minstrel show, or it was an individual matter, done either in the black community or in private. The dance instruction song 'crazes' seem repeatedly to have served the function of both teaching and licensing whites to do black dance movements wholesale, in public spaces in mainstream Euro-American culture, to African American music.[23] That an African American movement style, done to a 4/4 beat, was utterly alien to whites accounts for the necessity of these songs' explicating not only steps, but also aspects of dance style, even bodily style. (It must be noted, however, that the dances are doubly coded, for embedded in the instructions are often allusions to aspects of black culture – particularly to religious experience – that would not necessarily be understood by the average white listener.) The repeated infusions of black style into white mass culture, which dance instruction songs enable, have allowed for temporary resolutions of racial conflict to take place on a deeply embodied cultural level, paralleling shifts in political and legal strata. The (as yet uncompleted) democratisation of American culture has depended, in part, on the Africanisation of American culture. And the dance instruction song has been both a reflection and an agent of that process, although this has not been unproblematic, as we will discuss below.

23. 'Public spaces', however, were, and to some degree still are, segregated: 'American Bandstand', the television show which did the most to spread new dances in the United States, was initially restricted to whites.

TAXONOMY: STRUCTURE AND FUNCTION OF THE DANCE INSTRUCTION SONG

In order to analyse the dance instruction song in more depth, it is useful to establish a taxonomy of the structure and function of the songs and their component parts. For example, some songs do little more than urge the listener to perform the dance by naming it, like Rufus Thomas' 'The Dog' and Van McCoy's 'The Hustle'. However, the majority of the songs begin with the premise that the listener has to be instructed in at least one or more categories –

not only in the steps, spacing, timing, or other particulars of the dance, but in the style as well (that is, in a specifically African American dance style). Although in this section we concentrate on the directions given in the lyrics, a great deal of instruction in these songs takes place through aspects of the musical as well as verbal text.

In the beginning stages of the waves of the 1920s and 1960s at least, the detailed instructions of the songs seem to indicate that the white mass audience/participants needed tutoring in all the moves, postures, and rhythms of black dance. However, in each wave, as it progressed, the songs begin to assume some mastery of the black dance style, naming only figures or other coded instructions; sometimes they even assume mastery of previous dances, naming them specifically as comparative references, as we will illustrate below.

Most of the song structures, despite their apparent simplicity and their repetitions, are quite complex. They contain information about the quantitative and qualitative content of the dance – its steps, gestures, and style – but also, they make reference to its novelty, popularity, and/or venerable history; to the dance's psychological affect; to other practitioners of the dance; to the dancer's agency; and to aspects of teaching or learning the dance. They may also make reference to religious practices, sexual pleasure, or altered states of consciousness. Sometimes the songs use the dance as a mask or metaphor for those other experiences; sometimes they overtly frame the dance as a social activity connected with courtship; but at other times they simply offer the listener the chance to learn the dance, with no strings attached.

(Strangely, the wording of the instructions given in Irene and Vernon Castle's 1914 book, *Modern Dancing*, seems very similar to that of dance instruction songs, perhaps suggesting that in the process of learning these dances from African Americans, they also absorbed the pedagogical rhetoric.[24])

The dance instruction songs usually begin, almost obligatorily, with a formulaic *exhortation* to learn or perform the dance. These range from the paternalistic ('Listen while I talk to you/I tell you what we're gonna do' ['Shake']) to the pedagogical ('C'mon baby want to teach it to you' ['Mashed Potato Time']) to the factual ('Come on let's stroll, stroll across the floor' ['Stroll']); from the encouraging ('Come on baby, do the Bird with me' ['Do the Bird']) to the wheedling ('Come on mama, do that dance for me' ['Come on Mama']) to the aggressive ('Hey you! Come out here on the floor/Let's rock some more' ['Baby Workout']) to the tender ('Come on baby, let's do the Twist … Take me by my little hand/And go like this' ['The Twist']).

It's striking that when inviting the listener to do the dance, narrators of the dance instruction song often sweeten the offer with the promise that the dance will be easy to do. Sometimes, this assurance comes in the form of pointing out that other people have already mastered the dance: 'I wish I could shimmy like my sister Kate'; 'My little baby sister can do it with ease'; 'Goin' to see little Susie/Who lives next door/She's doin' the Pony/She's takin' the floor'; 'You should see my little sis/She knows how to rock/She knows how to twist'; 'Mama

24. Mr and Mrs Vernon [and Irene] Castle, *Modern Dancing*, World Syndicate Co., by arrangement with Harper and Brothers, New York 1914. Reid Badger, *A Life in Ragtime: A Biography of James Reese Europe*, Oxford University Press, New York and Oxford 1995, describes the relationship between the Euro-American Castles and James Europe, their African American bandleader, and names black dancers such as Johnny Peters and his partner Ethel Williams, who taught the Castles African American dances.

Hully Gully, Papa Hully Gully, Baby Hully Gully too'; 'Pappy knows how ...'. These are aspects of the formulaic part of the song that reflexively calls attention to its *pedagogical function*. In fact, in 'Loco-Motion', Little Eva makes literal the connection with learning, simultaneously guaranteeing user-friendliness, when she remarks that the dance is 'easy as a line in your abcs'. And the many allusions to little sisters also seem to literalise the idiom that these dances will be child's play. At least as early as 'Doin' the Scraunch' (1930), Robert Hicks (aka Barbecue Bob) promised that 'Ain't much to it an' it's easy to do'.

But these references to teaching and learning also come simply, without any warranties of easy mastery: 'Bobby's going to show you how to do the Swim'; 'C'mon now, take a lesson now'; 'Now if you don't know what it's all about/Come to me, I'll show you how/We'll do it fast, we'll do it slow/Then you'll know the Walk everywhere you go'. As the song progresses, words of encouragement and positive feedback are frequent: 'Oh, you're lookin' good, now'; 'That's the way to do it'; 'Well, I think you've got the knack.'

Related to the promise that the dance will be user-friendly and the coaching offered by way of positive feedback is the part of the song – not obligatory but still quite frequent – that speaks to *psychological affect*, either that of the listener or that of the narrator. In 'Finger Poppin' Time', Hank Ballard sings 'I feel so good/And that's a real good sign', and in 'Bristol Stomp', the Dovells predict, 'Gonna feel fine' and conclude the song by noting 'I feel fine'. Sam Cooke, in 'Shake', exclaims 'Oh I like to do it ... Make me feel good now', and Little Eva, in 'Loco-Motion', guarantees, 'It even makes you happy when you're feeling blue'. The lyric 'Twist and fly/To the sky' is one of many invocations of euphoria in 'Do the Bird'. There is a connection here, to be sure, between the kinetic pleasure of the dance and other forms of ecstasy – sexual, romantic, drug-induced, and religious.

On the other hand, a few songs tell of failures to learn the dances, but always within special circumstances: some blame their partners, as in 'My Baby Couldn't Do the Cha Cha', or in Buddy Sharpe and The Shakers' 'Fat Mama Twist', where the singer's girlfriend is too fat to do it. In other songs, the singer is culturally unprepared for the dance: in Frankie Davidson and the Sapphires' 'I Can't Do the Twist', the singer (in a fake Spanish accent) confesses he can't do it, though he can do all of the Latin dances; Benny Bell & His Pretzel Twisters' 'Kosher Twist' follows much the same pattern, but in Borscht Belt dialect.

Sometimes, at or near the beginning of the song, the narrator makes references to the *popularity, novelty, and/or venerability* of the dance. Although the Stearns consider this aspect of the song a symptom of commercialisation and decline, we see it quite otherwise. This is an African-derived practice, clearly in the tradition of the African American praise song. (Indeed, some of the dance instruction songs – like the 'Ali Shuffle' – also function as praise songs for other objects than the dance itself. Similarly, in 'It's Madison Time', both Wilt Chamberlain and Jackie Gleason are celebrated with a step.) 'Down in Dixie, there's a dance that's new', Barbecue Bob announces in 'Doin' the

Scraunch'. Blind Willie McTell's 'Georgia Rag' sets the scene 'Down in Atlanta on Harris Street', and insists that 'Every little kid, that you meet,/Doin' that rag, that Georgia Rag … Come all the way from Paris, France/Come to Atlanta to get a chance … Peoples come from miles around/Get into Darktown t' break 'em down'. In 'Loco-Motion', Little Eva notes that 'Everybody's doing a brand new dance now', while in the background the chorus exhorts 'Come on baby, do the Loco-Motion'. In 'Popeye', Huey Smith and the Clowns tell us that 'Everywhere we go, people jump and shout/They all want to know what the Popeye's all about'. In 'Peppermint Twist', Joey Dee and the Starliters announce, 'They got a new dance and it goes like this/The name of the dance is the Peppermint Twist'. In 'The Bounce', the Olympics assert, 'You know there's a dance/That's spreading around/In every city/In every little town'. And in 'Hully Gully Baby', the Dovells characterise the dance's popularity somewhat ominously: 'There's a dance spreadin' round like an awful disease …'. Perhaps in 'Mashed Potato Time', Dee Dee Sharp puts the praise of the dance most succinctly: 'It's the latest/It's the greatest/Mashed Potato/Yeah yeah yeah yeah.' She then goes on to trace the roots of the dance and to bring the listener up to date on its vicissitudes. Similarly, 'The Original Black Bottom Dance', 'The Bristol Stomp', and 'Popeye' provide mythic accounts of origins.

Once the dance has been invoked and/or praised, the lyrics indicate the *steps, gestures, and postures*. Usually this information is stated in the imperative mode, as a command – 'Just move your body all around/And just shake' ('Shake'); 'You gotta swing your hips now …/Jump up, jump back' ('Loco-Motion'); 'All right, now, shake your shoulders now/All right, wiggle your knees now' ('Hully Gully'); 'You just shake your hips and close your eyes/And then you walk,' ('The Walk'); 'Shake it up baby' ('Twist and Shout'); 'Now you sway at the knees like a tree in the breeze/Then buzz around just like the bumblebees' ('Scratchin' the Gravel'); 'Oh, shout you cats, do it, stomp it, step you rats,/Shake your shimmy, break a leg,/Grab your gal and knock 'em dead' ('Shout You Cats'). Sometimes, however, the instructions are more in the manner of a description: 'Round and around/Up and down' ('The Peppermint Twist'); 'We're moving in we're moving out' ('Baby Workout'). And occasionally, this is stated as an invitation: 'Now turn around baby, let's stroll once more' ('Strolling'). At times, the narrator actually counts out the sequence: 'One, two, three, kick/One, two, three, jump' ('Peppermint Twist'); 'Oh my mama move up (first step)/Honey move back (second step)/Shuffle to the left (third step)/Wobble to the right (fourth step)' ('Baby Workout'). In Charles LaVerne's 'Shoot 'Em Up Twist' a freeze is ordered every time a gunshot is heard on the record.

One subcategory of this part of the dance is what might be termed *calling the figure*. As in contra dancing or square dancing, the narrator instructs the dancers to perform a phrase or move that itself has already been named, either during the current dance or by common knowledge because it exists in other cultural arenas (like dog paddle or back stroke, or hula hoop, or 'a chugga-chugga motion like a railroad train'). 'It's Pony Time' is a very good example of first teaching, then calling the figure. The narrator explains: 'Now

25. 'Gee' and 'haw' (or 'hoy') are commands used for horses or mules in the South. Their use in the 1950s and 1960s suggests that the influence of rural-based 'animal' dances was still vital.

you turn to the left when I say "gee"/You turn to the right when I say "haw" '. Then he sings, 'Now gee/Yeah, yeah little baby/Now haw'.[25] Or, in 'It's Madison Time', the narrator commands, 'When I say "Hit it!" I want you to go two up and two back, with a big strong turn, and back to the Madison'.

As suggested earlier, one way of calling the figure is actually to invoke another dance already popular and, presumably, known and available as a standard measurement. The dance may then simply be repeated: 'Let's Twist again/Like we did last summer'. Or, in a *mise-en-abyme* structure, the song may direct the listener to do other dances as part of the dance being taught (as noted above in 'Jonah's Band Party' and 'Original Black Bottom Dance'): 'Do that Slow Drag 'round the hall/Do that step the Texas Tommy' ('Walkin' the Dog', 1917); 'When I say "Hold it!" this time, I want everybody to Gully .../When I say hold it this time I want everybody to Sally Long' ('Fat Fanny Stomp'); 'Do the Shimmy Shimmy' ('Do the Bird'); 'Do a little Cha-cha, then you do the Buzz-saw' ('Hully-Gully'); 'Do a little wiggle and you do the Mess Around' ('Popeye'); 'Hitchhike baby, across the floor' ('The Harlem Shuffle'); 'We Ponyed and Twisted' ('Bristol Stomp'); 'Think we'll step back now/And end this dance with a Shout' ('Baby Workout').[26] Indeed, Bradford's 'Bullfrog Hop' is a veritable catalogue of other dance titles:

26. As we will discuss below, 'The Shout', contrary to what its title might suggest by way of vocalisation, is actually an AfricanAmerican religious dance. See Lynn Fauley Emery, *Black Dance in the United States from 1619 to 1970*, Dance Horizons, New York 1980.

27. Stearns and Stearns, *op.cit.*, p104.

> First you commence to wiggle from side to side
> Get 'way back and do the Jazzbo Glide
> Then you do the Shimmy with plenty of pep
> Stoop low, yeah Bo', and watch your step
> Do the Seven Years' Itch and the Possum Trot
> Scratch the Gravel in the vacant lot
> Then you drop like Johnny on the Spot
> That's the Bullfrog Hop.[27]

Sometimes, the called dance may serve as a model from which to deviate. For instance, in 'The Swim', Bobby Freeman explains how to do it: 'Just like the Dog, but not so low/Like the Hully Gully but not so slow.' 'The Walk' mentions the Texas Hop, the Fox Trot, the Mambo, and the Congo, but all as dances that are now out of fashion. In a very complex example, Junior and the Classics' 'The Dog', the dancer is asked to 'do' various breeds of dog – the poodle, the scotty, *et al.*

Oddly enough for songs that were usually distributed over nonvisual channels such as radio or records, sometimes the lyrics indicate that the narrator is also demonstrating the dance along the visual channel, as in 'The Swim' – 'Kind of like the Monkey, kind of like the Twist/Pretend you're in the water and you go like this' – or as in 'The Twist' – 'Come on and twist/Yeah, baby twist/Oooh yeah, just like this.'[28] The radio or record listener has to fill in the visuals, based on a general knowledge of the appropriate vocabulary and style.

28. There is an obvious sexual meaning here, to be discussed below.

This indication of visual demonstration seems to make reference to earlier times, when dance instruction was routinely done as part of live entertainment in black vaudeville and tent shows, as described above. Long before he became a recording artist, Rufus Thomas was a member of the Rabbit's Foot Minstrels, a black vaudeville group that showed its audiences the latest steps. 'I sing, I do a step or two, and I'm a comedian', Thomas later described his act.[29]

On the recordings, the residue of a live show with visual demonstration is evident during the musical break, when the time seems right either for the listener to watch the narrator demonstrate the dance (saving the breath he or she would otherwise need to sing) and/or for the listener to practise the movements just learned. Then, when the lyrics are repeated after the musical break, the listener does not find the repetition boring or redundant, because he or she is ready to test the progress made during the (nonverbal) practice time against the instructions once again.

This is nicely illustrated in the Pearl Bailey/Hot Lips Page version of 'The Hucklebuck', in which, partly because of the duet form and the dialogic patter, we have the distinct sense that Bailey is teaching Page how to do the dance. In fact, even before she begins singing, Bailey formulaically initiates the dance event by confiding in Page that she has learned a great new dance. According to their conversation, they're in a club, and not only do they comment on the abilities and looks of the musicians, but also Bailey at one point complains that Page is dancing right on her feet. This song seems to record a performance within a performance, for certain lines cue the listener also to set up a scene visually that puts Bailey and Page onstage in the the club, teaching the audience how to do the dance. That is, in the fictional drama of the song they are a couple getting together on the dance floor in a club, but in the frame they are the featured club performers singing the fictional romance narrative. In any case, they repeatedly sing the chorus together, exhorting the listener to do the dance and describing the steps and other movements:

> Do the Hucklebuck
> Do the Hucklebuck
> If you don't know how to do it, boy you're out of luck
> Push your partner out
> Then you hunch your back
> Start a little movement in your sacroiliac
> Wiggle like a snake
> Waddle like a duck
> That's the way you do it when you do the Hucklebuck.

As the band plays in between the stanzas, and Bailey and Page trade patter, it is clear that they are *doing* the dance, especially when Bailey scolds Page: 'No, not now! I'll tell you when. Right here!'

As noted earlier, dance instruction songs teach not only the quantitative aspects of the dance (the steps, postures, and gestures), but also the qualitative aspects. One of these aspects is *timing*. For instance, 'The Walk' is very specific

29. Quoted in Roger St. Pierre, liner notes, Rufus Thomas, *Jump Back*, Edsel Records ED 134, 1984.

in teaching the proper timing for the moves. Walking may be an ordinary act, but turning it into a dance requires the proper rhythmic sequence. So Jimmy McCracklin notes that 'We'll do it fast, we'll do it slow', and later regulates the speed even further as he marks the exact moment in the music when the dancer should take his or her step: 'You'll then walk/And you'll walk/*Now* you walk ...'. In 'The Harlem Shuffle', Bob and Earl often qualify a step by indicating its proper speed (which, of course, the slow and steady music underscores): 'You move it to the right (yeah)/If it takes all night' and they frequently admonish the dancer: 'Don't move it too fast/Make it last ...'. In 'Slow Twistin'', reminiscent of the 'Slow Drag', Chubby Checker and Dee Dee Sharp recommend: 'Baby baby baby take it easy/Let's do it right/Aw, baby take it easy/Don't you know we got all night ... Let's twist all night!/You're gonna last longer, longer/Just take your time ...'[30] The music, especially its percussive beat, plays an important role in all the songs in indicating timing.

30. Again, there is an obvious sexual reference here.

Another qualitative aspect of the dance is its *spacing*; this too serves as an aspect of instruction. Again in 'Slow Twistin'', Chubby Checker and Dee Dee Sharp advise the listener that all one needs is 'Just a little bit of room, now baby.' Spacing refers not only to ambient space, but also to levels of space, as in 'The Swim': 'Just like the Dog, but not so low ...'. It also refers to relations with one's partner, which can be difficult to negotiate. In 'The Walk', the narrator warns, 'But when you walk, you stand in close/And don't step on your partner's toes.' Several songs recommend, once one has learned a step, doing it in 'a big boss line' or 'a big strong line'. In 'Loco-Motion', Little Eva instructs the listeners, once they have mastered the step, to make a chain. This clearly invokes earlier African American vernacular and communal roots, when the dances were done as group folk forms, rather than as couple forms in the dance hall.

Yet another aspect of style is the category of *energy use* – what Laban movement analysts refer to as effort qualities, such as strength and lightness, boundedness and unboundedness, directness and indirectness. This too is a stylistic characteristic that the dance instruction song sometimes teaches. For instance, 'The Loco-Motion' tells us to 'Take it nice and easy, now/Don't lose control', while in 'The Shake', Sam Cooke gives us quite a few clues: 'Shake shake with all your might/Oh if you do it do it right/Just make your body loose and light/You just shake.' In 'The Duck', Jackie Lee gives some sense of the energy invested in the dance when he describes performing it as 'like working on a chain gang' or 'busting rocks'. Less easy to characterise are other references to *overall style*: the many songs that recommend, for instance, that the dance be performed 'with soul'.

31. Morton Marks, ' "You Can't Sing Unless You're Saved": Reliving the Call in Gospel Music', in Simon Ottenberg, (ed), *African Religious Groups and Beliefs*, Archana Publications, Meerut, India 1982, pp305-331.

One of the oldest forms of African American dance instruction is that given by the instruments themselves. The role of drums, for instance, in 'talking' to dancers, or in signalling states of possession is a well-known phenomenon, both in Africa and the Americas.[31] The role of instrument as caller or instructor is not so well understood in American dance music, but its presence is undeniable. Barry Michael Cooper describes both horns and singers calling instructions to dancers at Washington, DC go-go dances in the 1980s.[32] And dance music critic Michael Freedberg suggests that instruments enact gender roles, both in the blues and in dance music performances.[33]

Dance instruction songs vary in the amount of choreographic information they impart, and they obviously serve a range of functions. Some actually teach the dance from scratch; some serve as prompts or mnemonics, recalling for the listener previously demonstrated and learned dances; some serve to co-ordinate ensemble dancing; some merely praise a dance or exhort the listener to perform it. But it is possible for a dance instruction song to 'notate' all ten elements in the taxonomy: exhortation; pedagogical function; psychological affect; popularity, novelty, and/or venerability; steps, gestures, and postures; calling the figure; timing; spacing; energy use; and style. Thus the amount of information can be quite complete.

32. See Barry Michael Cooper, 'Kiss Me Before You Go-go', Spin, June, 1985, pp65-67.

33. Michael Freedberg, 'Dust Their Blues', The Boston Phoenix, 16 October 1992; and 'Rising Expectations: Rick James Gets Down', The Village Voice, 11 October 1983.

DOIN' THE HERMENEUTICS

Certain aspects of the dance instruction song have nothing to do with learning or remembering to perform the dance. In fact, sometimes even what serves as explicit instructions seems also to have subtextual, metaphoric, or 'secret' meanings. So, while the dance instruction songs have partly served to teach the rest of the world African American dances and dance styles, they also allude to other aspects of knowledge and experience. Some of these allusions are highly coded in terms of African American custom, emerging for white consumers and participants only through familiarity with African American history and culture. That these references are also formulaic and appear repeatedly in the songs, in succeeding generations, shows the extent and tenacity of their roots. They are often unrecognised, sturdy traces of long-standing cultural traditions.

Some of the metaphors of African American dance instruction songs are merely pedagogical in function, since traditional dance language lacks names for the steps. So 'mashed potatoes', 'ride your pony', 'walk like a duck', 'walk pigeon-toed' and the like are means of directing the dancers away from the received, conventional steps of western dance.

Not all the extrachoreographic references have to do with experiences that are uniquely African American. Often, social dancing serves as a metaphor in these narratives for other kinds of partnering – either romantic or sexual. And, since dancing – especially to slow music – often involves sustained body-to-body contact between partners, the metaphoric leap can be but a tiny one. When white teenagers danced the Twist, they were accused of moving in overly erotic ways and raised the ire of their parents. The lyrics of 'Slow Twistin'' are full of double entendres, underscored by the male-female vocal duet: 'Don't you know we got all night ... Let's twist all night!/You're gonna last longer, longer/Just take your time ...'. Perhaps the extreme case is Ronnie Fuller's 'Do the Dive', where cunnilingus appears to be the move taught. In some songs, however, the dance serves not as a metaphor for sex, but as a love potion. Performing the dance itself is guaranteed to bond the partners romantically, as in 'The Bristol Stomp': 'We'll fall in love you see/The Bristol Stomp will make you mine, all mine.'

The ecstatic body consciousness of sex, however, is easily conflated with that of another high – from drugs or alcohol. The word 'trance' does not only show up in these songs because it rhymes with 'dance'. Thus, in 'Do the Bird', as we have seen, it is not clear whether romance or drugs, or both at once, are in effect when the singer urges:

Come on take me to the sky above (fly-y-y-y-y)
Come on baby we can fall in love (fly-y-y-y-y)....
(Do the bird do the bird) You're a-crazy flying
(Do the bird do the bird) You're going to fly higher.

Similarly, the lines 'Let's go strolling in Wonderland', or 'Baby, let's go strolling by the candy store', in 'The Stroll', also ambiguously suggest some kind of euphoria, whether sexual, drug-induced, or religious.

And yet 'Doin' the New Low-Down', while acknowledging rapture – even invoking dreams and trances – specifically rejects other, non-dance forms of euphoria, either chemical or sexual, insisting on a surface reading: for 'It isn't alcohol/No yaller girl at all! Thrills me, fills me with the pep I've got/I've got a pair of feet/That found a low-down beat ... Heigh! Ho! doin' the New Low-Down'.

Another line in 'Doin' the New Low-Down' invokes a crucial category of cultural invocations: specifically African American signs of *religious* references. 'I got a soul that's not for savin' now', this song's narrator admits, since his feet are 'misbehavin' now'. But more often, dance and religion are seen in the dance instruction song not as exclusionary opposites but as integrally linked. In fact, the frequent references in the songs to black religious practices, in particular the shaking or trembling associated with religious possession, suggests that many secular African American folk dances or social dances are derived directly from religious dances; they may even be the same dances performed in a different context. These are movements that originated in sacred rituals in West Africa, were associated with Yoruba, Ashanti, Congo, and other West African spirits, and shaped the syncretic worship formations of the African American church. In fact, instruction in appropriate physical response among Afro-Protestants is seen when ministers direct the congregation verbally ('Everybody raise your right hand and say "Praise Jesus!" '); and in eighteenth-century Cuba, among Afro-Cuban religious orders, when leaders directed initiates to 'open their ears, stand straight, and put their left hand on their hip.'[34]

Thus the Eagle Rock, mentioned in many of the songs beginning with 'Ballin' the Jack', and described by the Stearns as 'thrusting the arms high over the head with a variety of shuffle steps', actually took its name from the Eagle Rock

34. Ramon Guirao, *Orbita de la Poesia Afrocubana, 1928-37*, [Talleres de ucar, Garcia y cial], Havana 1938.

Baptist Church in Kansas City. According to musician Wilbur Sweatman, worshippers at the church 'were famous for dancing it during religious services in the years following the Civil War', and the Stearns note that although the Eagle Rock eventually adapted itself to rent parties and other secular venues, 'it has the high arm gestures associated with evangelical dances and religious trance.'[35]

35. Stearns and Stearns, *op.cit.*, p27.

Similarly, the Shout often crops up in the steps invoked by dance instruction songs, from 'Twist and Shout' to 'Do the Bird' to 'Baby Work Out'. Also known as the Ring Shout when done in a group form, this was not a strictly vocal performance, but a religious dance with chants. It involved a rhythmic walk or shuffle in a circle, tapping the heels, swaying, and clapping as one advanced. In several accounts, observers noted that the shouters moved increasingly faster, working themselves into a trance.[36]

36. See Emery, *op.cit.*, pp120-126. Also see Jones and Hawes, *op.cit.*, pp45-46, for the distinction between religious and secular shout steps.

Indeed, Jones and Hawes explicitly make the connection among child en's ring plays, adult secular dances, and religious ring shouts in the African American tradition. They include in their chapter on dances the religious ring shout 'Daniel', which includes lyrics, sung by the leader, strikingly reminiscent of several dance instruction songs:

Walk, believer, walk,
Walk, believer, walk,
Walk, I tell you, walk,
Shout, believer, shout,
Shout, believer, shout,
On the eagle wing,
On the eagle wing,
Fly, I tell you, fly
Rock, I tell you, rock
Fly the other way,
Shout, I tell you, shout,
Give me the kneebone bend,
On the eagle wing,
Fly, I tell you, fly
Fly back home.[37]

37. Jones and Hawes, *op.cit.*, pp144-45. After each line sung by the leader, the group responds, 'Daniel', and performs a mimetic action.

Finally, the all-over body trembling called for and described in various songs – and known as the Shake, the Shimmy, and the Quiver, among other dances – bears a striking resemblance to the movements seen, especially among women, during religious possession in gospel churches.[38] Terms like 'workout', 'work it on out', 'rock my soul', 'turn the joint out', and 'tear the house down', as well as the instruction to 'go down to the river' ('The Duck'), all make explicit reference to ecstatic forms of African American religious worship.

38. See Stearns and Stearns, *op.cit.*, p105, on the various titles of the dances.

In addition to these markedly African-derived dance practices, yet another set of associations reveal the presence of African cultural practices in dance

39. William Moore, 'Ragtime Crazy', quoted in Oliver, *op.cit.*, p33.

40. In fact, the earliest recorded dance calls for European set dances and dance suites were performed by African Americans. See John F. Szwed and Morton Marks, 'The Afro-American Transformation of European Set Dances and Dance Suites', *Dance Research Journal*, Volume 20, Number 1, 1988.

41. This has complex crosscultural repercussions, especially since, as several theorists have argued, black music and dance (on both sides of the Atlantic) are key agents in the articulation of cultural memory. See, for instance, Paul Gilroy, *The Black Atlantic: Modernity and Double Consciousness*, Verso, London 1993.

42. Conveniently collected together are the following sets of dance songs without dances: *It's Finking Time!: 60s Punk vs. Dancing Junk* (Beware Records LP Fink 1); *Bug Out Volume One: Sixteen Itchy Twitchy Classics* (Candy Records LP4); *Bug Out Volume Two: Sixteen Itchy Twitchy Classics* (Candy Records LP5); *Land of 1,000 Dunces: Bug Out Volume 3* (Candy Records LP 7). A selection from the three Candy discs is available as *Best of the Bug-Outs* (Candy CD7).

instruction songs. Although the songs do give choreographic directions to the dancer, space is often made for *improvisation*. Thus, in 'Shake', we are told 'Dance what you wanna'; in 'The Swim', we are assured 'Do what you wanna, it's all right'; in 'The Loco-Motion', we are told 'Dance what you wanna'; in 'The Swim', we are assured 'Do what you wanna, it's all right'; in 'The Loco-Motion', we are instructed 'Do it holding hands if you get the notion'; and in 'It's Pony Time', we learn that 'Any way you do it/You're gonna look real fine'. These lyrics not only reveal improvisation as a standard component of African American dance, suggesting that during the musical break it will be perfectly appropriate to 'go crazy folks for a minute'.[39] They also suggest, in a deeper vein, the metaphoric meaning of that improvisation. That is, the songs promise more than simply feeling good; they imply freedom and agency.

It should be acknowledged that the cross-cultural pedagogy of dance has been neither static nor one-way. Hip-hop, go-go, and ska are only the latest African American dance forms assimilated by white America. On the other hand, European dances like the quadrille have been absorbed, albeit in modified form, into the African American repertory.[40] For instance, the Stroll involves forming two facing longways rows of dance partners, as in a European contra dance configuration. But there is a difference. When each couple goes down the column of space between the rows, they improvise virtuosic inventions in a characteristically African American vein.

One way to understand dance instruction songs is as a kind of summing-up of a musical period. There is considerable self-consciousness about them, and by the time the songs are commercially available it is likely that the original people involved with the dance have moved on to other dances, or will soon do as popularisation sets in.

What is striking about most of these songs is that they offer a thin reading of the dance that lay behind them. Especially among Euro-Americans there is a tendency to reduce a complex physical-verbal-musical phenomenon to the merely verbal. Thus the Shout is often discussed as a kind of folk song. And the same reduction has been worked on rap, where the dance components of the form are almost always ignored in favour of the verbal.[41]

THE DECLINE OF THE DANCE INSTRUCTION SONG

At the end of the 1960s popular music was developing at a remarkable rate. Yet, dance *per se* was not the focus of forms such as psychedelic music, heavy metal, and art rock. Increasingly, songs about dances became not merely wanna-be dances, but conceptual dance instruction songs – songs about dances that didn't exist. The genre became something of a joke. *Mad Magazine*'s 'Let's Do the Fink', by Alfred E. Newman, which came with illustrated dance steps, was typical.[42] At the same time, however, black and Latin music continued a commitment to 'the beat', so that when the white gay community encountered strongly grounded dance music in clubs and ballrooms in the 1970s, it seemed a totally new phenomenon. It was as if rock had never happened.

When dance music made its comeback as disco, it did so with a vengeance. New dances were developed apace, but instructional songs were minimal at best, with exhortation and novelty/praise functions carrying the weight of the lyrics. The names of dances were repeated rifflike in songs: 'Do the Hustle', 'Do the Jaws'. Professional dance teachers returned, and a ballroom formality replaced the home-made, self-help atmosphere of many earlier dance eras.

The 1990s are certainly a time of acute racial tension and heightened race awareness in the United States. And yet, dances are being invented and reinvented at a slower rate, and no dance instruction song craze has emerged thus far in this generation. The Electric Slide, one of the few to have appeared in recent years (accompanied by a song of the same name by Marcia Griffith [1989]), was immediately challenged by an older generation of dancers as a thinly disguised remake of the Madison, especially as it, too, emerged from the Baltimore-DC area.[43] Similarly, the Lambada was attacked as a commercially fabricated generic Latin dance, and its accompanying song debunked as plagiarism. The current generation of African American kids still knows some dance instruction songs, like the currently popular 'Tootsie Roll' by The 69 Boys. But these have not crossed over into the mainstream. In hip hop, one of the few distinctive music forms of the current era, MCs (especially in the early days of the form) may direct dancing and crowd behaviour, but usually in an improvised rap, with routinised calls, and seldom in the form of a fully structured song for a distinctive dance. Madonna's appropriation of Voguing from the black gay community in the early 1990s was a sudden, singular – and spectacularly popular – resuscitation of the genre, but it did not spark a new wave.[44]

Dance instruction songs are still with us, though, in truncated, restricted forms. Country and western line dances – a remarkable case of cultural lag – still retain something of the calling of steps used in black popular dancing of the late 1950s and early 1960s (at least in the instructional videos), and aerobics and jazzercise do struggle mightily to get the feel of the discotheque into their routines. But there is a sense here of the end of an era. Two items of nostalgia – 'Time Warp' (a camp parody of 'Ballin' the Jack') from *The Rocky Horror Picture Show* (1975) and the commemorative scenes from John Waters' 1988 film *Hairspray* indicate that for the mainstream, the dance instruction song is truly a relic from the past.

CONCLUSIONS

There is a school of mass culture criticism, most notoriously represented by Adorno, that condemns popular music as an opiate.[45] The dance instruction song, however, clearly contradicts that position. Far from assuming a docile listener, it galvanises audiences into action with both its swinging beat and its lyrics. It is a dialogic form, requiring interaction between artist and auditor. Thus, even though the form of dissemination – especially after the invention of the phonograph – has been mass production or broadcast, the dance

43. Lena Williams, 'Three Steps Right, Three Steps Left: Sliding Into the Hot New Dance', *New York Times*, 22 April 1990.

44. On Madonna's appropriation of Voguing, see Cindy Patton, 'Embodying Subaltern Memory: Kinesthesia & the Problematics of Gender and Race', in Cathy Schwichtenberg (ed), *The Madonna Connection: Representational Politics, Subcultural Identies, and Cultural Theory*, Westview Press, Boulder, CO 1993, pp81-105.

45. See Theodor W. Adorno, *The Culture Industry: Selected Essays on Mass Culture*, edited and with an introduction by Jeremy M. Bernstein, Routledge, London 1991.

instruction song does not promote passivity. Rather, it provides a means for individual agency and creativity, especially with its improvisational component. Moreover, it insists that listener response can be bodily, not just intellectual, participation. And, unlike the Castles' gendered ballroom choreography instructions, the dance instruction songs make no gender distinctions in the movements. In fact, unlike the Euro-American style of couple dancing, where the man leads and the woman follows, in the pedagogy proposed by dance instruction songs, women and even girls are often cited as authorities.

The question arises as to whether people actually *listen* to the lyrics and, further, whether listening to the lyrics enables people to learn to do the dance. Several theorists of popular culture claim that people screen out the words in popular music and hear only the rhythm or the emotional contours.[46] And many cultural critics condemn the lyrics of popular songs, claiming that since the words are banal and predictable to begin with, auditors don't need to pay attention to them.[47] The dance instruction song seems unlike other genres of popular music, in that here it *is* important to listen to the words, and not just to sense the beat, melody, or emotional content of the song. This is not to say that the words alone supply the entire set of choreographic instructions, for as we have pointed out, the music also directs the dancer. But the words *are* important, even if not all of them need to be heard or understood, because the dance is 'overdetermined'. That is, listeners may not hear or comprehend every single word (and indeed, not every song makes every word clear enough to understand). But, given the various ways people learn to dance, the redundancies, both in terms of the repetition of the lyrics and the parallel teaching across various channels – verbal, rhythmic, melodic, and visual – allow for successful instruction.

The dance instruction song is laced with esoteric references to African American culture – especially to ecstatic religious experiences – that have been inaccessible to most Euro-Americans. Nevertheless, during the course of the twentieth century the dance instruction song, while keeping black vernacular dances alive, has had a mass appeal to white audiences. Through the dance instruction song, white bodies have learned – and loved – black moves, from the practice of performing separate rhythms with diverse body parts, to stances like akimbo arms and bent knees, to specific movements like all-over body quivers or hip rotations. Despite the recondite allusions, there is enough accessible material in the songs, both in the music and the lyrics, for Euro-Americans to learn the dances and the dance style. The genre has become part of mainstream American culture.

We want to close by raising the issue of cultural appropriation. On the one hand, the dance instruction song, besides its own formal pleasures, is an attractive genre for all the reasons we have already mentioned – not only its preservation of vernacular black dance, but also its dialogic character, its role in the democratisation and Africanisation of American culture, and the economic opportunities it has created for African American musicians. By introducing an African American bodily habitus into mass white culture, thereby stirring

46. In 'Why Do Songs Have Words?' (in *Music for Pleasure: Essays in the Sociology of Pop* [Routledge, New York 1988]), Simon Frith cites two such theorists: David Riesman, 'Listening to Popular Music', *American Quarterly* 2 (1950); and Norman Denzin, 'Problems in Analyzing Elements of Mass Culture: Notes on the Popular Song and Other Artistic Productions', *American Journal of Sociology* 75 (1969). And Frith notes that this was the typical view of sociologists of rock and pop music in the 1970s.

47. Frith, in 'Why Do Songs Have Words?', traces this view back to 1930s Leavisite mass-culture criticism.

up racial, generational, and sexual threats, it has even been subversive. But on the other hand, the dance instruction song *crazes* have been problematic, for they commodified and naturalised the dances, appropriating them for white culture without fully acknowledging their cultural source – their African roots – and sometimes totally detaching them from black bodies and black communities. The dance instruction song crazes created the impression that these dances have no roots – that they always have been and always will be. We hope that this article will in part redress that misperception.[48]

48. The authors would like to thank Roger Abrahams, Robert F. Thompson, Noël Carroll, Laurence Senelick, Michael McDowell, David Krasner, Gerri Gurman and her Memorial High School dance class, Amy Seham, Toni Hull, Juliette Willis, and Margaret Keyes, as well as Brooks McNamara, Richard Schechner, and the faculty and students in the Department of Performance Studies, New York University, for their help with this article.

'WHEN THE BIG TIMES COME': THE CASE OF FRANK NORMAN

John Stokes

People whispered that I had been ruined by success, but were unaware how ruined I had already become through failure.[1]

1. Frank Norman, *Why Fings Went West*, Lemon Tree Press, London 1975, p22.

UP WEST

Halfway through *Fings Ain't Wot They Us'd T'be* there is a rock-and-roll song, the only one in the show:

> When the big times come
> I'm gonna have me some
> I'm gonna do the fings
> My Daddy never done.
> I'm gonna get rich quick,
> And you're a lucky chick
> If you're around when I'm
> Big Time!
>
> No more Woolworth raids
> And showing off wiv blades
> Trips to Notting Hill
> For punches-up wiv spades
> Let all the other yobs
> Have tupp'ny ha'p'ny jobs
> I'm hearing Big Ben chime …
> Big Time!
>
> Big guys are cool
> Just like an icicle.
> I'm gonna fix this chain
> Back on the bicycle
> I'm gonna use my wits
> Instead of just my mitts
> So long! Small-time crime …
> Hullo! Big Time!
> I'm gonna be *so* big![2]

2. Samuel French, 'When the Big Times Come', London, pp42-3. Adam Faith later recorded the song, a follow-up to his hit, fitting epitaph to the Macmillan years, 'What Do You Want If You Don't Want Money?'.

For a brief moment you might think that this was a satirical musical like Wolf

Mankowitz's *Expresso Bongo*, where mockery of the music industry competes with the energy of its product.[3]

The sharper comparison, though, would be with Christopher Logue's *The Lily-White Boys*, directed by Lindsay Anderson at the Royal Court Theatre in the same years *Fings* moved from the Theatre Royal in Stratford East to the Garrick Theatre in the West End.[4] *The Lily-White Boys* employed the modern jazz of Bill Le Sage and, since Logue had studied with the Berliner Ensemble, it was stuffed with neo-Brechtian techniques. By conflating *Arturo Ui* with *The Threepenny Opera*, applying the result to the contemporary English scene, Logue set out to reveal an overall corruption. In *The Lily-White Boys* the 'big time' is made up of the parallel processes of politics, industry, the City, and entertainment, a series of greasy poles that are assaulted by the play's heroes, a group of young delinquents, as they gradually come to realise where the action really is:

> **Ted:** Another thing; do we ever make any big money?
> **Musclebound:** We do all right Ted.
> **Ted:** A couple of pound here, a couple of pound there! Who's making the big money? Real big money; the thousands and the tens of thousands and the hundreds of thousands? Who's making that eh? I'll tell you; it's the legitimate people.
> **Razzo:** (shocked) I'm surprised at you, Ted. A lot of people do very well on the crook.
> **Ted:** And a lot of people get put away for ten years. But if you got a legitimate business – you get away with it.[5]

Throughout *The Lily-White Boys* each episode is interspersed, in good Brechtian fashion, with short lyrics underlining the political message. 'The Song of Innocent Prosperity', for example, which has the kind of straightforwardly satirical thrust a Royal Court audience had come to expect:

> We're the lucky generation,
> Born in times when good men thrive,
> Britishers of nineteen-sixty,
> What a year to be alive!

Fings is different. It's set in a Soho *spieler* frequented by low-life of varying generations and backgrounds. Fred Cochran, an ageing gangster, attempts a comeback, but ends up becoming respectable; Sergeant Collins, a corrupt policeman, retires from the force in order to take over Fred's gambling operation; and Tosher, a ponce facing hard times, loses one of his girls only to find another, even younger. The reversals are not even moral, let alone political.

Bart's 'Big Time' rock-and-roll song remains incidental to this plot because it is performed by a group of teddy boys and girls who, however grand their

3. Saville Theatre, opened 23 April 1958.

4. 27 January 1960, with Albert Finney, Philip Locke, Georgia Brown and Shirley Anne Field.

5. *The Lily-White Boys* was never published. Quotations are taken from a licensing copy of the manuscript in the Lord Chamberlain's Collection in the British Library dated 22.1.60, No.535, p14. Logue's *Songs from The Lily-White Boys* were published by the Scorpion Press in 1960.

plans, remain a chorus. In any case, 'Big Time' is structurally overshadowed by the famous title song which, framing the main action, is sung first at the end of Act One, Scene One and then again at the end of the evening. In the first rendition 'Fings Ain't Wot They Us'd T'be' does have one or two menacing lines: 'Once in golden days of yore/Ponces killed a lazy whore'. The reprise is far less threatening:

6. Frank Norman, *Norman's London*, Secker and Warburg, London 1969, p203. Hereafter *Norman's London*.

7. Unless otherwise stated information about the early productions of *Fings* and quotations from those involved are taken from the following broadcasts: 'Ewan MacColl', BBC TV, 1990; 'Joan Littlewood', *Omnibus*, BBC TV 1994; 'Lionel Bart', *South Bank Show* 1994; 'Lionel Bart: Reviewing the Situation', compiled and produced by Carol Smith, Radio 2, 1994; 'Theatre Workshop', introduced and compiled by Howard Goorney, Radio 4, 1995. The main printed sources for the history of Theatre Workshop are: Dympha Callaghan, 'Shakespeare at the Fun Palace: Joan Littlewood', in *Cross-Cultural Performances. Differences in Women's Re-Visions of Shakespeare*, University of Illinois Press, Urbana and Chicago 1993, pp108-26; Howard Goorney, *The Theatre Workshop Story*, Methuen, London 1981; Michael Coren, *Theatre Royal: 100 Years of Stratford East*, Quartet, London 1984; Joan Littlewood, *Joan's Book*, Methuen, London 1994. Hereafter *Joan's Book*.

8. See Ewan MacColl, *Journeyman*, Sidgwick and Jackson, London 1990, p268.

Fings ain't wot they us'd t'be.
It used t'be fun –
Dad and ole' mum –
Paddlin dahn Southend.
But now it ain't done.
Never mind chum,
Paris is where we spend our outings.
Monkeys flying rahnd the moon –
We'll be up there wiv 'em soon.
Fings ain't wot they used ter,
Fings ain't wot they us'd t'be.'

The sheet music on which the hit recording was based has these verses plus some additional lines about singers 'backing themselves with three chords only!'. 'Once we danced from twelve to three/I've got news from Elvis P. Fings ain't wot they used t'be': not only are 'ponces' and 'whores' nowhere to be seen, but teenage music is relegated to second place, its subversive beat lost in the familial jollity of a Cockney knees-up.

For all those involved, *Fings* was 'Big Time' indeed. The show opened at Stratford on 15 February 1959 and was revived there on 22 December. On 11 February 1960 it transferred, winning the *Evening Standard* Award for Best Musical, running at the Garrick for just over two years, bringing the writer Frank Norman 'an average £200 a week'.[6] Income from the show briefly changed the fortunes of Joan Littlewood's Theatre Workshop company,[7] while the popularity of the songs, bolstered by a hit single of the title tune, consolidated the career of their composer, Lionel Bart. And, of course, *Fings* established the names of a whole raft of performers, Barbara Windsor, Yootha Joyce, James Booth, Miriam Karlin, Glyn Edwards among them. Barbara Windsor still thinks that *Fings* changed the face of British musical and made her kind of career possible. In 1960, with four West End musicals running at once (*Oliver, Lock up Your Daughters, Blitz* as well as *Fings*) Bart, he now says, felt 'part of the pavements of London'.

Yet for some observers, and even for some of those who were directly involved, *Fings* has become an uneasy memory. Ewan MacColl, a founder of Theatre Workshop, thought that *Fings* confirmed the forebodings he had felt in 1953 when the company had decided to give up touring working-class areas around the country and settle in London.[8] *Fings* represented 'the nadir ... the low point' of the company's history. Even Littlewood has confessed that, despite her enthusiasm for the work of Norman and Bart, she felt disappointment when the Stratford audience preferred their style to the poetry of her own favourite writer, the Jacobean playwright John Marston.[9] Norman himself often protested in his later years that the production, particularly after it had been changed from three acts to two and travelled to the West End, was very far indeed from his original conception.

9. *Joan's Book*, p546.

Quite how obvious that conception might have been when Norman's manuscript first arrived at Stratford it is hard, probably impossible, to say. Littlewood recalls a 'big sagging packet',[10] though she has also referred to '18 pages of script'. Bart has spoken of a 25 page document written in a 'kind of dyslexic way' called 'Fings Ain't Like They Used to be'. On the other hand Norman later maintained that there had been '48 pages of script',[11] and that like Brendan Behan and Shelagh Delaney he 'had provided enough meat for a feast'. Nevertheless Miriam Karlin still insists on 'a few sheets of loo paper', while James Booth, who played Tosher, and who, according to Littlewood, was the first to show enthusiasm for Norman's work, maintains that 'there was no play' and that Littlewood wrote much of the dialogue. Too many subjective memories, too much vested interest, even today.

10. *Joan's Book*, p539.

11. Norman, *op.cit.*, p50.

The Lord Chamberlain's Collection of playscripts in the British Library contains two early typescripts. One is dated 9 February 1960, less than a week before the first Stratford opening, the other has neither date nor stamp, but would seem to come from a later stage, conceivably the December revival.[12] There are also two published texts: one appeared from Secker and Warburg in 1960, the other is a French's acting edition also produced in 1960. For the most part these are very similar. The French's edition adds its customary advice for would-be producers about sets and movement and has much fuller stage directions, probably reflecting the show as it was eventually performed at the Garrick. There are also one or two changes which show how the production was adapted to make it more intelligible to a West End audience.

12. Lord Chamberlain's Collection. Licence dated 17 February 1959. No.1733.

So, for instance, the Lord Chamberlain's licensing copy opens with the prostitute's song, 'G'Night Dearie', which leads to a single exchange with Collins, the local sergeant, after he has complained about the difficulties of making an arrest. The published texts, however, open with an extended prologue scene set on VJ night:

> The entire company are on stage dancing wildly to a 'Hokey-Kokey'. A banner is stretched across the stage with the words, 'WELCOME HOME FRED' written on it. The company are dressed in various service uniforms. Fred Cochran comes on stage, everyone cheers. Two men bring on another banner inscribed 'FROM DARTMOOR'.

When the stage finally clears there's a short pause until

> ... a banner is drawn across the stage, reading 'TEN YEARS ROLL BY'; the band play a slow beat. teddy boys and girls wander on in a straggly line, and stare at the audience with contempt.

After a brief exchange the teds are replaced by Collins and the prostitutes, and 'G'Night Dearie' takes over as before.

These typescripts may not tell us much about the very earliest stages of the production (they certainly don't clarify the problem of exactly what Norman first sent down to Stratford), but they are helpful in that they show how *Fings* evolved through established methods. In this collaboration nobody was inessential; but they all had past histories.

In 1959 Joan Littlewood had more than twenty years of intensive work in the theatre behind her, years in which she had developed a volatile, constantly changing set of directorial principles. The Theatre Workshop ensemble, which she had founded with Ewan MacColl and Gerry Raffles in 1945, was nothing if not adaptable. Richard Harris speaks of her 'flirting' with Stanislavski and Laban. Brecht, however much she may have dismissed his influence later on, clearly counted for something once.[13] Lionel Bart, along with many others, has plausibly described the company style as *commedia dell'arte*. And this is backed up by Miriam Karlin, who created the role of Lily, Cochran's partner, when she says that working for Littlewood was the first time she felt she could 'legitimately improvise' – and stresses the word 'legitimately'.

'Actor-artists' is what Littlewood says she was looking for, and what, for the most part, she found. The considerable development in the role of 'Horace Seaton', the camp interior decorator in *Fings*, is almost certainly due to the inventive contribution made by the actor Wallace Eaton, while 'Redhot's' prolonged business with a suitcase packed with stolen gear surely originated in the imagination of Edward Caddick, helped perhaps by memories of Harpo Marx. Ad libs are inevitably hard to identify once they have been incorporated into a script, while many chance remarks go unrecorded – a problem that dogged the Lord Chamberlain throughout the run of *Fings*.[14]

Certainly there was nothing very systematic about Littlewood's ideas. Over the years 'the Littlewood actor mutated from a Laban athlete, into a classical realist, a clown technician, a spontaneous character improviser, a street trader; anyone who could get up and hold a crowd, and finally the crowd itself', as Irving Wardle has put it.[15] The only real constant was spontaneity: faith in the expressive power of the body ('Everything is in your feet') and in the natural energy of working-class speech.

That spontaneity still had to be worked for. Barbara Windsor later discovered that she had won the role of Rosie, one of the prostitutes in *Fings*, not through her audition, but because on her arrival at the Theatre Royal she had confided to a cleaning lady, as one Cockney to another, that she wasn't particularly keen on the part anyway. The 'cleaning lady' turned out to be Littlewood, who was so impressed by Windsor's own Shoreditch style that Rosie was swiftly changed from an Irish immigrant into a local London girl.[16]

Littlewood also had a way of asking her actors to try out each other's parts. Windsor again:

On the first day of rehearsal, Joan said, 'This script's no good ... we'll make

13. See *Bertolt Brecht in Britain*, Nicholas Jacobs and Prudence Ohlsen (eds), TQ Publications, 1977.

14. See Frank Norman, *The Guntz*, Secker and Warburg, London 1962, pp139-41. Hereafter *The Guntz*.

15. Irving Wardle, review of *Joan's Book* in *The Independent on Sunday*, 3 April 1994, p20.

16. Barbara Windsor, *Barbara: The Laughter and Tears of a Cockney Sparrow*, Century, London 1990, pp37-8.

it up as we go along.' I looked at her as if she'd gone bonkers, I was used to being told what to do. She had us all ad-libbing and generally playing silly buggers. I really thought she'd flipped her lid when she asked me to play Tosher, James Booth's part. 'I want you to go and find what his problems are.'

Littlewood's aim was a double defamiliarisation: the spontaneity achieved by having actors rely on their own resources was extended even further once they were required to imagine a range of perspectives on a single situation.

Trust in the actor's imagination even controlled set design. John Bury's partially exposed interior for *Fings*, a typical workshop design of the period, encouraged 'spontaneity' because it allowed for the actors to move directly from the close communal environment of the *spieler* down to the forestage, where they could establish a speaking rapport with their audience. Bury himself has spoken of how he and the other Theatre Workshop designers took 'the elements we needed out of naturalism and out of realism ... creating our own form of settings'. Transitions had to be quick. Theatre Workshop's long established expertise in this area is reflected in the early typescripts of *Fings*, which indicate how ambient effects can be economically achieved. So, for instance, early in Act 1:

RIVER BOATS HEARD AGAIN AS GAME RESUMES. THE CARD GAME RITUAL IS HEARD OUTSIDE. A BUS DRIVER WALKS BY BRISKLY, WHISTLING. THE GIRLS WATCH. A CAT RUNS ACROSS ROAD. THE GAME FINISHES. THE WATCHERS DISPERSE. TED COLLECTS – STRETCHES.[17]

17. Lord Chamberlain No.1733, p1.

However flexible its methods, the professed aim of Theatre Workshop never really faltered: 'Popular Theatre', productions whose energy would reflect the potential of their working-class audience. This ideal is still being maintained in the programme note to the December 1959 revival of *Fings* presumably written by Littlewood:

It is said to be a sign of the declining morals of the time that there are now so many successful plays with low life settings – THE HOSTAGE, A TASTE OF HONEY and FINGS AIN'T WHAT THEY USED TO BE – to mention only three of our own recent productions that are set outside Mayfair drawing rooms.

Unfortunately the argument does not really stand examination. Playwrights have always turned to the underworld when *le haut monde* was too rigid and dull to provide theatrical interest. The Georgian era, when the aristocracy were 'the wild ones' of the generation, brought us Restoration Comedy, but Plautus and Terence in Ancient Rome, the wandering companies of the *Commedia dell'arte* in medieval Italy, and Shakespeare, Jonson and Marston in Elizabethan England all turned away from 'respectable' life for the subjects of many of their works.

If Tosher in FINGS AIN'T WOT THEY USED T'BE wore tights and spoke in poetical fashion he would be perfectly at home on the Old Vic stage, whilst if Falstaff were played as a modern ponce and Mistress Quickly and Doll Tearsheet as modern brothel-keeper and whore, the old ladies would soon find the Old Vic was not what it used t'be. Perhaps that would not be a bad thing either.[18]

18. Programme note for the revival on 22 December 1959.

Lionel Bart had grasped this vision immediately. Born in the East End in 1930, Bart came to Stratford East via St Martin's School of Art; the '2 I's' coffee bar in Dean Street, Soho (which led to his writing hits for Tommy Steele and Cliff Richard); Denmark Street, where he got to know the music publishers; and King's Cross, where Unity, the left-wing theatre, had its base. At Unity he had most recently been involved in *Wally Pone*, a musical about a gangster based on Jonson's *Volpone*, but set in contemporary Soho. The opening song for *Fings*, 'G'night Dearie', was imported from this project which had run for ten not very successful weeks the previous year.[19]

19. Colin Chambers, *The Story of Unity Theatre*, Lawrence and Wishart, London 1989, pp350-1.

When journalists made cultural connections with other Jewish writers from the East End – Wolf Mankowitz, Arnold Wesker, Harold Pinter – Bart was happy enough to go along on the grounds that they were all 'realists'. 'People like me', he told Herbert Kretzmer in 1960, 'who came from the gutters of the East End, we haven't got time for all that surface chi-chi like *Salad Days*. We have seen too much that is true and real. Look at Wesker. All that guts and reality, man! Look at Pinter. You know what it is? It's a search for truth. That's what it is.'[20]

20. Interview with Herbert Kretzmer, *Sunday Dispatch*, 3 July 1960, p2.

Bart's particular 'search for truth' was geared to writing for performance. 'I never write into a void. I always know just who I am writing a song for. I work to his individual style and audience. I put myself in his shoes.' If necessary Bart would perform his songs himself. For the first couple of weeks of the initial run of *Fings* it was the composer, disguised as a busker in an old First World War greatcoat and boots found under the stage, who delivered, unaccompanied, the menacing 'Meatface' rhyme:

> Who left his old girl in the lurch?
> Meatface! Meatface!
>
> Who made a rude noise in church?
> Meatface! Meatface!
>
> When there's a fight, his day's well made ...
> He's a proper villain wiv a razor-blade

Bart's understanding of individual performers was responsible for some of the most successful moments in *Fings*: the ballad 'Where do Little Birds Go?' for instance (half Marie Lloyd, half Rose Murphy), specially written for Barbara Windsor. An earlier song, still visible in the typescripts, called 'A Place in the

Old Country' (presumably written when Rosie was still Irish) seems to have disappeared altogether, despite some wry lines:

> I remember a cottage in County Kildare
> And there's nothing so green as the grass growing there
> When I'm closing my eyes that's the picture I see …
> And it's oh, for a place in the old country …
> I found work as a waitress in Lyons Corner-House
> And I lives on a diet – enough for a mouse –
> But the tips were much larger in Piccadilly …
> And it's oh, for a place in the old country!

Bart's best lyrics are rooted in the London he knew. The witty 'Contempery' number, originally sung by Miriam Karlin, makes a point about Cockney aspirations even more pointedly than the title song. It's a comic version of Mick's famous dreams of 'teal-blue, copper and parchment squares' in Pinter's *The Caretaker*.[21]

Where does this leave the contribution of Frank Norman? Everywhere and nowhere. However much its 'original conception' was subsequently redirected by the combined interventions of director, composer and cast, *Fings* undeniably had its origins in Norman's own experience, and in a style of writing he had brought to the fore with his first book, *Bang to Rights*. When this had appeared the previous year it had attracted attention as much for the supposed authenticity of its 'Cockney' style as for the revelations of its subject-matter.

Not that Norman was a Cockney by any conventional definition. Born out of wedlock in Bristol in 1930, a series of would-be adoptive parents eventually decided not to take him on and he was placed, aged seven, with Dr Barnardo's, who moved him from institution to institution in and around the home counties. On his release in 1946 Norman worked the dodgems with a travelling fair, and then gravitated to Soho, where he survived by doing odd jobs in small-time gambling dens, and by petty crime. A number of short prison sentences finally culminated in three years 'corrective training' imposed for using a stolen cheque book. It was this that had formed the basis for the first and triumphant book, an insider's record of constant surveillance and daily bullying, of profound homelessness.

'Everybody wants to belong somewhere. I belong nowhere', Norman told Herbert Kretzmer in 1960.

> My mother and father were never married. I knew my old man. He had a fruit stall. I took his religion – Catholic.
>
> I never knew my mother. She married a cabbie the same year I was born. I was sent to a kid's home, something like that. My mother's got three kids now. Like I say, I've never seen her. No, I don't want to meet her again. What for? I'd hate it.
>
> I don't know if she even knows I'm alive. It doesn't matter either way. I

21. *Plays Two*, Faber, London 1991, p58.

22. *Sunday Dispatch*,
14 February 1960, p2.

never knew I was illegitimate until I was 14. A trick cyclist may say it affected my life. Maybe that's true. It doesn't matter.[22]

The success of *Bang to Rights* meant that when Norman (at the suggestion of Penelope Gilliat) sent his play manuscript to Stratford East in 1959 he had already had some knowledge of the worlds of publishing and journalism. The theatre was new to him:

> ... I just stood by not saying all that much and watched the whole thing take shape under the hand of Joan Littlewood. From time to time I was dragged onto the stage to ad lib some dialogue, but was given the slingers almost straight away for not being all that good at the acting game.[23]

23. There are further accounts of rehearsals of the first production by Norman in *The Guntz*, pp34-5; *Norman's London*, Secker and Warburg, London 1969, pp147-56; *Joan's Book*, Chapter 46 *passim*.

In Littlewood's revised version of Norman's script petty theft and illegal gambling are all-pervasive, but are treated in an entirely lighthearted, matter-of-fact way. The director, no more than the author, had little interest in stressing parallels between crime and capitalism in the Brechtian manner of *The Lily-White Boys*. The slumming aristocrats who visit Cochran's *spieler* to gamble are simply, comically, absurd.

Similarly the representation of prostitution in *Fings* is largely genial. Although the recommendations of the Street Offences Act 1959, which had been designed to keep prostitutes out of sight, are shown to be ineffective, there is no indication of the kind of heated controversy that grew up in response to the Act. (Would driving the sex trade underground lead to the increasing power of the ponces? Or, quite the reverse, would the women be freed from the kind of organisation run by the notorious Messina brothers?[24] Would the 'hostess' racket be any kind of improvement?) Littlewood did encourage James Booth to play Tosher as 'a new character, young and lively' – whereas Norman had written him 'as an old geezer' – but her aim was to sharpen the confrontation with Collins, the corrupt sergeant, rather than to say anything about the changing face of Soho.[25]

24. The notorious Maltese family who ran a Soho vice racket in the 1950s get a single brief mention in the play.

25. *Joan's Book*, p541.

Even so there may be a clue here to an essential point of difference between writer and director: their representation of Soho's past. In the printed text, the stages of Fred Cochran's career are precisely dated: started on crime in 1929, had one-armed bandits in the Mile End Road in 1932, by 1937 had five *spielers*, sold clothing coupons in the early years of the war, and so on. The trouble with the ad libbing that Littlewood encouraged was, as Norman complained later, that it broke this carefully patterned chronology:

> ...some of the actors overdo it and start adding lines which have nothing whatever to do with the play such as remarks about Krushchev, Tony Armstrong-Jones, the Lord Chamberlain, the Duchess of Argyll, Franco, parking meters, Debs Delights, Football Teams, the Weather and even myself, also anything topical which might get a laugh. I reckon this is a bit dodgy because the action of the play (as far as I am concerned) took place

over ten years ago, and the characters in the play would in fact have no interest what ever in the aforementioned people, object or subjects.[26]

26. *The Guntz*, p75.

Norman always saw Soho as an accurate locus for measuring social change – that had been the starting-point for *Fings*. 'It's different now around these streets,' he told Kretzmer as they strolled up Dean Street in 1960, 'There don't seem to be no bums around any more. Ten years ago all kinds of geezer got carved up and the bums had somewhere to go. Today, if you want to go on the bum in Soho you're on your own.'

By treating Soho in this way Norman was not alone among the writers of the 1950s: Peter Wildeblood, Bernard Kops, Colin MacInnes and Colin Wilson all took much the same approach. Later on, despite the success in Stratford and at the Garrick, despite a flat in Hampstead, Soho remained Norman's beat. *Stand on Me: A True Story of Soho* published in 1959 is very similar in parts to *Fings*. In 1966, together with Jeffrey Bernard, Norman compiled *Soho Night and Day*, a valedictory picture-book, and the area is featured throughout *Norman's London* of 1969. In 1974 he told Daniel Farson, a fellow frequenter of Muriel Belcher's Colony Room, that he had written a comedy called *Rough Trade*, which was 'really more about the decline and imminent fall of Soho than it is about club life'.[27]

27. Daniel Farson, *Soho in the Fifties*, Michael Joseph, London 1987, p51.

Norman's mixed feelings about Soho, his deepening nostalgia for a past that was certainly mythologised if not exactly mythical, explain why 'my conception of *Fings* was and still is a bit of a nasty story about a has-been gangster who is trying to make a come back, and how he doesn't make it on account of "things not being what they used to be".'[28] In the Littlewood revision Fred Cochran does 'make it': he survives a razor fight (which takes place off-stage), he becomes successful when he turns the *spieler* into a fashionable night-spot, and the show ends in celebration with his wedding to Lily. All this, claimed Norman in 1962, 'was a load of schmaltz which had very little to do with what I had written about'.

28. *The Guntz*, p74.

When Bart later described *Fings* as a 'totally organic' show he must surely have meant in its creative process rather than in its constituent parts. For all that, Littlewood, Norman and Bart did share one vital attitude: generosity towards their audiences. The friendly direct address of which *Fings* makes frequent use – 'It's going to be lovely' Horace Seaton tells the audience at the end of the second act – is a symptom of this deliberate rapport. It is impossible to imagine a Theatre Workshop show concluding with the final line of *The Lily-White Boys*: 'Goodbye folks', says 'Ted', also to the audience: 'It was nice meeting you ... See you all in hell! And if you get there first – keep the home fires burning.' 'I don't hate anybody,' said Frank Norman in 1960. 'I'm not like John Osborne and Christopher Logue who are always cramming hate into their writing. It's embarrassing to watch them on TV. They're always having a go at somebody.'[29]

29. *Sunday Dispatch*, 14 February 1960, p2.

30. Littlewood has frequently been accused of sentimentality and nostalgia. See, for example, Daniel Farson, *Sacred Monsters*, Bloomsbury, London 1988, pp126-7 and Lindsay Anderson quoted in Coren, *op.cit.*, p40.

Ironically, it was this ineradicable populism that made it difficult for Theatre Workshop to criticise the 'big-time' Toryism of the 1950s in any kind of focused way.[30] Expressing the voice of the people would have to be an end in itself.

Fortunately the sheer variety of those popular voices did alert the company to the expressive opportunities offered the working class through entertainment – whether supposedly traditional in the manner of the music-hall – or brand new, like rock-and-roll. Variety was in itself a sign of changes in the composition, experience and outlook of their audience. From now on, with the coming of TV, of pop, of 'affluence' (however selective that might have been), working-class authenticity would be a mode of performance, of testing and of adaptation. No wonder that its creators look back at *Fings* in apprehension. It prefigures so much: from *Till Death Do Us Part* to *Birds of a Feather*, from *Steptoe and Son* to, inevitably, *EastEnders*.

FURTHER DOWN THE LINE

'I'm contemporary ... aren't I? I really do live at the same time as myself, don't I?'

Shelagh Delaney, *A Taste of Honey*

'In the theatre of those dear departed days when every actress had roses round her vowels and a butler's suit was an essential part of an actor's equipment, the voice of the Cockney was one long whine of blissful servitude', wrote Joan Littlewood in the introduction to the published edition of *Fings*.

Cockney is as Cockney sounds. Norman may have been a novice when it came to acting and improvisation but he knew something about what Lionel Bart liked to call 'English as she is spoke'. *Bang to Rights* and *Stand on Me* were both printed apparently as he had written them: ungrammatical and, in the case of the first book, misspelt. Though this was probably the publisher's idea, Norman had gone along with it, explaining in a preface to *Bang to Rights* that 'the spelling was part of the book and should remain as it is now'. A Cockney glossary entitled 'A Bit about Slang'[31] had also helped in the launching of his reputation: a mixture of rhyming slang,[32] Yiddish, prison argot and recent Americanisms, a farago of solecisms and send-ups. In the books this heterogeneity is coupled with consistent errors, and not only of spelling.

'Error', according to modern linguistic theory, should be considered at best as 'a neutral term'.[33] In Norman's case, because the medium of production (the published book) normally respects the conventions, the term may quite accurately describe a deliberate transgression. Norman's fractured, ironic, self-aware language, with its calculated attempt to catch the public notion of Cockney speech, may have served a commercial impulse, but nevertheless, like Littlewood's campaign to purge the stage of refined diction, it was socially affirmative. 'Error' attempted to reclaim the metropolis for those who lived there, took it back from the possessive gaze of the professional *flâneurs*.

When you survey the city from a distance, what you see tends to be what you hear. Here, for example, is a passage from Richard Cobb's introduction to a reprint of Norman's *Banana Boy*, published as recently as 1987. Norman, says Cobb,

31. First printed in *Encounter* in 1959, reprinted in *Norman's London*.

32. Rhyming slang, a major component of Norman's style, is said to have been first written about in the 1850s and to have come into fashion the previous decade. See Julian Franklyn, *The Cockney*, Deutsch, London 1953, p295.

33. 'To the psychologist and linguist, speech errors and errors in writing are not mistakes in the social sense, but pieces of evidence that allow a reconstruction of the theory that went into their writing. "Error" is a neutral term'. Carolyn Steedman, Introduction to *The Radical Soldier's Tale*, Routledge, London 1988, p23.

has the knack ... of bringing out the dreary, yet semi-comical, banality of trolley-bus-terminal topography on the northern edges of London – Enfield, Dalston, Ponders End, and the ever-persistent Waltham Cross ... the dim, seedy borderlands between the vast city and that indefinable county: Herts. Some of the worst years of his childhood had been in Bedford, followed, briefly, by Kingston-upon-Thames, then Herts; and his surburbia is funny, totally un-assuming, pathetic, and rather sad.

Why Hertfordshire should be 'indefinable' or why North London should be 'anonymous' when Cobb has just named its constituent areas is unclear. But then topography is here being defied in the interests of the kind of appropriative musing that can, at the same time, easily shade into plebeian romanticism: 'funny ... and rather sad'.[34]

Cobb posits a connection between language and landscape. 'Frank Norman is not only a very visual writer, especially when describing the anonymous wasteland on the northern rim of London, he also knows how to use his ears, which are well attuned to the vagaries of cockney speech'. It follows that Cobb should see Norman's 'ever-watchful, quick-footed, wry humour' as simple resistance to a doomed environment (the predictable 'wasteland') rather than as the product of a social experience that undoubtedly had its communal elements. When Cobb quotes Norman on how 'On Saturday afternoons the local talent, both boys and girls, congregated outside Woolworth's in Waltham Cross High Street', he seems oblivious to what this might imply.

Cobb's well-intentioned tribute to Norman's style obscures its real origins, which were historical and well known to its author. As *Stand on Me* insists:

I am that dreaded thing that people do not like to accept, 'a product of the war'. When I should have been in school I was sitting in air raid shelters, and therefore when I left school at the age of fourteen I was double backward, and in fact could not read and write at all.

Once again historical awareness is crucial. Compare the previous passage by Cobb, the academic historian, with this by the 'illiterate' Barnado's boy writing on exactly the same topic: outer London.

The Cockney accent has now spread as far afield as Stevenage in Hertfordshire and Bromley in Kent, for the housing in town is rapidly reaching saturation point. Old and young are persuaded by their local councils to move from their squalid homes in Paddington, Islington and Limehouse but all are reluctant to move to the shiny new houses in the suburbs, where the air is fresh and the grass green. They prefer by far to remain where they are amid the squalor, coal-dust and grime, for that is where their roots are and they have no wish to tear them up. Who can blame them for that? The more I look at London the less I seem to know it.[35]

34. This is the same criticism of Cobb that Adrian Rifkin has voiced about his (and others') work on Paris: that here is a version of the city 'that refuses any kind of politic(s) – except the unspoken one that controls their texts, the politics of the freedom of the *flâneur*, to master the appearances of things.' Adrian Rifkin, *Street Noises: Parisian Pleasures 1900-40*, Manchester University Press, Manchester 1993, p23. Norman was no *flâneur*.

35. *Norman's London*, pp255-6.

If, in 1960, Frank Norman could no longer 'know' London, who could? Certainly not the sociologists, though they, unlike Cobb, were at least prepared to ask questions.

Post-war London was much scrutinised by academics. Not surprisingly. Out of bomb sites tower blocks were rising; 'New Towns' pushed against 'Green Belt'. The city was changing its shape, as cities must. The most celebrated investigations of subsequent social change were produced by Michael Young and Peter Willmott, who conducted a series of investigations into urban life based on comparisons between established communities like Bethnal Green and suburban developments in Essex.[36] What they discovered were changing values – though their own ideological preconceptions made it easier for them to identify social positives in Bethnal Green rather than further out.

Past surveys ('Study has been piled upon study')[37] of working-class life, they claimed, had created an impression that working-class families are 'unsuited, unsocial and unhappy'. But this judgement was inaccurate and confused, in that it suggested that life was the same in 1957 as when it had 'evoked such righteous horror from Mayhew, Booth and Rowntree'. Whereas

36. *Family and Kinship in East London*, Routledge and Kegan Paul, London 1957 and *Family and Class in a London Suburb*, Routledge and Kegan Paul, London 1960.

37. *Family and Kinship*, pp19-20.

there is no confusion in Bethnal Green. People are well aware of the change which has come upon them in the course of a few decades. Indeed it is because the comparisons they make between the old and the new are so much a part of their mentality, the source of much present exhilaration and perplexity, and because the influence of the old is so clearly written upon the new, that the contrast properly belongs to an account of the impressions we have formed of present-day life.

Working people are as acutely aware of change as anyone else, probably more so. As Young and Willmott pointed out – and in 1957 this was already rather labouring the obvious:

The popular press, the cinema, the radio, and now the television have put new models, drawn from other classes and other parts of the world, before the local people, creating new aspirations and new ideals.

More importantly, they recognised how these 'new models' had deeply affected the rhythms of domestic life:

George, twenty-three and still single, rushed about, washing in the kitchen, combing his hair and fixing his tie in front of the mirror above the fireplace, preparatory to 'going out with boys'. By the wall, near the door sat the nineteen-year-old Jean and her boy Freddie, holding hands, looking at the television when they took their eyes off each other, and giggling occasionally at the rigmarole of extraordinary questions.

In the suburbs, by contrast, Young and Willmott discovered lives based on status and possessions (the materialist bogey of 1950s sociology). The comparison between Bethnal Green ('Bethnal Greeners are not lonely people: whenever they go for a walk in the street, for a drink in the pub, or for a row on the lake in Victoria Park, they know the faces in the crowd', and 'Greenleigh', the suburb (' "it's the television most nights and the garden in the summer" ') is unavoidable.

Like Bethnal Green, Stratford East, where Theatre Workshop operated, is working-class, halfway down the Central Line, eight stops from Oxford Circus, eight stops from Debden, one of the newer suburban developments noted by Willmott and Young. Already in the early 1950s, when the company first arrived, Stratford was changing, its traditional industries dying, its High Street a rat-run for cars heading for Epping Forest, even further out. It was becoming more and more of a transitional area, which is why critics and commentators never ceased to marvel that the theatre was only a minute's walk from the tube station.

They, of course, were travelling east, returning west, and, as postmodern geography reminds us, perception of place depends upon angle of approach. What if you travelled into Stratford the other way around? What if you left by travelling in the direction that so many East Londoners had already followed or planned so to do? What was the message of *Fings* for you?

There's no need to question Theatre Workshop's claim to have built up a local audience since all the evidence suggests that, against enormous odds, it was extraordinarily successful in doing just that. This was a community interested in, and informed about, the wider world, conscious (how could it be otherwise?) of the impermanence of buildings, the changing nature of social groups. Accordingly Theatre Workshop conceived of an audience that would be largely local in habitation, and in its sense of itself, but wide-ranging in its interests and knowledge. The company could be confident of such an audience because over the years it had observed the modern urban world and knew that most theatre was hopelessly out-of-step. It's what Littlewood meant when she complained in the note to *Fings* about a stultifying bourgeois tradition that had all 'the charm of an aged Peter Pan'.

One way in which Theatre Workshop responded to the new circumstances was by refusing to confine its repertoire to the obviously relevant: Brendan Behan's *The Quare Feller* and *The Hostage* were not exactly London plays, nor was Shelagh Delaney's *A Taste of Honey*, nor for that matter were plays by Molière and Hasek. *Fings*, though, like Wolf Mankowitz's *Make me an Offer*, 1959, and Stephen Lewis' *Sparrers Can't Sing*, 1960, *was* a London play, a play about London in flux. That is why Norman's 'Cockney' dialogue was so powerful, not because it was permanent and indigenous, quite the contrary, but because it was the conscious product of a time that no longer knew its social place, of a place that only knew that times were changing. *Fings*, the 'Cockney musical', is one of the forms – nostalgic, ripe, displaced – in which that awareness found theatrical expression.

In their second book on East London, Willmott and Young offer a spatial image of the metropolis, recording that in the Essex suburb of Woodford,

> Although people talk about travelling 'up to town' in this social context 'out' means 'up', up the 'ladder', up 'in the social scale', 'up in the world'. It was as though, in the mind's eye, people had turned the whole of East London on its side like a geological exhibit in a giant-sized museum. There deep down in the social strata were Bethnal Green and Stepney and there at the top Woodford and Wanstead. To clamber up the slope was success, to remain at the bottom, failure ...[38]

38. *Family and Class*, p4.

By this reckoning Joan Littlewood's London would have Stratford at the top and Shaftesbury Avenue somewhere near the bottom. Frank Norman, though, always played time against place, held the whole of London up to his own changing view.

THE GUNTZ

In later years Norman returned continually to the experience of *Fings* because he felt it important that the record should be set straight. Survival depended on his maintaining his original talent; failure would cast doubt over his previous career. Theatre Workshop had, for a 'serious writer', been the best and the worst of places:

> ... there was the impossibility of identification between what was originally on the page and what was being passed off on the stage as the author's work. This of course gave rise to a situation in which a playwright with a natural aptitude for drama would never discover how good he really was, while a writer with no knowledge of the theatre, but enough gumption to slap down an idea, would find himself saddled with a reputation out of all proportion to his talent.[39]

39. Norman, *op.cit.*, p22.

'Seriousness' and 'talent', 'aptitude' and 'knowledge' are the watch-words now. Long ago, in *Stand on Me*, Norman had written about Bill, a would-be painter who had remarked that there were times when he felt as if he would masturbate into the paint so that he could be sure he had put everything into his work. Only later had Norman grasped the personal relevance of his friend's unusual thought:

> At the time I was greatly shocked by what he said, because it doesn't follow that just because you are a thief and maybe a few other things as well, that you are also corrupt, in fact nothing could be further from the truth. I was dead innocent in a lot of ways and things like this always shocked me, but now that I am a little older I am beginning to understand what he was talking about, even though it may be going to extremes just to put yourself

into something. I also realise now that Bill was nowhere near as intelligent as I had thought him to be, but he was sincere in whatever he did whether he was writing or painting; for sincerity has nothing whatever to do with ability or talent.[40]

40. *Stand on Me*, pp73-4.

Once sincerity had been cast aside, performance, artifice, pretence even, became part of being Frank Norman. He eventually came to accept the inevitability of his image as 'scar-faced ex-jailbird, illegitimate son of a costermonger', and built it into parody interviews.[41] A story went around (said to have originated with Bernard Levin) that he was the son of an aristocrat, educated at Eton and Cambridge.[42]

41. *The Guntz*, pp163-4.

42. *The Guntz*, p121.

Performance was part of being a personality, which was in turn part of being a writer. Walking the streets of Soho with Norman three days after the West End opening of *Fings*, Kretzmer cleverly turns the interview into *faux* Chandlerese:

> expensively suited, he walked to his glinting Lagonda. In the wet, hurrying streets, nobody paused to recognise him. Not even the policeman untangling the angry traffic on the corner of Shaftesbury Avenue.

Like other journalists, Kretzmer quickly cottoned on to Norman's game:

> 'I've never been married,' he announced resolutely ignoring the fact he was married nine years ago ... 'I have no family and that lark,' declared Frank Norman, who has a daughter to whom he is devoted.'

At the same time as Norman's writing became more meticulous, and more conventionally literate, it remained introspective. In *Banana Boy*, published in 1969, memory and observation are played off against each other. Middle-aged and drunk, Norman returns to Onslow Square where he remembers spending time in the care of a charitable aristocrat. The building is nowhere to be found. Later his recollections of swallows that fed out of his hand compete with memories of being ordered to unblock lavatories.

Could any theatre ever have accommodated that private void? Littlewood had managed it for Behan with *The Quare Fellow* in the very early 1960s, but once again, her approach had moved on. In 1964 Norman returned to the Stratford with *A Kayf Up West* set in 1949: 'a great rambling, panoramic documentary of Soho's lower depths during the post-war years'.[43] Only a few scenes were set in the 'kayf' and the script demanded, among other things, for the recreation of Kew Gardens, the barrier at Waterloo station, a London park. There were forty-six speaking parts: one stage direction reads 'A troupe of West Indian immigrants dance on.' To cope with the problem and to demonstrate her belief in natural talent Littlewood called in some local teddy boys who got distinctly annoyed when told they could not smoke on stage.[44] Little wonder that *Kayf* failed to interest any West End managers. It wasn't even a musical.

43. Norman, *op.cit.*, p81. Also see Barry Humphries, *More Please*, Penguin, Harmondsworth 1993, pp237-8.

44. See Irving Wardle's review of *Joan's Book*.

It was a topographical play that, unlike *Fings*, not only asked for full-scale semi-realistic effects but a more self-conscious use of theatricality (the characters introduce themselves to the audience at the start).[45] Conventionally picaresque, the story opens with Tommie, the hero, hitching a lift to London where he falls in with a bunch of out-of-work actors, tarts, dope-pushers. As a result of a misunderstanding he ends up in jail. While inside he loses his girlfriend, Jess, who becomes a full-time prostitute. On his release they break up, and the show concludes with a repeat of the first scene in which another young boy wanders into the café, much as Tommie had done at the start:

45. *Kayf* was never published: quotations are taken from the typescript in the Lord Chamberlain's Collection. Licence dated 10 March 1964, no.4080.

> **Boy:** (Sitting. To Jess) I bin walking all night.
> **Jess:** Where'd you come from, kid?
> **Boy:** Thames Ditton.
> **Jess:** Ain't that funny – I come from Kingston.

As always the vastness of the metropolis creates the smallest, the most complete, the most diverse of worlds. The really powerful parts of *Kayf*, though, are the prison scenes which have something of the quality of *Bang to Rights*, the book in which Norman had first expressed his authoritative views on the contradictory nature of justice.

With *Insideout*, which Ken Campbell directed at the Royal Court in November 1969, Norman again returned to prison life.[46] Lindsay Anderson, who, together with Anthony Page, was running the Court at the time, described Norman's extreme sensitivity about working with others, but remembered the play as 'well received'.[47] It certainly reads well. The stage directions have a new confidence: Norman knows what he wants to say, knows how that might be theatrically expressed. It's a play without a set that relies on the rhythms of institutionalised speech: 'the standard ritual of turning PRISONERS into convicts (coldblooded and inhuman)'. According to the criminologist C.H. Rolph, *Insideout* 'horrified all but those who go into the prisons and see for themselves.'[48]

46. Published in *Plays and Players*, February 1970, pp61-78.

47. *Bang to Rights*, un-numbered page. Also see *Why Fings Went West*, pp95-100.

48. Introduction, *The Lives of Frank Norman*, Penguin, Harmonds-worth 1972, p9.

Somehow the impetus foundered. *Costa Packet*, a musical about package holidays, directed by Joan Littlewood in 1972 with songs by Alan Klein, was Norman's last play to be staged. It ran at the Theatre Royal for ten weeks, but there were decisive rows and in Littlewood's autobiography *Costa Packet* goes unmentioned.

SEXTON BLAKING

> I was sometimes referred to in the press as the Cockney Brendan Behan and later the Cockney Jean Genet. I do not recall ever seeing the compliment reversed.[49]

49. Norman, *op.cit.*, p22.

For most of the 1970s Norman concentrated on novels, usually comedy thrillers. When he died of Hodgkin's Disease in 1980 at the age of 50, his career as a writer was at an uncertain stage, the material repetitive, the ambition reasonably intact. It is not easy to predict what the outcome might have been.[50]

In 1977 he had collaborated with his second wife, Geraldine Norman, sale-room correspondent of *The Times*, on a book about the painter Tom Keating, who had become famous for his skill in recreating the styles of the masters. *The Fake's Progress*, has a foreword, jointly ascribed to husband and wife, followed by 'Tom Keating's Story. As told by Frank Norman'.[51] Affection and respect for Keating are evident throughout the biographical section, and a strong degree of identification. Both men had working-class origins: Keating had a taste for rhyming slang; Norman was a self-described 'Sunday painter'. The book closes with an essay by Geraldine Norman on 'Art Trading and Art Faking' which defines successful faking as the combination of technique and inspiration. A need for technique is obvious. Why should fakers need inspiration? Because they must communicate on a level commensurate with that of the original artist.

By these criteria Frank Norman emerges as a true artist, a genuine faker. The man whose criminal career came to an end when he was arrested for imitating other people's signatures became a writer by standing up for himself. Reproducing Cockney speech as it was commonly thought to sound, he developed his technique to the point where he could turn out journalism, novels and plays that were widely accepted as his own. Inspiration was there too. By acting out his life in his writing Frank Norman became an original.

50. For various memories of Norman, including those of Geraldine Norman, see *The Times*, 10 January 1987, p7.

51. *The Fake's Progress*, Hutchinson, London 1977.

EMBODYING THE NATION: GENDER AND PERFORMANCE IN WOMEN'S FICTION

Gill Frith

National identity is the hot topic of the 1990s, but literary and social historians seem to be having trouble putting gender on this newly-emerging map. In his introduction to *Literary Englands*, David Gervais comments: 'I have not discussed any English women writers. When I thought of doing so I began to wonder if their concern with "Englishness" were not of a different order'. Quite so. It is. But I am not satisfied that the difference lies, as Gervais suggests, in a concern that is 'less public and less geared to nationalistic attitudes'.[1]

Nationalism, says Benedict Anderson, is 'an imagined political community', a community whose members 'will never know most of their fellow-members, meet them, or even hear of them, yet in the minds of each lives the image of their communion'.[2] The community's homogeneity, and the boundaries to that homogeneity, are sustained in the mind through shared ceremonies and commodities, replications which reassure each member 'that the imagined world is visibly rooted in everyday life'.[3] I shall be looking in this essay at novels by women writers which both 'place' women in the 'imagined political community', and work towards envisaging a community *beyond* the everyday, beyond the constraints of the existent 'imaginings'. I want to demonstrate the ways in which nation and gender work together in women's fiction by looking at female 'performativity' in novels written during two periods of cultural crisis, periods when gender roles were the subject of intense public contestation and debate: the 1840s and the 1970s/1980s.

The 1840s saw the publication of a number of novels which interweave nation and gender by depicting a relationship between a young English woman and a woman who is part-Italian. In Geraldine Jewsbury's *The Half Sisters* (1848) and Georgiana Fullerton's *Grantley Manor* (1847), the two women are half-sisters; in Elizabeth Sewell's *Margaret Percival* (1847) and Grace Aguilar's *Woman's Friendship* (1850), they are friends. The 'mother-text' of all four novels is clearly Mme de Staël's *Corinne* (1807), a novel whose impact on British women writers cannot be overestimated. Although Maggie Tulliver in *The Mill on the Floss* failed to finish it, its general reception is captured more accurately in *The Half Sisters*: 'The first reading of 'Corinne' is an epoch a woman never forgets, and Alice never lifted her head till she had come to the last line in the last page of the volume ...'[4]

Corinne's fictional British 'daughters' of the 1840s were completed before the 1848 revolutions, but they do reflect the political, social, and religious ferment of the decade. It was a time, said Elizabeth Sewell, when 'everyone seemed waking up to a sense of unfulfilled duties'.[5] It was also a strangely contradictory

1. David Gervais, *Literary Englands: Versions of 'Englishness' in Modern Writing*, Cambridge University Press, Cambridge, 1993 ppxiii-xiv. For an alternative viewpoint, see Terry Lovell, 'Gender and Englishness in *Villette*' in Sally Ledger, Josephine McDonagh and Jane Spencer (eds), *Political Gender*, Harvester Wheatsheaf, Hemel Hempstead, 1994, pp37-52.

2. Benedict Anderson, *Imagined Communities: Reflections on the Origin and Spread of Nationalism*, rev. ed., Verso, London 1991, p6.

3. *Ibid.*, pp35-36.

4. Geraldine Jewsbury, *The Half Sisters* (1848), Oxford University Press, Oxford, 1994, p60.

5. *The Autobiography of Elizabeth M. Sewell*, Eleanor L. Sewell (ed), Longmans, Green and Co., London 1907, p80.

period for women. On the one hand, it was the decade in which the ideology which confined the middle-class woman to the confines of the home was consolidated; on the other hand, it was the decade which saw the seeds of the middle-class women's movement, and the changes in women's educational opportunities which were to accelerate over the next half-century. The same period saw the proliferation of conduct manuals which set out the terms of the middle-class Englishwoman's 'mission', the contribution which she could make to the good of the community; and they did so by appealing to origins: to the fixity and 'naturalness' of both gendered and national identity. I shall be arguing that the double identity, the hybrid origins, of the half-Italian heroine provided a means by which the woman writer could attempt to negotiate a position beyond that fixity. Once 'origins' are in doubt, nature is also thrown into the air.

It is in the 'half-sisters' plot that the question of origins is most pressing. *The Half Sisters* and *Grantley Manor* closely follow the model of *Corinne*. In all three novels, the half-Italian sister is illegitimate, either literally, or because she has been spurned by her biological father. She is also a 'performing heroine': she sings, acts, improvises, plays the piano publicly, on stage. She has a 'hybrid' personality: innocent and passionate, creative and domestic, autonomous and dependent. During the course of the novel she discovers and encounters her English half-sister, who conforms to the English domestic ideal. The two women fall in love with the same man, an Englishman.

'Foreignness' might simply be seen here as providing a licence for transgression: the non-British heroine can act out desires, adopt positions, realise talents which are illegitimate for women within the terms of the English community. But it isn't as simple as that, for two reasons. Firstly, and seemingly paradoxically, her performance is not represented as an 'act'. It is, rather, a public expression of her truest and deepest self, an externalisation which also mediates the aspirations and profoundest feelings of the community to which she performs. She performs, then, *for* the community: she pulls together its scattered members, articulates desires it didn't know it had, and gives a shape to its imaginings. Secondly, there is the question of what happens to her *after* the performance. The moment when the heroine reaches her creative peak comes relatively early in the novel. She is feted and adored by a (primarily male) audience which is putty in her hands. But this integration is followed by her gradual disintegration; she falls sick, becomes pale and emaciated, and loses her powers.

It may seem that nation is acting here simply as a trope for gender, providing a vehicle for questioning some of the Victorian constraints upon female identity and desire. But the very inextricability of the two terms – nation and gender – as they work together in the text means that, in pushing against the boundaries of gender norms, the narrative also pushes against the existing configurations of 'Englishness'. The contradictory position of the foreign woman who gives cohesiveness to the community but remains outside its boundaries directs attention to the fact that the shortcomings of the community are *national* shortcomings.

In *The Location of Culture*, Homi Bhabha urges us to 'locate the question of culture in the realm of the *beyond*'; to look beyond singular positions and unitary identities, and *at* the 'in-between' and the 'unhomely'.

> What is theoretically innovative, and politically crucial, is the need to think beyond narratives of originary and initial subjectivities and to focus on those moments or processes that are produced in the articulation of cultural differences. These 'in-between' spaces provide the terrain for elaborating strategies of selfhood – singular or communal – that initiate new signs of identity, and innovative sites of collaboration, and contestation, in the act of defining the idea of society itself.
>
> It is in the emergence of the interstices – the overlap and displacement of domains of difference – that the intersubjective and collective experiences of *nationness*, community interest, or cultural value are negotiated.[6]

6. Homi K. Bhabha, *The Location of Culture*, Routledge, London 1994, pp1-2.

7. *Ibid.*, p6.

Bhabha is describing a contemporary phenomenon, the new internationalism in which 'national' cultures are 'being produced from the perspective of disenfranchised minorities',[7] so it might seem impertinent to apply his arguments to Victorian fiction. But I want to do so because I think his words describe precisely what is happening in the half-sisters novels: 'origin' is displaced, and the 'in-between' serves to negotiate new signs of identity. I would suggest, however, that it is a prefigurative use of the 'in-between', a *fantasy* of shifting the boundaries of the legitimate, which can only be realised in fiction – and even the fantasy is circumscribed. The heroine's illegitimacy places her outside normal kinship structures and confers the power to go beyond the constraints of paternal naming. But although she performs *as* herself, she directs that performance *to* a man. Her fascination and flamboyance are mediated to the reader through the eyes of her present or future lover: it is for him, really, that she places herself on display. But she can't have him: his father's edict demands that he marry an English rose. Paternal prohibition gets in the way after all: her foreignness, her religion, her illegitimacy place her too far outside the boundaries of what the community can imagine. She cannot, ultimately, name herself or her desires. She can perform *for* the community, but the performance cannot be sustained *into* the community. It is beyond the limits of its collective imagination.

8. Joan Riviere, 'Womanliness as a Masquerade' pp35-44 in *Formations of Fantasy*, Victor Burgin, James Donald and Cora Kaplan (eds), Methuen, London 1986, p35.

9. See Judith Butler, *Gender Trouble: Feminism and the Subversion of Identity*, Routledge, New York and London 1990, and *Bodies that Matter: On the Discursive Limits of 'Sex'*, Routledge, London 1993.

The representation of the performing heroine in these texts might be explained in terms of Joan Riviere's configuration of the 'masquerade', in which 'women who wish for masculinity may put on a mask of womanliness to avert anxiety and the retribution feared from men'.[8] But the half-sisters' authors continually insist that their heroines are *not* assuming a mask: their performance is an expression of their truest self. Judith Butler's argument that identity is something we *perform* is more useful here, I feel.[9] To see identity as 'performativity' is to say that we may *feel* that we have an authentic self, that we act according to spontaneous desires, but in fact there is no essence, no 'real me', no original self. Identity is, rather, constituted within the prevalent cultural codes, regulations and discourses. Its daily re-enactment involves exclusion and choices by which the subject defines the limits of her performativity. But the performance of identity is not a theatrical act, adopted at will, 'by which the subject brings into being what he/she names'. Any attempt to take up a new, resistant or subversive, position is contingent: it can only reverse, mimic, parody or in some other way allude to the identities culturally available to the subject. 'This kind of citation will emerge as *theatrical* to the extent that it *mimes and renders hyperbolic* the discursive convention that it also *reverses*'.[10]

10. *Bodies that Matter*, p232.

The 'performing heroine' doesn't slot neatly into Butler's argument, since the representation of identity as a *staged* performance unsettles the question of regulation. The performer both does, and doesn't, produce herself. What is, normally, particular to a theatrical performance is that it is simultaneously spontaneous and rehearsed, natural and artificial, controlling and controlled. The performer *appears* to be expressing herself, unveiling her most intimate thoughts, inviting the audience into intimacy – but the script is not hers.[11] In the half-sisters novels, however, the narrative insists that the script *is* hers, even when she is performing a male-authored script: the performer constitutes herself. For this reason, I think it is appropriate to apply some of Butler's ideas to these novels: in particular, to the way in which the body of the performer changes its shape – expands and dwindles – during the course of the narrative. Butler asks, what contours the materiality of the body? She answers that we need to think of sexing practices 'not only as ones through which a heterosexual imperative is inculcated, but as ones through which boundaries of racial distinction are secured as well as contested'.[12] When gender performativity gets entangled with nationality, 'matter' gets complicated. I want to demonstrate how the materiality of the body in women's fiction shifts in accordance with national position and allegiance, by taking a close look at Mme de Staël's *Corinne*.

11. See Simon Frith, *Performing Rites. The Aesthetics of Popular Music*, Harvard University Press, Cambridge, MA, forthcoming, 1996.

12. *Bodies that Matter*, p18.

Corinne is ostensibly an affirmation of national diversity – or, rather, of the 'natural' diversity of 'imagined political communities':

> The art of civilization tends to make all men seem alike and almost be alike in reality. But our mind and imagination enjoy characteristic differences among nations: men are the same only in their insincerity and selfishness, diversity is the sign of everything natural.[13]

13. Germaine de Staël, *Corinne, or Italy* (1807), tr Avriel H. Goldberger, Rutgers University Press, New Brunswick 1987, p12. Further page references in the text are to this edition.

Diversity is located in Corinne and her English lover, Oswald Nelvil. Nelvil represents the 'best of Britishness'; courage, honour, duty, moral principle, wit, restraint. Corinne is the embodiment of Italy: warmth, passion, beauty, grace, spontaneity, culture. But the narrative is impelled by the need to bring the two together: by the desire for, and the impossibility of, union between the qualities – the collective imaginations – of the two nations.

At the start of the novel, Nelvil is locked in oedipal melancholy, mourning the death of his father, whom he had deeply (mortally?) offended by his plan for an unsuitable marriage. He arrives in Rome on the day of Corinne's greatest triumph: she is to be 'crowned' at the Capitol. All of Rome has gathered to celebrate her achievements: she is poet, singer, dancer, musician, fluent in many languages, an inspired and eloquent *improvisatrice*, and the loveliest woman in Rome. But her real accomplishment is to embody, to make material, the Italy 'which must be understood through imagination' (p17). Corinne not only pulls together the 'imagined community', but tells her audience *how* to imagine it, as the prince who pays public tribute at her 'crowning' makes clear:

> Corinne is the common bond shared by her friends; she is the impulse, the interest of our life; we depend on her goodness; we are proud of her genius. To foreigners we say: 'Gaze on her, for she is the image of our beautiful Italy; she is what we would be except for the ignorance, envy, discord and indolence to which our fate has condemned us' (p25).

The subject of Corinne's improvisation on the day of her coronation is 'The Glory and Bliss of Italy': her brilliant performance is observed through Nelvil's mesmerised eyes. What the narrative stresses at this point is her amplitude: 'Her arms were ravishingly beautiful; her tall full figure, reminiscent of Greek statuary, vigorously conveyed youth and happiness' (p21). She is dressed like Domenichino's Sibyl: she is not only the 'whole' of Italy, but *all woman* and, indeed, all women (it would be wearisome for the reader if I were to list all of the paradoxical qualities which De Staël attributes to her heroine). She is, like the sibyl, obscure: her origins and history are unknown. She has no patronymic, and even the name 'Corinne' is one she has chosen for herself. But even at this point, her repleteness, her autonomy, are placed in doubt. Nelvil observes that she is sometimes tremulous: 'it seemed to him that in the very midst of all the splendour and all her success, Corinne's eyes pleaded for the protection of a friend, a protection no woman can ever do without, however superior she may be' (p22). We might think again here of Riviere and the masquerade, but De Staël goes to great pains to stress that there is no 'mockery', no artifice, no coquettishness, no pretension or pretence in Corinne. There is no 'art' in her performance: she is entirely 'natural'. She acts what she *is*.

Italy and Corinne open up Nelvil's ability to feel: 'what if he could recover memories of his native land and at the same time gain a new life through the imagination; what if he could be reborn to the future and yet not break with the past?' (p33). They fall passionately in love. Corinne embarks on Nelvil's 'sentimental education' and takes him on an extended guided tour of Rome and Naples. She implants the paintings, buildings, music, theatre, ruins, literature and landscape of Italy into Nelvil's sensibility. He tells her (quoting Goethe): 'You are the one who will bring that feeling back to life ... Rome shown by you, Rome interpreted by imagination and genius; *Rome: a world quickened by feeling, without which the world itself is but a desert*' (p56).

Corinne's power over Nelvil and over language is confirmed when, at a ball, she performs a spontaneous and graceful dance which mixes 'modesty and sensual delight': 'as if she were improvising, as if she were playing the lyre or sketching faces, Corinne communicated her feelings directly to the souls of the spectators through her dance: everything was language to her' (p92). Nelvil falls to his knees; Corinne dances around him.

During the course of the rest of the novel, three changes gradually take place. Corinne is given a name: she proves to be half-English, the daughter of an English peer. Despite a desperate struggle to hold on to her autonomy, to 'sustain the brilliance of the life I have adopted' (p90) she becomes hopelessly dependent on Nelvil's love. Nelvil increasingly doubts whether his father would have approved his marriage to Corinne; these doubts are confirmed when he finds that the marriage had indeed been contemplated, that his father had vetoed it and wished him to marry Corinne's half-sister, Lucille. The pull of the father and the fatherland are too strong; he returns to England, and marries Lucille. These changes are embodied in the narrative in two ways: through the changes in Corinne's performance, and in her physique.

'Artfulness' and 'mockery' begin to enter Corinne's performances. When she plays the part of the heroine in Shakespeare's *Romeo and Juliet* (Italian story, English author), 'her hair was artfully interwoven with flowers and precious stones. At first, she struck the audience as someone new to them; then they recognized her voice and her face – but a face transformed, divinely expressing poetry alone' (p126). Later, Corinne plays an Amazon queen, ruling over men, in an Italian comic drama which allows for improvisation: 'Her hair, meant to look dishevelled, was nonetheless arranged with a care that revealed her keen desire to please, and her elegantly light and whimsical costume gave her noble face a singularly graceful air of coquetry and mischief' (p305). Corinne's audience, dazzled with her charm, rises to applaud her as the 'true queen': just as they did at the Capitol. But Corinne is now 'queening it' in a quite different way: 'this coquette crowned, this sovereign fairy portrayed by Corinne, blending anger with pleasantry, thoughtlessness with the desire to please, grace with despotism, seemed to reign over destiny as much as over hearts; and mounting the throne, she smiled at her subjects, imposing submission with gentle arrogance' (p306).

Corinne's teasing role-playing here is more reminiscent of Irigaray's account of the feminine 'masquerade' than Riviere's. Women, Irigaray suggests, 'make "visible" … the cover up of a possible operation of the feminine in language' by means of 'an effect of playful repetition'.[14] 'To play with mimesis is thus, for a woman, to try to recover the place of her exploitation by discourse, without allowing herself to be simply reduced to it'. But Irigaray's words suggest a degree of control which is not present in Corinne. Immediately after this performance, Nelvil declares his intention to return to England. Corinne falls unconscious, hitting the floor so sharply that blood spurts from her head. From this point onwards, Corinne's amplitude is progressively undermined. She loses control over her body, and over language. Her physique shrinks: she

14. Luce Irigaray, *This Sex Which Is Not One*, tr Catherine Porter, Cornell University Press, Ithaca, NY 1985, p76.

becomes pale, thin, and dishevelled, prone to fainting and tears. She is unable to read, and barely able to speak. The depletion of Corinne's body, and her diminishment into the subjugated position of the 'ordinary' woman, racked by the failure of love, are parelleled in the narrative by the gradual effacement of Italy from Nelvil's imagination. His 'inborn tendencies, habits and tastes' are reawakened; he comes to think of Italy with compassion, as a temporary 'dazzling apparition' and 'intoxicating wave' (p315).

Up to this point, there has been an interplay, but also a neat symmetry, between the terms Corinne/Italy/woman and Nelvil/England/man. But at the end of the novel, this symmetry is disrupted by the manner in which Corinne's death is 'staged'. In England, Nelvil falls seriously ill. Realising how desperately he misses Corinne, his wife Lucille self-sacrificingly arranges their departure for Italy. But the Italy he encounters is not the one he remembers, the Italy of his imagination: heavy snow, drenching rain and thick fog shroud its charms. On reaching Rome, Nelvil sees a recent portrait of Corinne, dressed in black:

> But what struck him most of all was the unimaginable change in Corinne's face. She was there before him pale as death, her eyes half closed, her long eyelids veiling her gaze and casting a shadow over colourless cheeks. Across the bottom of the portrait was written this line from *The Faithful Shepherd*:
> *A pena si può dir: questa fu rosa.*
> (Scarcely can one say: she was a rose). (pp404-5)

What Nelvil witnesses on his return to Italy is a complete inversion of both Corinne and the country she embodies: both have become grimly parodic *copies* of their former selves. The process continues when Corinne gives her final performance: veiled, barely able to move, breathing with difficulty, she sits in an armchair while the verses she has written in her solitude are sung by proxy, by a lovely young girl dressed in white and crowned with flowers. Again, the performance is observed through the eyes of Nelvil, who cannot tear his gaze 'from the shadow that he saw as a cruel apparition in a night of delirium' (p415).

In the final pages of the novel, Corinne orchestrates her own death. Nelvil is excluded from her death bed, but at the last moment, unable to restrain himself, he bursts into the room. Nelvil falls on his knees; Corinne points to the moon with her dying hand. Both gestures repeat earlier moments in the novel which took place at the height of their romance. Nevil is reunited, not with the 'authentic' Corinne whom he has renounced, but with the parodic copy into which she has reconstituted herself.

As Elisabeth Bronfen has demonstrated in her work on Anne Sexton, the woman who stages her own death is both subsumed and empowered by her performance.[15] Sexton was, in private life, a classic hysteric. Hysteria, Bronfen suggests, is a 'performative disease', in which psychic disturbance, a disorder not located in the body, is articulated through the language of the body, through the public staging of private trauma. At home, Sexton was a mess: but

15. See Elisabeth Bronfen, *The Knotted Subject: Hysteria and its Discontents*, Manchester University Press, 1996. My thanks to Elisabeth Bronfen for sending me her work on Anne Sexton, which has considerably influenced my approach in this essay. For the connections between hysteria and female performance, see Catherine Clément, *Opera, or the Undoing of Women*, Virago, London, 1989, and Elisabeth Bronfen, ' "Lasciatemi Morir": Representations of the Diva's Swan Song', *Modern Language Quarterly*, December 1992, pp427-448.

when she performed her poetry, played out her intimate anguish, *on stage*, she was entirely in control, mesmerising her audience with the flamboyant power of her physical presence.

The death of Corinne is, similarly, a 'consummation' in which she is at the height of her powers even as she is being 'consumed'. The manner of her death overturns the impetus of the narrative: Corinne/Italy is no longer subsumed/defeated by England/Nelvil. But what really disrupts the neat synchronicity of nation and gender is the shift in the relationship between the half-sisters as Corinne approaches her death. For most of the novel, the English Lucille is positioned as Corinne's opposite: she is blonde, reserved, silent, insipid, child-like, timid and domesticated. While Corinne shrivels, she blossoms. But in the final chapters, the narrative draws the two women together: both are tormented by their love for Nelvil. Corinne's loss of voice parallels Lucille's silence. Lucille loses her bloom, becomes pale and drawn, her eyes continually wet with unshed tears. Their shared airy disengagement from language and the body is confirmed by the epithet which is repeatedly used to describe both women: 'celestial'.

The relationship between nation and gender is realigned: the potential for union between nations shifts from heterosexual to same-sex bonds. Eve Sedgwick has identified a longstanding and extensive literary tradition in which homosocial bonding is mediated by a ritualised 'traffic' of women; women act as the conduit of a relationship in which the final object is the affirmation of male collectivity and power.[16] *Corinne* is an influential text in an alternative tradition in which nation and gender work together to affirm 'gynosocial' bonding through the exchange of a man. It is Lucille who orchestrates Nelvil's return to Italy and Corinne. But Corinne, in turn, delivers Nelvil back to Lucille, telling her 'May he live with you in happiness' (p418). After a proper period of wild mourning for Corinne, affection and duty prevail, and Nelvil becomes an exemplary husband.

The initial meeting between the half-sisters is mediated, however, by another female: Juliette, the young daughter of Nelvil and Lucille. In the last days of her life, Corinne takes over Juliette's education. For the miserably jealous Lucille, this interference is the last straw. She overcomes her timidity and goes to see Corinne, opening up 'a completely candid exchange' (p412) between the half-sisters. Nelvil finds Juliette 'holding a lyre-shaped harp made for her size, in the same way that Corinne held it, and her little arms and pretty expression imitated Corinne perfectly. It was like seeing a beautiful painting in miniature, with a child's grace tinging everything with innocent charm' (p411). It is clear that it is in the body of Juliette that 'union' between the nations will finally be accomplished.

Germaine de Staël had no particular personal allegiance to Italy. She was Swiss-Protestant by birth, and resident in France for most of her life. Her celebration of Italy in *Corinne* may be attributed to her disaffection with Napoleonic France, or to her recent visit to Rome with her lover, but her 'Italy' has a primarily symbolic function: it is a country of the mind which, the novel

16. See Eve Kosofsky Sedgwick, *Between Men: English Literature and Male Homosocial Desire*, Columbia University Press, New York 1985.

17. Examples include
Samuel Richardson's
*The History of Sir
Charles Grandison*
(1754), Mme de Staël's
Delphine (1802) and
Maria Edgeworth's
Leonora (1806).

fantasises, might be realised in the body. *Corinne* is, also, one major intervention in a war of the words which was waged during the course of the late eighteenth and early nineteenth centuries, in which novelists on both sides of the channel sought to establish who was the 'true' woman: English or European? Northern or Southern?[17] For Corinne, England is both the object of desire and the source of death: her girlhood years in Northumberland are presented as a kind of living death, in which her creative talents were stifled. She cannot 'breathe' in England. In the British 'half-sisters' novels of the 1840s, the Corinne plot is adopted and modified. What we find here is an attempt to interrogate de Staël's attack on English domestic ideology while negotiating a place for Italy within that ideology.

Georgiana Fullerton wrote *Grantley Manor* when she was on the point of converting to Roman Catholicism. Her purpose in the novel is not to validate the Roman over the English church, but to plead for a tolerant recognition of difference, a sympathetic understanding, between the two churches. In *Grantley Manor*, both sisters are legitimate. Again, there is a shared lover, but Edmund and Ginevra are secretly married before the novel starts. The marriage is kept secret at Edmund's insistence, because of his father's rigid opposition to Roman Catholicism. Like Corinne, Ginevra is an *improvisatrice* and an actress of rare talent, but the question of the 'woman of genius' is not the primary focus of this novel. Fullerton's project is to bring the two apparently contrasting sisters together. Ginevra is seen through Margaret's eyes as an object of mystery, foreign yet familiar. The plot proceeds through a series of misunderstandings, in which Margaret doubts Ginevra's piety and purity, but long before the truth is revealed, Fullerton has guided the reader to anticipate that Ginevra is really as pure and 'true' as Margaret herself.

Geraldine Jewsbury's *The Half Sisters* follows the Corinne model more closely, validating the illegitimate half-Italian 'woman of genius', Bianca, over the legitimate daughter Alice, the subdued product of the English bourgeoisie. Restricted to a life of listless domesticity and claustrophobic prosperity, Alice has a brief love affair, falls sick, and dies. Bianca, by contrast, joins a circus and becomes an acclaimed actress. But unlike Corinne, Bianca is absorbed into the English domestic world; she marries a wealthy English aristocrat, gives up the stage and directs her energies and talents to managing the household with magnificent dexterity. Jewsbury wants to show that England is redeemable; she twists the *Corinne* story to show the possibility and desirability of reform from within. What England needs is an infusion of 'illegitimate Italy'; the woman who can be passionate, creative *and* domesticated. What is interesting is what happens, in the process, to the representation of the performing female body.

Corinne moves from amplitude/autonomy to depletion/death; Bianca does the reverse. At the start of the novel, Bianca is fragile, reserved, unawakened; poverty and chance direct her to the circus. When she timidly takes on her first role, 'death' is exorcised: she plays the part of a dumb girl who is trampled by horses. It is a moment of transformation. Bianca feels a 'glow in her heart': 'She had got over her fear of the horses, and her "*death*" was very effective, and brought great applause'.[18] From this moment onwards, Bianca grows in exuberance and energy. But if the body is not subsumed, 'Italy' is: by the end of the novel, Bianca is leading an exemplary life indistinguishable from that of Lucille in *Corinne*.

18. *The Half Sisters*, p32.

In the nineteenth-century realist novel, the possibility of 'in-betweenness' is explored, but it cannot finally be maintained. I want to turn now to the feminist fiction of the 1970s and 1980s, to show how 'double identity' can be realised when a fantasy text is placed alongside the realist narrative. But first I need to take a brief look at the two prevalent narrative forms in the feminist fiction of this period.

The patchwork novel is the dominant 'consciousness-raising' form. Among the best-known American examples are Marilyn French's *The Women's Room* (1977) and Marge Piercy's *Braided Lives* (1982). British versions of this form include Fay Weldon's *Female Friends* (1975), Michèle Roberts' *A Piece of the Night* (1978), Anna Wilson's *Cactus* (1980) and Caeia March's *Three Ply Yarn* (1986). In these novels, the narrative shifts continually between past and present, interweaving the lives of several women (usually three), to uncover the hidden patterns of female identity and the bonds between women. The patchwork novel is a fictional call to arms in which the central issue is women's shared struggle against patriarchy, and although some patchwork fictions are lesbian-feminist in perspective, the emphasis is on political collectivity, rather than sexuality. It is a form which allows for the acknowledgement of differences between women – of race, class, nation, generation and sexual orientation – but the primary focus is on unity-in-difference, on the continuity and cohesiveness of women's experience.

In the mirror novel, there are two narratives. One is a 'realist' narrative which follows the logic of everyday life; the other is a 'dream' or fantasy text which offers access to an alternative, visionary ontology. This is not quite the same thing as 'magic realism', in which realism and fantasy are heterogeneously interwoven. In the mirror novel, the two texts are separate; they are lightly attached and appear to be following parallel paths, but each raises questions the other cannot answer and neither is finally validated as offering the whole truth. The fantasy text refracts and inverts the logic and impetus of the realist narrative, sometimes mimicking, sometimes subverting, its chronology and exegesis. Examples of this form include Michèle Robert's *The Visitation* (1983), Rosalind Brackenbury's *Sense and Sensuality* (1985), Alison Fell's *The Bad Box* (1987), Joan Riley's *The Unbelonging* (1985), Ellen Galford's *The Fires of Bride* (1986) and Emma Tennant's *Queen of Stones* (1982) and *The Bad Sister* (1978).

While the patchwork novel emphasises cohesion, the mirror novel foregrounds contradiction and disjuncture; both forms are informed by the desire for 'wholeness', but in the mirror novel this can only be achieved in fantasy. Mirror fictions are informed by a psychoanalytic understanding of female subjectivity as fragmented and in process: the split narrative reflects and explores the splitting of the female subject. In several of these texts, the protagonist is a woman who has in some way lost, or become separated from, her masculine 'other self'. Union can only be accomplished in the fantasy narrative, which commonly ends with a symbolic ritual of rebirth in which the protagonist is recreated as 'whole'.

For the purposes of this essay, what is most interesting is that the writers of mirror fictions are often women who have a double national identity, or are displaced from their country of origin. Roberts is half-French; Riley is Jamaican, but wrote *The Unbelonging* while living in Britain; Tennant and Fell are Scottish, but live in England; Galford is Jewish–American, but wrote *The Fires of Bride* while living in Scotland. In the case of those writers whose habitat of origin is in Scotland, the mirror novel takes a particular form: the fantasy narrative is a 'psychic' text in a double sense, in that it both allows for the release of repressed desires and fears, and invokes the rich Celtic heritage of the supernatural: witches, goddesses, stone circles, demonic or ghostly transformations and visitations.

The connection between the mirror novel and the experience of displaced or dual national identity doesn't seem difficult to identify. The double text allows for competing apprehensions of time and space, for the exploration of what it means to be 'in-between', for the idea of 'unhomeliness'. In a number of these novels, the fantasy text evokes and fulfils a yearning for the secret places of the lost childhood home which is denied expression in the real world.

But in Emma Tennant's *Queen of Stones* and *The Bad Sister*, the mirror novel takes a different form. Scottish history and cultural traditions impel the narratives, but the fantasy text takes the protagonists into a different symbolic, the country of psychosis. Judith Butler has commented that 'the symbolic ought to be rethought as a series of normativizing injunctions that secure the borders of sex through the threat of psychosis, abjection, psychic unlivability'.[19] Butler defines the abject as those 'unlivable' and 'uninhabitable' zones of social life which constitute the defining limit of the subject's domain. Tennant's novels take the subject *into* those 'uninhabitable zones'. As Tom Nairn has commented,

19. *Bodies that Matter*, pp14-15.

> 'Nationalism' is the pathology of modern developmental history, as inescapable as 'neurosis' in the individual, with much the same essential ambiguity attaching to it, a similar built-in capacity for descent into dementia ...[20]

20. Tom Nairn, *The Break-up of Britain*, p359, quoted in Anderson, *op.cit.*, p5.

Tennant's texts extend and invert this idea by making gender and nation work together: female neurosis is the pathology of unstable or conflicting national identity. 'Scottishness' is both evoked and transcended in a fantasy narrative which propels the protagonists beyond nation and gender.

In both *Queen of Stone* and *The Bad Sister*, the structural 'split' is between a male-authored and a female-authored narrative. The double text serves to challenge the apparent fixity of the gendered symbolic order: the validity of a male-authored, 'controlling' narrative is tested against the subversive questions posed by an alternative, female-authored text. While, overtly, the masculine text 'explains' the female text, what in fact happens is the reverse: the feminine text reveals the inadequacies of the masculine text's resources.

Queen of Stones is explicitly a rewriting of Golding's *Lord of the Flies*: a story of a group of children cut off from the outside world which culminates in the sacrificial murder of a short-sighted working-class victim. Golding's boys fall from the sky; Tennant's girls disappear into a white fog. Golding's boys play at being Lord of the Flies: Tennant's girls play Queen of the Castle. Melanie (Tennant's 'Piggy') becomes the sacrificial pawn in a struggle between two potential 'Queens of Stones' which is played out as a contest between nations: or, rather, through the ritualised performance of a struggle between competing fantasies of national identity.

The two rival 'queens' have long been involved in an elaborate dressing-up game. Red-haired English Bess has an obsessional identification with Elizabeth, the Virgin Queen; French Laurie is 'the martyr, the Catholic Queen';[21] every Scottish schoolgirl's romantic heroine, Mary Queen of Scots. Tennant takes the fantasy games of girlhood to their extreme limits, turning Golding's manichaean conflict between good and evil, civilization and original sin, into a ritualised fable of female adolescent development in which the psychic trigger is the onset of menstruation. The story of this 'bloody adventure' is framed by an interpretative commentary: a formal, meticulous dossier, complete with footnotes and bibliography, compiled from reports on the girls submitted by social workers, psychiatrists, teachers and a bishop. The purpose of this impressive paraphernalia, the editor tells us, is that 'the psychopathology of the developing female be more fully comprehended' (p33).

The text which Tennant is really rewriting here is Freud's *Dora*. The dossier includes, at intervals, extracts from a case-history of Bess written by her male psychiatrist. He quotes, from *Dora*, Freud's comments on the prevalence of homoerotic attachments among young girls, but initially, like Freud, he overlooks the significance of this insight, preferring to locate the source of Bess's neurosis in her hostility to her mother and her attachment to her father. Laurie's importance is finally recognised in the psychiatrist's narrative, when he reinterprets his evidence and sees, at last, that Bess and Laurie were locked, not just in a struggle of jealousy and hatred, but also in an affair of love. But the real nature of this relationship has been indicated to the reader long before, in the alternative, much more fragmented, feminine narrative. This consists of extracts from the girls' diaries, and brief moments when the narrative consciousness is located in one or other of the girls. This narrative contains odd gaps, unexplained happenings, fantastic coincidences: the question of whether Melanie had psychic powers, as she claims in her diary, is left open. The relationship between the two narratives suggests that there are areas in the opaque 'white fog' of female adolescent experience which cannot be explained within conventional ontologies, and for which there is no readily available language. The 'mystery' of femininity is located in the enigmatic Laurie, whose quixotic and alluring mixture of sophistication and innocence is identified with her 'foreignness'. In their dressing-up game, as Laurie records

21. Emma Tennant, *Queen of Stones* (1982) and *Alice Fell* (1980), Faber and Faber, London 1987, p145. Further page references in the text are to this edition.

in her journal, Bess's motto was *Semper eadem*, always the same; '*semper mutata resurgam* was mine. I come back always in a different shape, or guise, daughter of the Guise, queen from France, her sister and her enemy' (p123). Laurie's 'mixed' nationality – French by birth, Scottish by performance – signifies the possibility of going beyond nation, beyond fixed definitions of femininity, and the allure of an alternative performativity: chameleon, shape-shifting.

'Shape-shifting' is also a central theme in Tennant's earlier novel, *The Bad Sister* (1978), a contemporary rewriting of the 'half-sisters' story. This novel doesn't belong within the female literary tradition I discussed earlier in this essay: the illegitimate half-sister is part-Scottish, rather than part-Italian, and she is a film-critic rather than a 'performer' in the literal sense. But I want to end by looking at *The Bad Sister* because it raises useful questions both about the place of national identity in women's fiction and about the idea of identity as performativity.

Tennant's literary allegiance here is to James Hogg's *Private Memoirs and Confessions of a Justified Sinner* (1824), a central text in the Scottish literary canon. Hogg's novel is a tale about the psychological doubling of half-brothers which is, simultaneously, fantastic and pathological, at once a story of demoniac possession and a study in fanaticism and paranoia. This psychosocial drama is rooted in the Scottish landscape and derives directly from Scottish history, superstition, and political and religious struggles.

Tales of second-self doubling are conventionally seen as 'male Gothic' (Stevenson's *Dr Jekyll and Mr Hyde* and Edgar Allan Poe's 'William Wilson', for example), and, as Eve Kosofsky Sedgwick has demonstrated, *Confessions of a Justified Sinner* offers an intricate example of the ways in which the flux of identification, persecution and desire between the 'doubles' acts to affirm male homosocial empowerment.[22] Tennant's novel follows Hogg's closely, drawing freely and playfully on its structure and themes. But she appropriates and disarms its homosocial frame by feminising its form and plot. In *Confessions of a Justified Sinner*, Robert's paranoid journal is placed within an explanatory editorial narrative: the authors of both are male, as are the central protagonists. In *The Bad Sister*, the author of the psychotic journal is female. So are her doubles, or, to use the novel's terminology, 'shadows'. Whereas Hogg's novel is set entirely in Scotland, Tennant moves freely between Scotland and England. She turns Hogg's devil, Gilmartin, into a Scottish witch, Meg Gil-martin. What the journal conveys is the idea of 'another country', a 'gynosocial' landscape of the mind where the body is liberated, an imagined political community which transcends nation, time and space.

Nicci Gerrard has suggested that women 'write from the shadow side', able, 'as marginalised beings, to experience the present as alien and to position themselves in the imagined landscapes of future, fantasy and myth'.[23] Jane's journal takes us into the 'shadow side'. In her 'wild' narrative, Tennant probes the forbidden areas of female experience: rage, violence, possessiveness, rivalry, sexuality. As Jane puts it, 'The Muse is female, and a woman who thinks must live with a demented sister'.[24] But Tennant also hints at an alternative,

22. *Between Men*, pp97-117.

23. Nicci Gerrard, *Into the Mainstream: How Feminism has Changed Women's Writing*, Pandora, London, 1989, p162.

24. Emma Tennant, *The Bad Sister* (1978), Picador, London 1983, p63. Further page references in the text are to this edition.

less embattled world. Jane has a visionary glimpse of 'the witches Meg and I had been ... I felt the hatred. I felt to blame. And yet ... somewhere beyond that ... we had been happy together, in another country. We had been whole.' (p86).

At the centre of *The Bad Sister* is the journal of Jane Wild, a tormented and haunting narrative which is, it seems, partly real, and partly a psychotic fantasy. Jane's journal is enclosed by the 'Editor's Narrative', which applies a psychoanalytic lens to the journal, drawing on the evidence supplied by three men: a psychiatrist, a clergyman, and a close friend of Jane's father. *The Bad Sister* is an impossible novel to summarise, since almost every fact in both narratives is, at some point, placed in question. They *appear* to be as follows: Jane, the illegitimate daughter of a Scottish land-owner, was obsessively jealous of her legitimate half-sister. Jane was brought up in a women's commune in which all of the women took the surname Wild; she left the commune to live with her boyfriend Tony, but remained in contact with the women's leader, the charismatic Meg Gil-martin. Traumatised by the belief that her boyfriend was having an affair, Jane took to feminist terrorism and killed her father and half-sister Ishbel. Her body was found later on a Scottish hillside, with a stake through the heart.

Jane's journal, however, offers a very different version of the story. She says nothing of Ishbel's death. According to Jane, Meg Gil-martin is a witch and a vampire, who has initiated Jane into the cult, and on the night of the murder she takes her rival to Meg as part of a bargain: in return for her new victim, Meg has promised to use her psychic powers to make Jane whole. Jane is in search of the missing 'male principle', lost with the ending of childhood. Meg fulfils her promise. The journal ends, not with death, but with ritualised reunion: Jane is sailing in a ship towards a hillside where K, the missing male principle, 'I divided by<' (p110) is waiting for her.

The Editor's Narrative interprets Jane's case as one of psychotic transference. Jane's paranoid jealousy has become projected from her half-sister Ishbel on to her rival for Tony, Miranda; she killed Ishbel believing that she was killing Miranda. Meg the witch is a projection of Jane's intense dislike of her boyfriend's mother. If read as the product of a deranged mind, Jane's narrative supports this interpretation. But, as in *Queen of Stones*, the two texts cannot finally be fitted together. Clues are scattered through the novel to suggest that Jane's account is in fact true, and the journal has a vividness and intensity which carries far more conviction than the flat, pedantic editorial commentary. 'K', the name of Jane's masculine other, is explained by Meg as 'a bent line that comes in on a straight line and shoots it to pieces' (p85). In much the same way, Jane's 'bent' text shatters the 'straight' narrative which attempts to contain and explain it. As Jane tells a friend, 'This is about believing something different' (p72).

The other world which Jane enters through Meg's powers is never presented as anything other than strange, dangerous, even terrifying, but it is also liberating. Meg gives her 'something else in place of the bad sister, something that made me as strong and round as the beginning of the world' (p77). Jane escapes into a world of sharp, intense colours, and into a new skin. Her body shrinks and becomes androgynous; she is provided with different clothes, 'magic garments ... which transcend sex and wealth and individuality' (p69). In a series of nightly transformations, she crosses time and space to enter the experience of other women: she becomes a prostitute, an assassin, an oppressed Irish maid. With Meg's aid, she can fly, walk on air, 'see the world below the surface' (p73) and cross the boundaries of race, class and sexuality. She kills; she has incestuous, lesbian and sado-masochistic sex. The thrill is the release from the 'matter' of the body: Meg, 'reversing science' (p73), translates the known into the unknown.

On the night of the murder Jane goes, or imagines she goes, to a fancy-dress party; she finds herself in a room full of mirrors, surrounded by women dressed up as courtesans, witches and wives. These, the novel suggests, are the choices open to women. Meg gives Jane the chance to play with a 'different choice' each night. But as Jane discovers, getting 'out of yourself' carries the enticing but terrifying knowledge that you might not be able to get back. The cost of Jane's commitment to Meg is to become 'a living shadow, a walking living being without a shadow' (p78); towards the end of her journal, she looks in a mirror and can see no reflection.

The Bad Sister has been read as a homophobic attack upon radical feminism, and it is not difficult to see why;[25] the association of feminism with witchcraft and vampirism seems troubling in itself, and in this novel its representation is often harrowing. But *The Bad Sister* was written when the contemporary women's movement was still comparatively new and threatening, and radical terrorism was in the air. Certainly, it is not a comfortable novel, but I don't think it is an *attack* on feminism; rather, it is a heightened, surrealistic account of the *challenge* represented by feminism, which presents it as a new, disruptive and radically different way of seeing the world. The novel may be seen as an example of what Judith Butler calls 'the reworking of abjection into political agency' which, she suggests, may, but does not *have to*, reinstall the version it seeks to overcome. 'Rather, this is the politicization of abjection in an effort to rewrite the history of the term, and to force it into a demanding resignification'.[26]

Jane Wild is a film critic, disillusioned both with the drab London suburb where she lives and with the monochromatic avant-garde movies she reviews, which seem to her more grey than black and white. Meg, the feminist witch and muse, opens up a chance of 'seeing in colour'. As Tennant has commented:

> I don't think it's so much the case that women generically see things in a different way, as that years and years of being downtrodden has given women another eye: often, women see things in more detail, with more colour, and observe psychic states more closely, than the equivalent 'male' eye. The women's movement has opened a Pandora's Box as far as writing is concerned.[27]

25. See Paulina Palmer, *Contemporary Women's Fiction: Narrative Practice and Feminist Theory*, Harvester Wheatsheaf, Hemel Hempstead, 1989, pp142-144.

26. *Bodies that Matter*, p21.

27. Emma Tennant, 'A Pandora's Box for Writing' in *Delighting the Heart: A Notebook by Women Writers*, Susan Sellers (ed), Women's Press, London, 1989, p189.

In recent conversations with friends, and in reading work submitted by graduate students, I have noticed an increasing and disturbing 'rewriting' of the feminism of the 1970s. Yes, it was terribly necessary and worthy, they say, but rather too homogeneous, blinkered and bland: thankfully, postmodernism has opened things up, fragmented the category 'woman', made a space for the exploration of differences within – race, class, sexuality. This new orthodoxy writes out the political diversity, the antagonisms, the contentiousness, the pleasure, the confusion, the excitement and the *danger* of those times. I think *The Bad Sister* is worth returning to simply as a corrective: as a reminder that 1970s feminism was a shock to the system and that consciousness of the 'differences within' predates postmodernism. *The Bad Sister* is a 1970s text quite at variance with the type of feminist novel caricatured by Leslie Dick as 'positive role models and peppermint tea'.[28] Indeed, Tennant's novel uses many of the strategies now routinely attributed to postmodernism: purloinment and pastiche, multiple fragmentation, refusal of chronology and causality. But *The Bad Sister* is a postmodernist text which questions some of postmodernism's assumptions. It provides a salutary reminder that moving from a monochrome world to 'seeing in colour' is an exhilarating but destabilising process. At a time when popular appropriations of postmodernism are telling us that identity is just a game, that performativity is a position to be adopted and relinquished at will, it is useful to be reminded that breaking boundaries, 'recreating' the self, becoming *foreign* to oneself, can be elating but is also *scary*.

28. Leslie Dick, 'Feminism, Writing, Postmodernism' in *From My Guy to Sci-Fi: Genre and Women's Writing in the Postmodern World*, Helen Carr (ed), Pandora, London 1989, p212.

TELEVISION PERFORMANCE: BEING, ACTING AND 'CORPSING'

Karen Lury

I would like to thank
John Caughie and
Jane Sillars for their
helpful comments on
an earlier draft of this
paper.

There is always a pedagogical problem teaching television and even more so, perhaps in the attempt to teach television performance analytically. Be it as a flow of signification, or even as segmented process, it is always sensed that what is being taught about television is past, and that what remains is not the object/subject itself but the detritus of meaning. This is true of all temporally based media (it is true in different ways of both music and film) but explicitly so in television where so much (even in the age of the video recorder) can be missed and mis-remembered. Continuity mistakes, the newsflash, unloved sitcoms, the beginnings or ends of favourite programmes, are easily forgotten or simply stored and never watched. The historical and even the contemporary resource of television texts that are taught are often a bizarre bricolage of fragments, made up to be evidence, but which actually suggest more of teachers' and students' passions, and reflect more of their tastes and domestic living arrangements than television itself. Of those programmes that are saved, there will be numerous discrepancies and irritating omissions: we may have only one episode out of four in a dramatic serial, or retain a predominance of controversial documentaries and keep only excessive and indicatively sexist advertisements, which accumulate as providential or wasteful accidents, or which serve specific purposes. Importantly, these programmes and fragments are then also often studied in isolation. Not surprisingly, what is often first forgotten and ignored by students and teachers is what continues to be central to the television medium – that it is the flow of programmes which dictates in part both the style and substance of television. It is this flow or schedule (private or commercial) which enables the emotional shifts engendered by an evening's viewing. All of which relate to the significant embeddedness (the relationships generated and sustained by the viewing context, both social and textual) which characterises the television text and television performances.

Partly as a consequence of this, but in any case, what becomes increasingly impossible to transfer, or learn, is the experience of watching (not just how you watch, but how you feel, and why you feel, when you watch.) This is important for any assessment of television texts, but it is central in the assessment and analysis of performance which is so strongly encoded by extra-textual elements. The viewing experience is missed out not only because the domestic situation cannot be recreated in the classroom, or because the family dynamics and disinterested gaze of the so-called typical television viewer can be misrepresented (this is true (again) of all media that are characterised by their sociability): but for my concerns here, what is also lacking is a way to encapsulate in any useful form the kind of experience accrued by years of watching. It is, I want to suggest, the cumulation of viewing experience that informs television viewing in significant ways, ways that are specific to television as an aesthetic and technological form. It is the kind of experience which in some large part determines the pleasure and the meaning of television watching, and is not transferable because so much viewing is not rational or systematic, but is instead a knowledge built out of familiarity and happenstance. It is a process of accumulation: it is a developing inner voice or a false 'mental echo',[1] both emotional and cognitive, that is generated by expectation and repetition. Watching and interpreting television texts and television performances for me, at least, is articulated by an ongoing passive participation, and by the encroachment of years of television viewing. Knowledge, not so much out of desire, or curiosity, but of cumulation and accumulation. It is like hearing the beginning of a particular piece of music because of the order of tracks on a favourite album, so that you anticipate the first few notes of the next song after the last, and are then surprised when the tape playing in the shop, or the DJ's play list, doesn't go on to reproduce the sounds that are stubbornly playing in your head. It is an individual's experience, but it is also related to age (to *when*) you watched. (When, that is, in respect of decades, historical periods, fashions, of moon landings and political elections, but also mundanely, as in what time of day, and with whom you watched.) As I will go on to discuss, the expectations and assumptions generated by the kind of television experienced by the viewer inform their understanding and appreciation of performance, of the acting and appearing that occurs on the small screen; it frames both feeling and taste.

I am of the generation of British television viewers that grew up with the boyish antics of John Noakes on *Blue Peter* and I remember 'I'm free!' and 'Nice to See You, to see you Nice!' as catch phrases, repeated week after week. I am before *Neighbours* and *Byker Grove* and I remember *Top of the Pops* as an institution. I didn't find it odd (at the time) that Morecambe and Wise shared a bed, and I can see that Harry Enfield is like Dick Emery, just as Vic Reeves is like Eric Morecambe. Yet I have never, for example, seen an episode of *Leave it to Beaver* or *The Brady Bunch*, and I'm not sure I would recognise Dan Rather. I do, however, remember *The Partridge Family* and that *Star Trek* used to be on at 7.20 pm on Monday nights. (If these references seem parochial and idiosyncratic, then this just goes to prove my point.) I am surprised that I am less cynical and engage more with television than students who are just ten years younger than I am, many of whom have watched far less television than I, and perhaps more unfortunately, are resistant to watching more – not just because it is now work (and therefore suffers as reading and film watching does) but because they see little need; television aesthetics is 'easy'. A crude reading of John Ellis' *Visible Fictions*[2], for example, might suggest that in terms of aesthetics, television is like cinema, only smaller, less complex and less interesting. Television is only regarded as important for its social or political implications, and while MTV engaged film scholars temporarily, it often

1. This concept is indebted to Andrew Goodwin's reworking of Volosinov's concept of 'inner speech' which he elaborates in his book *Dancing in the Distraction Factory: Music Television and Popular Culture*, University of Minnesota Press, Minneapolis 1992, p12.

2. John Ellis, *Visible Fictions: Cinema, Television Video*, Routledge, London 1992. Revised edition, first published 1982.

3. See Goodwin, *op.cit.*
particularly the
chapter 'Silence!
Academics at work',
pp1-24.

meant that, as Goodwin has suggested, critics tended to look without listening (were, in fact, 'critics without ears') so that television, as a talk-dominant and 'glance'-directed form was misread, and overdosed on theory.[3]

One particular kind of performance plays with our expectations and experience, and thereby demonstrates clearly the nature and presence of the 'false echo' I am attempting to describe. Impersonators (from Mike Yarwood to Rory Bremner on British television) play with our expectations of how particular performers can be seen to *be* performing, and, literally how we think (or know) they will act. They reveal ongoing assumptions, and disrupt the seemingly disinterested 'speed-reading' that we use in our watching, and in our interpretation of television performance. Through exaggeration or by working from inappropriate scripts, the impersonator demonstrates the determination of meaning given by viewers to specific performances by a humorous subversion of our expectations. What happens is that the impersonator has drawn his or herself into another performer (by accent, dress, posture and to limited degree, setting) but the resulting performance refuses to fit the pattern or framework that the audience is expecting; we have drawn the wrong conclusions, and are forced to adjust our 'mind set', acknowledging our mistakes through laughter.

An impersonation is only successful if you know the original performance; it doesn't make sense, and is distinctly unfunny if you are unaware of the foibles, features and voice of the performer being parodied. Only experienced viewers will get the joke, and as I have stated, this is likely to be generationally specific, but it will also be determined by cultural context – who can really appreciate a Frank Spencer or Bruce Forsyth impersonation apart from a British viewer of a certain age? If this is true of impersonations then it is also true of the television performance itself: I have found that in attempting to describe or teach performance on the small screen I spend the majority of my time teaching about things that are *not* the performance (that is how and what actually happens) and instead, I have to fill in, and provide information so that students can begin to make sense of what is happening. This is true of all performance (film as well as television) but it remains important not to assume too much about anyone's knowledge or experience. The difficulties that arise from this are often at their most acute when we are looking at performances as parody or homage: students may only have witnessed Madonna in the video for 'Material Girl' playing Marilyn Monroe, and yet never have seen Monroe playing Lorelei in *Gentlemen Prefer Blondes* (1953); or equally they may not realise that Keanu Reeves in the Paula Abdul video 'Push, Push' is 'playing' James Dean, as Dean played Jim Stark in *Rebel Without a Cause* (1955). The problem is not just one of research; obviously, while it is feasible to research and reproduce specific moments or sequences of signification (and it is easier, as I have observed, in film than in television) it is harder to engender, or demonstrate their *significance*, whether emotional or social. What I am suggesting therefore, is that the kind of experience I am promoting is not just the accumulation of evidence (the seeing of films and television programmes, the set texts of media courses), but that it is also, in part, a social and emotional experience, weathered and fitted into the individual psyche. It is, after all, because it is so much our *own* experience, that we all feel able to make judgements about performance; to decide whether or not this or that performance was good or bad, and to discuss with authority the appropriate or inappropriate behaviour of celebrities and stars on and off screen.

So, if the analysis of acting and performance is like 'quoting the unquotabale',[4] how might we attempt to systemise our thoughts about, if not exactly the process of, television performance? In the first instance, I believe we might usefully work through a series of dualities that are informed by each other (and are, in other words, inherently incestuous) but which may be kept separate for the purposes of analysis.

The first of these is the difference between the television personality (such as weathermen and women, news anchors, game show hosts, daytime magazine presenters) and the television actor (the actor in television fictions, from serious drama to sit-com.) In Britain, many of these performers may be drawn from a theatrical background or tradition. This could mean that performers can be associated with performance styles and techniques that have their origins in contexts outside of television: in arenas such as the infamous 'Northern comedy club circuit' or Cambridge University's 'Footlights Revue', in regional repertory companies or the Royal Shakespeare Company, all of which carry with them different kinds of credibility and varying amounts of cultural kudos. It is still rare for performers to be known solely through television: although some actors may be primarily associated only with their television work (in Britain, this would include actors such as John Thaw, David Jason and Julia Sawahala) other performers may refuse television celebrity as a strategic attempt to avoid over-exposure (Eddie Izzard, for example, a successful British comedian, appears on chat shows, but has so far refused offers to star in a television series). Although we may not always be aware of an individual performer's specific heritage, it nevertheless does 'show up' when certain performers do or do not fit into particular performing contexts on television. (Although deriving from a mismatch of performance styles different to the ones I have so far suggested, a useful analogy might be the excruciating embarrassment, the experience of 'non-fit', felt by many viewers in Britain when watching the Royal Family present a special version of the slapstick television game show *It's a Knockout*.)

Inconveniently, of course, the personality and the actor are, almost characteristically on television, entangled, and individuals may oscillate from one position to another. The actor may peform as a celebrity when they guest on a game show, whereas the celebrity may act in a dramatic fiction. On top of this, obviously, the personality is also always in some sense 'acting'. (See, for example, the celebrity as journalistic performer in my typology below.)

As celebrity or actor, the television performer will also be split by the actuality of the recorded sound and image. Their performance will always be a mixture of embodiment and surface. The pro-filmic moment is as much a part

4. This phrase is from Gillian Skirrow's article, 'Women/Acting/Power' in Helen Baehr and Gillian Dyer (eds), *Boxed In: Women and Television*, Pandora Press, London 1987, pp164-184.

of television as it is of film, so that what is represented in two-dimensions on screen is also a demonstration that there was something (three dimensional, solid) *there* once, or even, since television is still at times live, something there now.[5] Performance on television (as in film) is therefore both an enactment and appearance, a duality brought together by the processes of recording and transmitting, which is enabled and coded by a sub-set of processes and techniques that are also worthy of a brief description here.

5. Here, I am arguing against claims that John Ellis has made concerning the absence of the photo-effect in television, which he discusses in his chapter 'Stars as a cinematic phenom-enon' from *Visible Fiction, op.cit.,* pp91-109.

Crudely we can see these as technique (which refers to the skills of the performer aligned to their *given* physiology) as opposed to technology (which refers to the process of filming and recording). We might summarise this duality like this:

TECHNIQUE	TECHNOLOGY
expression	make-up
intonation	costume/setting
gestures	editing
posture	lighting
KEYWORDS:	
range	production values
experience	professionalism

For clarity, it is convenient to set these elements up in opposition, but again, it is only in combination that they produce meaning. However, it is also worth noting that the influence of (or the significance given to) an individual technique or technology will be perceived as more or less important both within (and for) particular performative moments and practices. So that, for example, costume does not feature in quite the same way in Channel 4's *Who's Line is it Anyway?* as it does in the encoding of a performance in a dramatic ficiton such as the BBC's *Martin Chuzzlewit.* This is not to say that the performers in *Who's Line is it Anyway?* don't dress up or wear costumes that say something about their performances: I have yet to see Josie Lawrence wear a skirt, for example, and while certainly this is to do with the fact that she may want to move about with freedom (the show is based on improvisation), it also indicates something about her performative practice in this particular context, that is perhaps defined by her ability to be 'one of the boys' (or give as good as she gets) in the male dominated arena of the show.

The most complex opposition (and as argued by some critics) the defining characteristic of the television performer is the distinction between the actor and the character. It is often argued that these are notoriously blurred in television and that this is part of the pleasure for the audience, to believe that the actor *is* (or is at least like) the character he or she plays. So that Julie Goodyear, for example, who played Bet Lynch in the British soap opera *Coronation Street* has been seen to suffer romantic trials and tribulations over the years (just like Bet), yet due to her character's popularity and her longevity on 'the Street' she has succeeded (just like Bet) in establishing a position as matriarch and mother confessor (both on and off screen). In fact her success meant that she piloted an afternoon chat/discussion show as a potential rival to Esther Rantzen (and hence, even Oprah Winfrey); however, according to rumours, the 'actress' was unable to work convincingly without a written script so that the project was quietly dropped. Similarly, another 'Street' veteran, William Roach (who plays school teacher Ken Barlow) took *The Sun* to court when it accused him of 'being boring' resulting in an expensive blurring of the character (the dull and worthy Ken) with the actor, who employed character testimonials – that is, testimonials to his, not Ken's character – from other members of the cast to establish his (Roach's) wit and popularity.

While this blurring tendency is perhaps understandable in connection to soap opera stars (some of whom have been playing their roles for years) it may be explained in other cases for two main reasons. One reason may be that, as Ellis suggests, because the publicity concerning the performer tends to circulate only when they are appearing or about to appear on screen, so their profile as a 'persona' outside of the programme text is circumscribed, resulting in a temporal (as well as a literal) confusion of knowledges concerning the character and actor. The second reason is perhaps connected to casting, since television even more than cinema tends to cast according to 'type'. Type is distinguished amongst other elements, primarily by sexual characteristics, class connotations and physiognomy. On British television the policeman and the crook are easily distinguishable as types, with some actors confined to dramas of law and order both through physiognomy but also through years of association with related parts. John Thaw, an actor known in Britain for his policeman roles – Inspectors Regan and Morse – demonstrates this by his unsuccessful attempt to diversify into light romantic fiction with his performance in the BBC's disastrous *A Year in Provence*, a fault which has been swiftly remedied by his appearance as a barrister in the successful *Kavanagh QC*. His erstwhile partner, (Sergeant Lewis) played by Kevin Whatley, has instead been cast, not as policeman, but into a related professional type. He successfully kept the integrity of his role as Morse's Sergeant sidekick, gained a little intelligence and has moved across to a medical drama, *Peak Practice*, where he plays an energetic country GP. This kind of move is *not* atypical – medical and law dramas very often demand similar types – Nigel Le Valiant for example, in his move from the long running *Casualty* (where he played a consultant) has had an unsurprising success as a police surgeon (in *Dangerfield*), thereby neatly dovetailing both professional types in one character. More interestingly, the casting of *The Bill* (a long running cop opera produced by Thames TV) demonstrates the recycling properties of typecasting where performers who have played policemen in the series may return as 'crooks', or where crooks return as new policemen (indicating, perhaps, that even at the level of casting, these two worlds are deliberately integrated within the series, thereby serving as one of the few remaining signs of the programme's much vaunted realist ambitions.)

Clearly the typing of performers is both about appearance and audience expectations, and is again about fit. This is not, as I have already suggested, simply due to the potential photo-effect of the recorded image, but is also, in television, perhaps more to do with the habitual, almost visceral effect of viewing, so that the audience may feel discomfort when producers and programme makers attempt to cast against type. Typing can also be seen to function at a more subtle level: the casting of Todd Carty as Mark Fowler in the British soap *EastEnders* was successful, I would argue, because the type associated with this young actor (who for my generation of viewers had played the memorable Tucker Jenkins in the earthy children's drama *Grange Hill*) fitted with the character established by another actor earlier on in the soap's history. 'Mark', like 'Tucker', is typed as a lad, working-class, smart but not clever, attractive but not good looking; and as an added benefit, as Michelle Fowler's brother, Todd as 'Mark', would be playing many of his scenes with an actress also associated with *Grange Hill*, Susan Tully. While the experience I'm calling on here is my own, and specific to both my age and viewing tastes, and therefore known or understood by a limited number of the audience, another (much used example) might be the type-casting of Joan Collins in *Dynasty*, although I feel that the associations she carries with her not just as British (and therefore in an American context potentially wicked and bitchy) but also as a film star are not quite the same as the knowledges inspired (or ingrained) by the television experience.

Yet Todd Carty's performance is not just sustained by the associations that he as an actor carries with him from other parts. There is clearly something about his performance technique that fits with the overall performance style engendered and privileged by other members of the cast in *EastEnders*. There are obviously forms of styles of performance that are specific to television (although they may, as I have indicated above, stem from traditions outside of television). It may be useful therefore to outline a brief typology here of performance styles within which certain television performers work.

The first of these relates to the journalistic form of presentation, as performed by newscasters, reporters, and documentary presenters. There seem to be two distinct styles here. The first of these is represented by the newscaster or reader: this style is reproduced by the authoritative, modulated and static performances of newsreaders such as Michael Buerk or Jon Snow, which rely heavily upon the voice (usually deep, and retaining the RP accent of the traditional BBC announcer) and which are – mostly – immobile with the newsreader positioned behind a desk. Their hands, for example, are rarely seen and if seen, their movement may indicate a conclusion to the performance (the shuffling of papers at the end of the newscast) or a mistake (a televised report unavailable or miscued), which forces the reader to reach for an alternative story or script. When readers are obliged to question reporters and politicians both within and without the studio, both voice and posture may occasionally move to the mildly interrogative; what is expressed here is an urgency and liveness suggested through an increase in pace and voice level, and by the reader physically turning, or leaning forward to the interviewee. However, the dominant mode of the reader's performance is distinguished by the performer holding the look of the camera, resulting in an almost unblinking eye contact in his or her attempt to address the viewer directly at home. (This is, of course, an illusion sustained by the autocue, enabling them to look up and read from the script at the same time.)

In contrast to this, the second style of journalistic performance is that of the anchor of a magazine current affairs programme, or the presenter of a documentary series. In Britain this would include performers such as Jeremy Paxman, Peter Snow or Kirsty Wark on *Newsnight*, Robin Day and now David Dimbleby on *Question Time*, or David Attenborough presenting a natural history series such as *Life On Earth*. Though authoritative (and still predominantly masculine, and RP in accent) these performers are more mobile and excitable. Using a greater range of voice (from a whisper in David Attenborough's case, to the high pitched hysteria of an excited Peter Snow) these leaders or seekers are allowed much more space and time to perform: their hands are much more visible, and both Wark and Paxman, for example, use their fingers to point and ask leading questions. Similarly, Attenborough leaps and scrabbles in his 'natural environment', playing nervously, perhaps, with a family of gorillas or crouching down and in to the camera lens, so that he is absurdly close both to the watching audience and to the object of his attention, which might be, for example, a tiny Arctic flower. The 'seeker' therefore reaches and points to the animate and inanimate (flowers and politicians) in order to reveal the truth to the viewer at home. These performers have to force information from their surroundings, creating particular pressures which show up in their performance. The hysteria of Peter Snow as he manipulates graphics displaying voting predictions, or when he plays with tanks in a mock up of Desert Storm, is laughable (and so easily parodied) because we can see clearly here that most of the information that he is revealing is redundant, irrelevant, or in the case of a long election night special, not *there* (where he is pointing) yet. In these contexts, the seeker's excitability is a bid to keep our attention, but it is also a poor mask for their desperation. These performers may also develop verbal tics just as they develop familiar physical mannerisms – Jeremy Paxman's, 'Come off it' or 'With respect, Minister', as responses indicating his increasing irritation, mean as much (surprisingly considering their vastly different contexts) as the familiar riposte 'You plonker' as performed by David Jason as 'Del Boy' in the sitcom *Only Fools and Horses*. Over months and even years of familiarity with these tics and foibles, the audience may accept them in some sense as characters, allowing Jeremy Paxman for example, more leniency to be aggressive or cynical, as part of his expected and accepted performance, than would be admired, or allowed from another journalist performer, such as, say, Julia Sommerville.

Closely related to the journalistic style, are the performances of presenters such as Anne Diamond and Nick Owen (from the BBC's *Good Morning*), and of course, Richard and Judy of *This Morning*. Weaned on breakfast television and regional presenting, these performers are more relaxed than their journalistic contemporaries, yet like the journalist style, their performance is in some sense a cover-up. As a style, their performances embody contradictions; at once both knowing and friendly, open and polished, they both include and charm the audience. They welcome the viewer in, pretty much with open arms, particularly in the context of daytime magazine or breakfast shows where they are obliged to reveal more than their news associates, so that sometimes all of the body is on display and available to the viewer. (Something that was perhaps, to exacerbate the downfall of Fiona 'legs' Armstrong, a newsreader turned presenter, whose skirt length and its much publicised shortening, undermined her performance, making her visibly uncomfortable.)

While presenters may address the viewer at home, they also look at each other (play off one another, and visibly appreciate each others' performances) so that at moments they may enter into a music hall or vaudeville style, a comedic performance perhaps taken to its extreme in the stand-up performance of Chris Evans (originally in Channel 4's *The Big Breakfast*) who was generously supported by the giggling or 'corpsing' straightman (who in that context, was played by Gaby Roslin). Whether manic or relaxed, the presenter's skill is defined by control (hence in part the 'cover-up', which covers gaps, drops in pace or weak performances from guests) so that even seemingly radical performers such as Evans will openly admire mainstream, and seemingly conservative, 'professionals' such as Noel Edmonds or Michael Barrymore. As controllers, presenters are also acting as hosts and are therefore aligned to chat show and game show performers; Michael Barrymore and Noel Edmonds, for example, both currently perform in, and present both weekend and chat/magazine programmes, as well as straightforward game shows.

Because the presenter's performance style has obvious comedic and music hall elements, it is not surprising that numerous 'straight' comedians, have themselves had success as presenters – British comedians such as Bob Monkhouse, Roy Walker and the late Les Dawson effectively presented the lighter versions of game shows. Also unsurprisingly, the more authoritative pose or performance of the journalist style can be adopted and adapted in game shows that supposedly require a little more education – Jeremy Paxman's hosting of *University Challenge* is therefore unremarkable, just as Magnus Magnusson's (the host of *Mastermind*) occasional documentary presentation does not go against the grain of his performance style.

The music hall style can also be seen in the performances of numerous actors working both in sit-coms and soaps (it would seem that these two genres' similarities work at the level of performance as well as structure). Comedians, or comic actors do well in both genres. Mike Reid, a conservative stand-up comedian, was generally thought to have made a success of his straight role as Frank Butcher in *EastEnders*; similarly, comedian Russ Abbot has won plaudits from critics for his performance in the melancholy sit-com *September Song*. I would also suggest that the recent casting of the much loved film comedienne Barbara Windsor as Peggy Mitchell in *EastEnders* and Amanda Barrie as Alma

Baldwin in *Coronation Street* (both actresses are familiar from their 'Carry On' appearances and therefore carry associations and repeat gestures and inflections learnt from this particular version of British comedy) indicates the importance of 'music hall' and seaside humour in British soap operas. In large part, however, this is not just about a comic sensibility, it is also about class: the music hall, and therefore the music hall performance, has been traditionally associated with the 'working class performance', and is often identified through visible 'lower class' performance markers which allow for, and promote, vulgarity, exaggeration and pathos.

It is by this that the music hall performer is explicitly distinguished from the theatrical performer, who may have known – or is simply assumed to have – connections to the stage. Located within a high culture context, theatrical performers produce performances that in contrast to the music hall performer, are often assumed to be about expressiveness, subtlety, and which inspire empathy (but which are, of course, refined versions of the 'markers' I have previously identified in the music hall performance). The theatrical performer can be seen to *be* acting, and is usually to be found in a 'quality' context in television, such as the literary adaptation or the 'authored' drama. In these programmes, 'great' actors produce 'great' performances: (Sir) John Mills in *Martin Chuzzlewit* or (Dame) Peggy Ashcroft in *The Jewel in the Crown* are examples of this, indicating that a great performance is not necessarily a large one (in terms of screen time) but can, at moments, dominate the programme. John Mills' appearances as 'Chuffy' in *Martin Chuzzlewit*, for example, were both narratively and performatively disrupting – his 'presence' seemed much larger than his part. (It is also worth noting, as an aside, that while John Mills' performance may have stood out as theatrical, something of the patchwork of class and character types described by Dickens was rather neatly articulated by the range of performance styles incorporated into one programme-text. For the cast of *Martin Chuzzlewit* included sit-com stars, such as Julia Sawahala and Lynda Bellingham as well as other 'great' actors such as Sir Paul Schofield and even alternative comedians such as Keith Allen). Theatrical performances can also be seen from less 'great' performers; Robert Lindsay in *GBH*, or Bob Peck in *Edge of Darkness*, are both examples of theatrical performances that were mannered and expressive, and where we could, at certain points, see them, and appreciate them *acting*.

In contrast to this, there is another style of dramatic performance which is not about playing the part, as we can see perhaps in the theatrical style, but is about underplaying, and literally perhaps about being caught up in the medium. This, I would suggest, is one of the few instances in which the television performance can be aligned to the cinematic style, particularly, perhaps, the internalised yet busy style adapted from the Method technique which is currently employed by American film actors such as Robert de Niro and Al Pacino. This style is familiar to British viewers because of the high profile and relatively strong presence of American imports on British television screens. In large part, I think it may be specific to US television performances because of the more intimate connection between the American film industry and US television production, which is very much in contrast to the traditional connection of British television to British theatre. As a performance style, the cinematic performance is particularly prevalent in American dramas such as *Hill Street Blues*, *ER* and *NYPD Blue* and is enhanced (less covertly than the 'theatrical' style) by the 'technology' of television. Recently, on British television screens at least, the performance of David Caruso as John Kelly in *NYPD Blue* seems to me a good example of this particular style: his technique was characterised by 'method-like' twitches – he looks and doesn't look (mimicking a busy intensity, both anxious, needy and aggressive). At the same time, he appears to carry a burden, indicating both his acceptance of responsibility and his sensitivity, so that his posture is hunched, and when he speaks to others, his head is bowed indicating again, sensitivity, and intensity. (The implication being, perhaps, that he is *listening*.) Caruso's 'soft-hard' performance is reinforced by the technology employed by the programme, so that the quick, repetitive and fussy camera pans emphasise the look and non-look, while the crowding of shots, and the odd camera angles reproduce intensity. Most significantly, however, the character's hard-softness is in part a result of the mixture of a harsh *tele-noir* look recreation in the station (strong shadows and dark corners, performers framed in silhouette) and a soft, backlit glow in which Kelly is bathed for romantic situations. Is it Kelly or the lighting that we fall in love with? What would his performance be, without the lighting?

Finally, we might want cautiously to acknowledge the performance of ordinary people on television. How do they (we?) appear, and what can be said about their performance (if it can be called that?) *How* they appear may be determined by *where* they appear. And ordinary performers appear in diverse contexts: performing as an 'expert' or eye witness, as a victim or perpetrator in the news or documentary, as game show contestants, or simply as accident prone in home-made videos. Ordinary people perform in numerous contexts, and are, as other critics have noted, beginning to appear more and more frequently, and in a wider range of programmes. On British television one of the most interesting recent developments has been the *Video Nation* shorts, where, sandwiched between a dramatic serial and *Newsnight* (on BBC2) the same ordinary performer may appear and reappear (albeit briefly) as music enthusiast, lottery loser and/or political commentator.

Ordinary performers are likely to be both constrained and liberated in their performances. In certain contexts they will be more constrained than professional performers as they are more likely to be intimidated by the technology, and the mechanics of being 'on' television. From the audience's perspective, we may hold our breath, sharing their anxiety: we are alternatively with them and against them, anticipating or possibly willing disaster. Our worries concerning the ordinary performer will be related to the conventions of the programme-context. In the news interview or informal discussion programme we may fear that the ordinary person will freeze, look into the wrong camera lens, or refuse to understand or participate in the agenda of questions. In the game show we may be dismayed or inappropriately amused when we see the ordinary person fluster the host, or disrupt the carefully organised hierarchies of space taped onto the studio floor. For even in a people-centred game show such as *Blind Date* participants are confined to specific places and pathways, which are strictly patrolled by camera angles, floor managers and ultimately by Cilla Black, the host. *Blind Date* is a particularly useful example as it demonstrates another concern for the ordinary performer: the pressure to win sympathy and the work required to get the 'laugh'; an ability largely determined in this case by Cilla herself, who may support or undermine particular performers and performances. As with any successful performance, timing is crucial, and the viewing audiences are likely to be more conscious of 'dead air' (stumbles and pauses, mis-cues and breaths) from the ordinary performance, revealing (as others have noted) how much the apparently ordinary improvised talk of professionals is, in fact, carefully timed and scripted.

However, sympathy is not always guaranteed for contestants by a good performance as if they were professionals. One of the most common observations concerning *Blind Date* for example, is the unacknowledged, practised nature of the contestants' apparently spontaneous responses, which is often articulated by viewers as dissatisfaction or displeasure, relating to the absence of a looked for 'naturalness' in these moments, and more generally, from this kind of performer. The framing of the natural or ordinary performer must therefore be carefully managed in order to please an audience suspicious of a too obviously practised charm but nevertheless enamoured of both naive or natural candour and the activities of a real eccentric.

The eccentric is, of course, an extreme representative of the ordinary performer who is liberated rather than constrained by the television medium. This performer either satisfactorily conceals his sophisticated understanding of the television audience or is ignorant of their expectations. He or she may appear to the watching audience as a natural, as an original (literally extraordinary) and may be accompanied by strange pets, or simply manifest bizarre skills, mannerisms, unusual accents and/or opinions. In the appropriate context (in shows such as *That's Life!* or *Barrymore*) although they may be extreme, these ordinary performers are still not 'performing' – the audience believes (or wants to believe) that they *are* characters, extroverts discovered by the researcher and eventually, the camera. Ultimately, it appears, the audience does not want the ordinary performer to be polished – a too professional amateur may be read as pushy, embarrassing or desperate for fame. A too naked desire for celebrity on the part of the ordinary performer may, in fact, be dangerous: the notorious activities of 'The Hopefuls' on Channel 4's *The Word* (where 'hopeful' ordinary performers may place slugs in their mouths, or drink milkshakes of offal in order to appear on television) demonstrate how the viewer's distaste can resolve itself as a sadistic pleasure, as the ordinary performer is punished or humiliated for his or her 'unseemly' desire to perform.

I feel that the television audience may be anxious (and occasionally antagonistic) about ordinary performers for at least two reasons. Firstly, the otherwise accepted duality of character and actor is made problematic when we witness real people perform. For if real people convincingly 'put on an act' where can sincerity, authenticity and real emotion be located with any conviction? The collapse of the distinction between appearance and actuality does not need to be intellectualised to become a focus for legitimate concern. While acting may be pleasurable when we know we are watching a performance (it is after all, a 'skilful' activity) when an ordinary performer acts, we may become uncomfortably aware of how appearance and reality (the behaviour and the feelings) of the performer may be no more matched in the everyday than they are on screen.

Secondly, the audience may simply feel that the ordinary performer is being forced to perform, coerced into making a fool of themselves, and that their presence or image on screen has been manipulated by technicians, producers and bullying presenters. In other words, we empathise uncomfortably with their lack of control. There is therefore often an uneasy ambivalence in the appreciation of the ordinary performer. On the other hand we may anticipate disaster, and while we may (carefully framed) enjoy this, on the other hand we may also be pleasantly surprised when the ordinary performer wins, not just by giving the right answers but when he or she effectively 'takes control' of either the technology (the camcorder or the interviewer's microphone) or the performance context itself (that is the studio, the emotional or intellectual agenda).

It is likely to be difficult, then, to establish an encompassing definition of a good ordinary performer or a bad ordinary performance: it will be determined, in part, by context, and by the individual audience member's experience, and be revealed, perhaps, by the successful encouragement or release of their sympathies and/or anxieties. This difficulty brings me to the final opposition, or pairing, in the analysis of television performance, which is the perceived, and celebrated, difference between a good performance and a bad performance. I believe, as I've suggested, that one of the reasons we all feel able to make judgements about television performance is that the interpretation and appreciation of different performances is personal as much as it is critical, and cumulative as much as it is emotional. On top of this, however, I also feel that because of this, what we perceive as bad or good may have less to do with the actual performance (that is what actually happens) than with our desire to recognise emotional complexity and to acknowledge what we know to be virtuosity – or, at the very least, an expressive range. Descriptions of a good performance imply that what is most successful, or what is good about the performance is a matter of consensus concerning the recognition of a play or a register of emotion by the performer, that is consistent and believable in the context of their specific performance. This passes by or, more frequently, is seen to cross over the face of the performer. (This is particularly true in television performance where there is so much concentration on the medium-close up, and a privileging of the face, head and shoulders shot.) The play of emotions is one of the reasons that performance is so difficult to describe and almost impossible to freeze frame and point to on screen. It is, if you like, a living moment, and while television is distinguished to a large degree by its aspiration towards liveness and therefore perhaps should be the best context (outside of a theatre) for a good performance, this is qualified by the fact that it is difficult to achieve a mutual, communal recognition of an affective moment (we can hear canned laughter, for example, but we never hear the collective indrawing of breath inspired by television, and we never hear the sniffles that we might hear in the back row of the cinema). Because the television audience is mass and their tastes and histories are at once so important and conflicting, a consensus is only achieved (and then only partially) in retrospect, through tomorrow's papers or the ratings.

Meanwhile, the only secure marker of what might signify a bad performance in television may be, as in the theatre, the phenomenon of 'corpsing'. Corpsing is the forgetting of lines, giggling inappropriately or in other ways 'breaking the frame' of the performance. On television corpsing manifests itself as the inability to sustain the look of the camera, or the other performer, and this is extremely disturbing, as it is this look which is central to television performance (just as it is in film). Yet there are television performers whose accidental or rehearsed corpsing becomes a much loved part of their performance, most obviously the ordinary performer, who, as I have indicated, can dismay us by corpsing, but who we may also perversely celebrate as a result of their failure. More surprisingly, the corpsing of professional performers, may also be appreciated: Goldie Hawn's stutters and giggles in *Rowan and Martin's Laugh In*, or Dudley Moore's stifled smirks in *Not Only But Also* work as indicators of a pleasure in performing that seems to be true for the performer as well as the viewer, and as such they let the viewer in, subverting the bad performance into a good moment (a moment perhaps of apparently mutual recognition). Corpsing engenders a moment where the television performer reveals his or herself as truly live, uncontrolled and expressive. And it is this process of revealing that the audience almost greedily looks for, or hopes for, in much of television. For it suggests that form of direct communication, the existence of a real bond between performer and viewer, which television seems to promise, yet which it can rarely deliver.

Television performance, like the medium itself, is both seductive and a focus for anxiety. Articulating a series of dualities, it is inherently contradictory, linking deeply held emotions with a demand for critical detachment. And the corpse (by being both funny and grotesque) can speak loudly about this contradiction; it reveals our collusion with the television medium and the different kinds of performance it facilitates. By demonstrating that we have been seduced or fooled by performance, corpsing also reveals that the television performer is, after all, only human – being, as well as acting.

X Amount of Sat Siri Akal! Apache Indian, Reggae Music and the Cultural Intermezzo[1]

Les Back

1. Thanks to Steven Kapur for his endless patience and encouragement and I am also grateful to Roger Hewitt, Michael Keith, Flemming Røgilds, Vron Ware, Paul Gilroy, Ko Banerjea, Sadie Plant, John Solomos, and Anoop Nayak for advice and critical comments. Special thanks to Parminder Bhachu for sisterly inspiration and crash lessons in Punjabi.

Standing at the Crossroads
  I tried to flag a ride
Mmm, the sun going down, boy
  Dark gon'catch me here

Robert Johnson, *Crossroads Blues – Take 2*

X amount of sat siri akal
X amount of salam 'l' acum
  Fe all the Muslim raggamuffin posse
X amount of time ca any time we come is excessive
  Amount of lyrics have fe rhyme
Ca all the people round the world say the love reggae music fe real
I want you know say any time we come in a combination style
  Fe reveal reggae music everyone should a feel

Apache Indian, *Fe Real*

The multiple *must be made*.

Gilles Deleuze and Felix Guattari, *A Thousand Plateaus*

The title of this article is drawn from the lyrics of the Birmingham-based musician Apache Indian. The phrase signifies a greeting. Its two components bring together the lexicon of the African-Caribbean and south Asia. *X amount* has its origins in the language of the reggae dance hall and it means a quantity beyond calculation: *sat siri akaal* is a Punjabi salutation. Apache himself was raised in the multi-ethnic area Handsworth, Birmingham, born of Hindu Punjabi parents from Jalandhar. He performs and expresses himself through snatches of Jamaican patois, Punjabi and a unique form of English which is being generated by groups of young people who are growing up alongside each other in Birmingham.

Apache's music is a cultural crossroads, a meeting place where the languages and rhythms of four continents intermingle producing a culture that cannot be reduced to its component parts. Rather, it needs to be understood in the context of the global passage of linguistic and cultural forms and the localities where they converge: the culture is simultaneously both local and global. In this essay I want to try and explore these processes through a discussion of the cultural crossroads from which Apache Indian's music emerges and the implications this has for conceptualising identity and contemporary culture.

As Paul Gilroy has commented, the metaphor of the crossroads might provide an 'appropriate conceptual vehicle for rethinking the dialectical tension between cultural roots and cultural routes'.[2] Recently the understanding of the passage of culture through space has been based on the idea of flows.[3] The challenge is how to keep sight of the histories which propel these cultural flows while remaining open to the new possibilities that emerge at the crossroads where unforeseen things happen. This is perhaps the tension to which Gilroy alludes that is between cultural roots that fix and ossify and *routes*[4] which allow passage, transcendence and lines of flight.

The concept of the crossroads alone cannot provide an adequately detailed theoretical tool to unpick what happens at the conjunction of cultural routes. Here I want to introduce the notion of rhizome as elaborated in the writings of Gilles Deleuze and Felix Guattari.[5] For Deleuze and Guattari rhizomes offer an alternative to the vertical root/tree structure of dichotomous arborescent thinking. Through adventurous growths and rhizomes horizontal connections can be developed between things that have no necessary relation with each other.

Cultural rhizomes[6] form places where political and cultural connections can take place through the creation of a 'throng of dialects, patois, slangs and specialised languages'.[7] A rhizome has no beginning or end, it is always in the middle. The usefulness of the notion of rhizome is that it provides a way of describing forms of cultural interbeing. What I want to argue here is that the proximity of the children of African and south Asian diasporas in Birmingham is leading to what I shall refer to later as an *intermezzo culture*. Before going on to do this I want to outline the origins and character of black musical cultures in Britain.

REGGAE BLUES TO BHANGRA BEAT: THE EXPRESSIVE CULTURE OF THE DANCE

In the post-war era black people encountered racism most starkly in the housing and labour markets, but comparable divisions also appeared in the institutions of working-class leisure. As Simon Jones points out:

> The same racism that operated in the job and housing markets also operated to bar black workers from many white working-class leisure institutions, such as pubs, clubs, dance palais and bingo halls.[8]

Faced with a racially debarred urban culture black workers had to find alternative forms of leisure. The emergence of black-owned clubs and religious organisations such as mosques and temples provided a context in which black workers could socialise without encountering racism.[9] Within Afro-Caribbean communities music was central to many of these leisure activities.[10] The

2. P. Gilroy, 'It's a family affair' in G. Dent (ed), *Black Popular Culture*, Bay Press, Seattle 1992, pp305.

3. See U. Hannerz, 'Culture Between Centre and Periphery: Towards a Macroanthropology', *Ethnos*, Vol 54, III-V, pp200-216, 1989, and *Five Nigerians and the Global Ecumene*, paper given to the SSRC Symposium on 'Public Culture in India and Its Global Problematics', Carmel, California, April 26-30 1989.

4. I. Chambers, *Border Dialogues*, Routledge, London 1990.

5. G. Deleuze, and F. Guattari, *A Thousand Plateaus: Capitalism and Schizophrenia*, Athlone Press, London 1988.

6. See also K. Mercer, 'Back to my routes: a postscript on the 80s', *Ten 8*, 2(3), 1992, pp32-39.

7. Deleuze and Guattari, *op.cit.*, p7.

8. S. Jones, *Black Culture, White Youth: the Reggae Tradition from JA to UK*, Macmillan, Basingstoke 1988, pp33.

9. See D. Hiro, *Black British: White British*, Eyre and Spottiswoode, London 1971, and C. Gutzmore, 'Carnival, the State and the Black Masses in the United Kingdom', *The Black Liberator*, 1 December 1978, pp8-27.

10. D. Hinds, 'The "Island" of Brixton', *Oral History*, Volume 8, 1, 1980, pp49-51.

emergence of a black British reggae sound system scene is linked to the exclusive practices operated in white working-class leisure. By the beginning of the 1980s sound systems operated in all the major regions where black communities lived. A politically engaged form of Rastafari was the dominant ethos within a reformed black working-class culture.

These expressive musical cultures are produced through the interaction between the audience and the performers. In sound system culture the consumption of the music becomes a collective celebratory event where listening is an active process.[11] The call and response, or *antiphonic*, nature of this culture has its roots in a long history of folk art originating from Africa.[12] The end result is a democratic process of mechanically reproduced art which converges with the participator elements in lyrical performance: 'Lines between self and other are blurred and special forms of pleasure are created as a result'.[13] The dance provides an alternative public sphere, a unifying context for the sharing and celebration of collective experiences.

During the mid-1980s the sound system and the microphone provided a platform from which black young people could rewrite and document their own history.[14] The physical and social reality common to the audience and the performers alike made the music relevant and accessible. The hegemony of politically focused forms of reggae music shifted during the end of the decade as innovations entered the culture. In particular the impact of synthesised rhythms, like Wayne Smith's 'Under Me Sleng Teng' moved the nature of dance-hall culture in a new direction. DJs would come to rely on digitally produced rhythms which were sparse and hard-hitting.

There are direct parallels between the development of sound-system culture and the emergence of new south Asian musical cultures in Britain during the 1980s. In particular, forms derived from *bhangra* served similar functions to those of the reggae dance hall. The dance and song genre bhangra originates in the Punjab and it 'Celebrates the robust and energetic punctuated rhythms and iambic meter of the double-sided drums *dhol* and *dholki*, the supple directness of Punjabi language, and the pleasures associated with its main social occasions, the harvest festival *bhaisakhi*'.[15] Within the context of Britain bhangra music has been re-invented. Bands like Alaap in West London's Southall district incorporated sound sampling, drum machines and synthesisers to produce the new form called *bhangra beat*, also known as 'Southall beat'. In the Midlands other influences from hip hop and house music have been incorporated producing *northern rock bhangra* and *house bhangra*.

The development of these robust and rich new forms has been read as a focal point for an incipient British Asian youth culture. Bhangra created an overarching reference point cutting across cleavages of nationality (Indian, Pakistani, Bangladeshi and others), religion (Sikh, Muslim and Hindu) and cast/class. One distinctive feature of this culture was the so called 'daytimer', a live event which took place during school hours to compensate for the young Asians' inability to attend night-time clubs. The function of the daytimer is described here by Mac, singer with the group Dhamaka:

11. P. Gilroy, 'Hip Hop Technology' in P. Ayrton, T. Engelhardt and V. Ware (eds), *World View*, Pluto Press, London 1985.

12. See R Finnegan, *Oral Literature in Africa*, Oxford University Press, Oxford 1970, and P. Oliver, *Savannah Syncopators*, Studio Vista, London 1970.

13. P. Gilroy, 'Sounds Authentic: black music, ethnicity and the challenge of the changing same', *Black Music Research Journal* 11(2), 1991, p113.

14. L. Back, ' "Coughing Up Fire": Sound Systems and Cultural Politics in South East London', *New Formations*, Summer 1988, pp141-52.

15. G. Baumann, 'The Re-Invention of bhangra: social change and aesthetic shifts in a Punjabi music in Britain', *Journal of the International Institute for Comparative Music Studies and Documentation (Berlin)*, Volume XXXII(2) 1990, p81.

Daytimers reinforce our culture and values, girls dress in *sulwaars* (*salwaar-kamiz*, the traditional dress of Punjabi women), boys can come in turbans and get no hassle. The music is our music, and it's their show, not a 'goray' [white] gig or a 'kale' [black] show. Do parents want for kids to go out to gora shows? Would they rather have Asian kids disowning and abandoning their culture, to become Sharons and Garys tomorrow?[16]

16. *Ibid*, p87.

The connection of bhangra with a youthful sense of Asian unity is also expressed in the following quote from Komal, one of the lead singers of the East London bhangra group Cobra:

I can remember going to college discos a long time ago, when all you heard was reggae, reggae, reggae. Asians were lost, they weren't accepted by whites, so they drifted into the black culture, dressing like blacks, talking like them, and listening to reggae. But now bhangra has given them 'their' music and made them feel that they do have an identity. No matter if they are Gujaratis, Punjabis or whatever – bhangra is Asian music for Asians.[17]

17. *Ibid*, p91.

The emergence of bhangra in the 1980s signalled the development of a self-conscious and distinctively British Asian youth culture which expressed the primacy of an Asian identity. The result was the development of an alternative public sphere for young Asians which was comparable to the reggae dance hall. However, by the early 1990s complex fusions of reggae and bhangra had emerged. This went far beyond any crude sense of mimicry alluded to in the quote from Cobra cited above. In particular, the popularity of the MC Apache Indian has come to symbolise this innovation. Apache, formerly a sheet metal-worker from Handsworth, takes his name from his Indo-Jamaican idol, the Wild Apache Supercat. Equally, in London's East End, Bengali youth operate sound systems and appropriate rap and reggae lyrical styles.[18]

18. The emergence of Bengali sound systems is reported in *Artrage*, Summer 1991.

'GROOVEALLEGIANCE': LIMINALITY AND SUBALTERN SOUNDSCAPES[19]

19. P. Gilroy, ' "After the Love Has Gone": Bio-Politics and Etho-Poetics in the Black Public Sphere', *Public Culture*, Fall, pp1-27.

In addition to providing sites for cultural affirmation, the dance halls and clubs can also be characterised as liminal spaces. For example, towards the end of 1992 Apache Indian and the black south London reggae singer Maxi Priest collaborated on a tune called 'Fe Real'.[20] (I will come back to the significance of this tune later.) Apache Indian and Maxi Priest performed a small number of PAs (that is, a live vocal performance rendered over a backing track) together. The first show was scheduled to take place in the unlikely setting of Peterborough. Peterborough has a small Afro-Caribbean and south Asian population and it is about 100 miles from Birmingham. I set off from Birmingham with a friend about 9.30pm. As we drove through countless stereotypically English villages, I reflected on how the places I was travelling through related to what I was going to see at my destination. It struck me, here

20. Maxi Priest/ Apache Indian, 'Fe Real', White Label TENRDJ416.

I was, a white Englishman with a profound love of the sensibilities of black music, passing through caricatures of England on my way to witness another version of what 'Englishness plus' might mean. We arrived at the La Vistos Nightclub just before midnight. The description that follows of what I saw there should not be read as a simple realist narrative. My intention here is to attempt to represent – albeit in an inevitably flawed and partial way – the sublime energy and joy of what it was like to bear witness to the appearance of a new transcultural congregation.[21] I am not asking you to necessarily believe me; but rather to read this as an urban poem:

21. After J. Clifford and G. Marcus, *Writing Culture: The Poetics and Politics of Ethnography*, University of California, Berkley 1986 and J. Clifford, *The Predicament of Culture: Twentieth-Century Ethnography, Literature, and Art*, Harvard University Press, Cambridge 1988.

La Vistos is a classic 1970s night-club with a full complement of glitz and neon. It could have been in any provincial town. The club was complete with revolving light rigs, strobes and a terminal that breathed dry ice over the heads of the people on the dance floor. It could have been 1976 and John Travolta might feasibly have been preening himself in the toilets. But this was not just a white disco scene. Forty per cent of the audience were black and Asian. It was almost as if the rituals of the dance hall and the kitsch disco cultures had seamlessly fused. The fault-lines showed but they were not totalising, as if for one brief moment the divisive identities of race and nation were up for grabs. It was a carnival of identity, a place where time and social designation seemed temporarily suspended under the omnipresent groove of the drum and the bass. One could feel things opening up.

Before Apache and Maxi took the stage the DJ proclaimed a dance competition. 'I have a bottle of champagne for the best dance hall shaker'. *He stood on top of a stack of speaker cabs and rode the rhythm, finger outstretched scanning the dance floor for crucial moves. Shabba Ranks offered a rhythm and it was almost impossible to stand still. The DJ presided over the swaying mass of people. First up was a black woman in her forties. In the corner a white woman moved to the rhythm in a way that was indistinguishable from her black friends. Her white boyfriend looked on disapprovingly. She turned her back on him and moved with a mass of people of all shades. The DJ recognised the shattered binary and proclaimed her, as the dance hall massive tore up racial boundaries.* 'Yes, yes, nuff respect – come here sister!' *The white sister picked up her prize, she took it over to her disapproving boyfriend and put it on the table in front of him.*

Three black women had been dancing with their white friend when one of them beckoned an Asian man. The pair moved in unison locked in motion at the hip, yet not touching. Another division was exploded in an expression of Afro-Asian unity. The DJ called them. The black woman took the bottle, she turned, a path was cleared on the dancefloor and the two partners slowly worked their way towards one another as if the music drew them together.

Last up was a black man in his thirties winning his bottle through sheer commitment rather than style. The DJ passed judgement – 'This man has been dancing his ass off all evening, come here brother'. *As I scanned the dancefloor I could see some white men on the periphery trying to find a groove, stiffly jerking their bodies like a car that turns over but will not start. Others stood unimpressed demanding that the DJ* 'Get on with it and play the music'. *Both for those whites who embraced the rhythm or those who were unable to be possessed by it there was no escape. The Next fashions and the Dorothy Perkins dresses all moved – however awkwardly – to the beat of a different drum.*

The lights went down and Apache took the stage. 'This one is dedicated to all the Indian raggamuffin posse – X amount of sat siri akal, X amount salaam alakum for all the Muslim posse'. *While the microphone failed him, Apache led the crowd through a tour of his hits. A group of Afro-Caribbean young men looked on unimpressed. One young man wearing a turned around baseball cap with X showing stood, arms folded, surveying the scene. His friend moved and swayed with the dance-hall massive composed of Asian, black and white but he stood motionless. Apache paused* 'I am going to bring out a friend of mine now'. *Maxi Priest strolled on stage. He proceeded to sing snatches from his hits through this awful sound system with such beauty that would have melted the 'whitest heart'. After the vocal overture Maxi addressed the crowd:* 'This tune that we have recorded is for the India people. In it I try to sing in Indian'. 'Fe Real' *begins. Apache proclaims Maxi in Punjabi –* 'Maxi Ji'. *As the tune draws to an end Maxi sings his Punjabi lines over and over again. The black young man standing on the side of the dancefloor is still unimpressed but as one of his friends grabs him and pulls him onto the floor the group move in unison to a new style. The tune draws to an end to frantic whistling as the crowd shout a chorus of approval* 'Bo, bo, bo!' *I looked at my watch and it was 2.30am.*

There are a number of things that I want to emphasise with regard to this story. First, it demonstrates the degree to which the dance offers a place where social divisions can be temporarily suspended. I think that the notion of liminality is useful here.[22] Liminality refers to a state of separations from the mundane aspects of life usually associated with a rite of passage. As Turner points out, liminality is not merely about assigning identity, it can also relate to the inversion and transformation of public roles.[23] In Turner's later work he deployed a concept of liminoid social contexts.[24] Liminoid contexts resemble liminal states, they are marginal, fragmentary, outside the central economic and political process. However, I have not deployed this notion here because I feel it implies a degree of stability and fixity which does not adequately reflect the intermezzo nature of the cultural processes I am describing. Equally, I do not want to characterise these social forms as in anyway 'deviant'. There is a danger that Turner's notion of 'liminoid social forms' may lend itself to such a reading. In this sense I want to argue that the alternative public sphere of the dance can produce liminal ethnicities.[25] Equally, I want to argue that what results from this is the opening up of new identifications. These processes are not completely autonomous from external forces and divisions but I am arguing that these dialogues can result in the development of new *intermezzo cultures*. The notion of 'intermezzo' features in the work of Deleuze and Guattari and draws appropriately on a musical metaphor.[26] Its literal meaning is a short dramatic musical performance serving as a connecting link between the main divisions of a large musical work. Here I am using this as an analogy

22. V. Turner, *The Ritual Process*, Routledge & Kegan Paul, London 1969.

23. V. Turner, 'Liminality and the Performative Genres', in J.J. MacAloon (ed), *Rite, Drama, Festival, Spectacle: Rehearsals Towards a Theory of Cultural Performance*, Institute for the Study of Human Issues, Philadelphia 1984, p26.

24. V. Turner, *On the Edge of the Bush: Anthropology as Experience*, University of Arizona Press, Arizona 1985.

25. This notion is developed further in L. Back, *New Ethnicities and Urban Culture: Racisms and Multiculture in Young Lives*, University College Press, London 1996.

26. Deleuze and Guattari, *op.cit.*, p25.

to refer to a space which links social collectivities producing cultures of interbeing and mutual identification. The prime one I am concerned with here is the fusion of elements of south Asian culture and the rituals of the reggae dance hall.

Through the call and response between performer and audience these new cultural forms are endorsed. There are two examples from Apache's musical collaborations which demonstrate this process. During the promotion of 'Fe Real' Maxi Priest and Apache performed at a celebration held in Leicester of the religious festival Diwali. The event drew an audience of 8000 Hindus. Apache, remembering the show, comments on its significance:

> It was a nice warm kind of evening. They had 8000 Asian kids on the streets. We never realised it was going to be that big. When we went on stage Maxi did his Indian [Punjabi] chorus, when they saw him singing that, it meant so much. The Maxi Priest thing was a huge thing – it is all to do with us being a very self-contained people and thinking that people around us don't want to know what is happening. They see a black person wanting to use the language, wanting to come aboard what Apache is doing. Then it is like Maxi is an international star singing in Punjabi and then the Asian youth check it as – 'yeah people do want to know about us.' It was special.[27]

27. All quotations from Apache Indian used in the following sections are drawn from interviews conducted since 1990.

The music in this setting addresses a specific Asian constituency, and was embraced and in turn legitimated. Similar processes occured when Apache performed at prestigious reggae venues. Notably he was acknowledged during a televised performance at the celebrated black London venue the 291 Club winning over many of his detractors. In 1991 he was voted Best Newcomer at the British Reggae Industry Awards. In these kinds of contexts the music is being authenticated by a distinctly African-Caribbean constituencey. Apache comments here on an experience of playing an African-Caribbean venue in Southall where he performed his tune 'Arranged Marriage', in which he takes himself through a marriage, and the dance-floor rouser 'Chok There' (which means 'lively up'):

> I did a show, a reggae show for Daddy Ernie from Choice FM at Tudor Rose, Southall – black crowd, 99% black crowd. Before I did 'Arranged Marriage' I said 'Boy I am looking for a girl for my arranged marriage who will dress up in a sari and come to Delhi,' and all the black girls threw up their hands. When I was singing 'Chok There' I had two thousand black people singing out 'Chok There'.

These constitute powerful moments where social and musical conventions are being played with and transgressed: an African-Caribbean performer singing in Punjabi to a south Asian audience, and an African-Caribbean audience singing Punjabi with an Asian artist. The result is an exciting tangle of rhizomorphous connection, a *sound block* that no longer has a point of origin but forms a conjunction.

Borrowing from the conceptual language of Deleuze and Guattari, these intermezzo cultures constitute a kind of *cultural body without organs*. A state of fusional multiplicity is established and music provides a smooth surface on which the distinctions and social divisions within the dance hall can be blurred. The body without organs (BWO) is a difficult concept to summarise; what it constitutes is a state of fusional multiplicity, with indeterminate organs, or with temporary, transitory organs.[28] BWO needs a principle of production in order to achieve what is referred to as a *zero intensity*. In the context of what I have been describing a zero intensity is achieved by music and the banishing – however temporarily – of racism. Complex and challenging cultures reside in this sonorous interjacence which cannot be comprehended in terms of simple racial binaries. The infectious rhythms of the music have the potential to suspend the social divisions which exist outside the dance and enable new forms of expression. Within these subaltern soundscapes different truths about the politics of race can be spoken, nurtured and circulated.

28. Deleuze and Guattari, *op.cit.*, p183.

THE HANDSWORTH TRANSLATION: 'BHANGRAMUFFIN', APACHE INDIAN AND AFRO-ASIAN DIALOGUE

Apache Indian – aka Steven Kapur – released his first record entitled 'Movie Over India' in 1990.[29] By January/February 1991 'Movie Over India' topped both the reggae and bhangra charts. The new form was dubbed *bhangramuffin* after its ragga counterpart. The first point to make about Apache's biography is that his relationship to reggae music cannot be separated from his broader involvement in multi-racial peer groups and the wider black community. Apache grew up in the multiracial district of Handsworth of Hindu parents from the Punjab. At school his closest friend was a young black man and reggae music captured his imagination from a very early age:

29. Apache Indian, 'Movie Over India', City to City SUNREC 001A.

> I remember this record shop in Handsworth, it was called Rough Groove Records, or something, and I always wanted to go into the shop, but there were always so many black people hanging around the shop and I was almost frightened to go in. But I slowed down as I passed by because I loved the music.

His early preference was roots reggae performed by Bob Marley and Burning Spear. Despite early feelings of ambivalence towards going into black record shops he continued to identify with the music and the physical culture which surrounded its performance.

> I was so much into reggae by the time I was fourteen. I remember I cut up one of my wardrobes to try and make it into a speaker box. I had this big wardrobe in those days and I dragged it out into the garden. I cut three holes in it. I didn't even know what size they were. I wanted to fit speakers in

the holes. I painted the whole thing black inside and out and that was my speaker box. But you could never use it as a speaker box because the wood was too thin. When my parents came back – Jesus Christ. That was probably me trying to get close to reggae and I wanted to do something. So I just cut up my wardrobe and put three holes in it and the speakers never did fit.

Apache was inducted into sound system culture by a young black man of Caribbean parentage called Sheldon who ran 'Siffa' sound system. Sheldon introduced him to important people within Birmingham's reggae scene and later he became his brother-in-law. By the time he was sixteen Apache was working with a sound system in the Birmingham area. He invested in his own set, calling it 'Simeon', the dread name given to the month of May – the month in which he was born – by Rastafari. Apache joined forces with Sheldon under the name of 'Sunset'. By the age of 18 he had his own amps and speaker boxes and was learning the culture of the dance hall. The next crucial step was his decision to become a 'van man'. He raised the money to buy a Luton van and ended up driving some of Birmingham's premier sound systems all over the country. By this time he had also followed his male relatives into a job in a local engineering factory where he was employed as a welder.

His involvement with dance hall culture intensified when he met a prominent Birmingham soundman called Wooligan who ran 'Orthodox 38' sound system.

When I met Woolly I realised that I met someone who was as crazy about the music as me. If you go to his house he eats off speaker boxes. He sleeps in a speaker box. It is in his blood. I was the van man and I just loved to drive to the dance – just to be around the sound. What happened was that one night, it was in Slough, his DJ and the people who were supposed to chat never showed up. So I started chatting on the mike. Somebody said 'Who is that chatting? It's the van man, van man doesn't chat, van man drives the van'.

This marked the end of a long induction into the culture:

Even down to loading the van. There is an art to loading a van. If you put too many boxes on one side the van will be unbalanced when you drive fast down the motorway. This was also the stage when I started to learn patois. People asked me how did I learn patois? Did you have to sit down and study it? Being in a sound [system] driving hundred of miles with a bunch of guys falling asleep at 4.00 am in the morning – that was my education, that was my school.

His identification with reggae and black style was taken to serious lengths. At sixteen he started to grow dreadlocks. Reflecting on this, he explains his desire to grow locks as an extension of his love and identification with reggae music and dance-hall culture. His experience of having locks was highly formative with regard to his own sense of politicisation. He describes an incident surrounding a shopping expedition on Handsworth's main street – Soho Road.

> I remember I walked in [to a shop] and as soon as I walked through the door people started to talk in Punjabi. They saw my locks and they checked me as a black guy. I can't remember exactly what the shopkeeper said but it was something like 'watch out this black guy is going to tief [thieve] something' ... This made me realise, it opened my eyes to what was happening in the street and what people like Bob Marley were saying about what black people go through and what tribulation meant. What made it worse was that it wasn't white people who were saying these things.

Apache talks about a period where he felt that he was effectively 'passing' as African-Caribbean. This was part and parcel of an identification with a culture but also a wider community. It was also about learning what the culture stood for historically and politically.

> I know it is a serious culture. I know it is a serious thing. I look around and see people playing with it today and I tell them this is a serious, serious thing. It has roots which go back a long way and you have to respect that. It means a lot to black people and I found that out being around black people. Me having locks was nothing cultural, it was me just trying to get closer to the music that I loved. I cut off my locks out of respect but I will always have my locks in my mind.

The significance of this story is that it shows that Apache's initiation into this culture was part of a long standing dialogue. Similar experiences have been documented elsewhere with regard to black culture and white young people.[30]

It is no surprise then that Apache's early records dealt with the central theme of translation. 'Movie Over India' provided rudimentary lessons in Punjabi and patois. It might have never been made had not Apache been able to convince his cousin to give him some studio time. The second single, which was not officially released because of problems with bootlegging, continued the theme and was called 'Come Follow Me' and featured the Birmingham MC Mikey G.[31]

Apache adopted a style which took everyday phrases from both cultures and used them interchangeably and in elaborate combinations. A good example of this is *O Chok there fut air* which in Punjabi means raise the floorboards. This idiom would be used along side creole grammar and phrases like *fe real*, *X amount* and *big up* which all have their origins in dance hall culture. The emerging language, what Apache calls Indian patois, is an urban *lingua franca* which provides a suture between communities while acknowledging specificities of their African and south Asian origins. This is the 'Handsworth translation'; it makes sense in the Birmingham context, but it also resonates with global reference points. Tunes like 'Movie Over India' and 'Come Follow Me'

30. See R. Hewitt, *White Talk, Black Talk: Inter-Racial Friendship and Communication Amongst Adolescents*, Cambridge University Press, London 1986; and S. Jones, *op.cit.*

31. Apache Indian 'Come Follow Me' City to City CTC 1001A.

take the listener on an imaginary journey through diasporas from Jalandhar and Bombay, to Kingston/Jamaica and back again to Handsworth. It is not just a matter of making Punjabi and patois mutually intelligible but it is also about plotting the nodal points of an *inter-diaspora imaginary*.

IDENTITY AND RACIAL AUTHENTICITY

This intermezzo culture is scrutinised both within the African-Caribbean and south Asian communities. Sonia Poulton writing in Britain's black music paper *Echoes* comments that 'The fascination of Apache Indian's music is his fusion of bhangra and reggae, but that doesn't make him a reggae artist'.[32] Poulton sees Apache's mode of cultural expression as a limited form of impersonation. In the same vein the prominent black British MC Tipper Irie reviewing 'Fe Real' in *Echoes* questioned Apache's suitability to collaborate with Maxi Priest. Equally, during a recent visit to a mainly Asian school in Slough, he was asked whether he was black or Asian! After a similar visit to a youth club in Stoke-on-Trent an egg was thrown at him.

Incidents like these immediately beg a whole range of questions relating to the nature of racial/ethnic authenticity. These objections are connected to a version of absolutist identity politics which – for whatever reasons – seek to protect claims over African and Asian modes of cultural production and expression. However, are such moves missing the radical potential of creative intermezzo cultures? Paul Gilroy suggests that '... the most important lesson music still has to teach us is that its inner secrets and its ethnic rules can be taught and learned ... black music cannot be reduced to a fixed dialogue between a thinking racial self and a stable racial community'.[33] He goes on to suggest that the notion of antiphony – of call and response – needs to be modified. The point that I would make is that a variety of social groups can respond to the call of black music. It is always important to raise the thorny question of who holds the power in this process of inter-cultural traffic. The crucial dimension here is the way the antiphonic dialogue between the performers and the audiences provides the arena in which the legitimacy of these forms can be established and their political valency scrutinised.

It is important to stress the plurality of south Asian musics and the variety of resources and inflections which young Asians have embraced. There is a dearth of insightful writing into the long history of musical creativity in south Asian communities in Britain and their participation in soul and reggae cultures. The limited comments offered here are only intended to point to some of the important developments. Signs of these dialogues can be seen with the swelling numbers of Asians following established reggae sound systems such a Jah Shaka.[34] Equally, the Coventry-based producer Bally Sagoo is combining bhangra beats, ragga and hip hop in his *Wham Bam* collections with richly syncretic results. His work includes swingbeat mixes of the Muslim Qawwali singer Nusrat Fateh Ali Khan[35] and ragga versions of classic Punjabi folk. Bally Sagoo's *Essential Ragga* album sold 50,000 copies and featured

32. Quoted in *The Independent*, 19 September 1991. See also *Caribbean Times*, 10 September 1991.

33. P. Gilroy, *The Black Atlantic: Modernity and Double Consciousness*, Verso, London 1994, pp109-110.

34. *The Voice*, 28 May 1991.

35. Bally Sagoo/ Nusrat Fateh Ali Khan, 'Magic Touch', Oriental Star SC 5130.

singers like Rama alongside the white MC Cheshire Cat.[36] The extent of his success went unnoticed until he was signed by Sony Records in 1994. A whole wave of south Asian musicians are beginning to emerge and include Bradford's Fun ^ da ^ mental, Leicester's indie rock band Cornership, the Kaliphz (meaning messenger in Arabic), Asian Dub Foundation, Hustlers HC, State of Bengal and Sasha, a major contributor to Multitone's bestseller *Ragga for the Masses*. The diversity of these forms of expression confounds the simple characterisation that bhangra is the prime form of expression of south Asian youth culture. These musical cultures provide a context to challenge dominant stereotypes, express translocal connections and find a voice that does justice to the social location and agenda of their British Asian exponents. These artists lay claim to Englishness while parodying the racial exclusivity present within the cultural rhetoric of national belonging.

36. Bally Sagoo, *Essential Ragga*, Oriental Star SC 5141.

It is equally important to realise that African-Caribbean musicians are answering the call of the musics of the south Asian diaspora. For example, a young band called XLNC from Wolverhampton are developing a unique 'combination style'. At the core of their music is bhangra beat, yet their bass player Derrick is of Jamaican parents. They cover the reggae classic 'Red Red Wine' but in the form of a traditional Punjabi song 'Lwt Ke Le Gaye' (meaning, she swept me away). Similarly, the Southall-based African-Caribbean singer Mixmaster Ji combines lyrics sung in impeccable Punjabi with dance beats. This antiphonic exchange makes the music a junction box for cross-cultural flows resonant with the sounds of reggae, house, techno, soul and Indian folk.

Apache Indian faces a range of pressure to place himself within a singular definition of 'identity', to reterritorialise himself as either black or Asian, Hindu or Sikh, English or Indian. Yet his music and experience confound such segmentations. On a recent tour of India he was asked about his religion; echoing Gandhi he replied 'I am a Hindu, a Sikh, a Muslim, a Jew – anything you want me to be'.[37] He reflects:

37. *New Musical Express*, 7 August 1993, p47.

> That was my way of saying to people if you are going to ask me a stupid question then I am going to come back at you like that. When I really sit down and think about it I am not Jamaican, I am not fully Indian: I am a mixture of everything. I also feel very English. I think that the fusion of culture is something that is going to become a normal thing and whoever is fighting it is fighting a battle that they are going to lose. How can you stop fusion? You can never stop it.

The types of 'fusion' that Apache's music personifies are not arbitrary. What his music demonstrates is a series of departures, identifications which traverse a number of continents then return and pause at Birmingham's cultural crossroads only to re-depart again. These migrations are made possible by the infrastructure of global culture industries but their significance cannot be simply reduced to their status as a commodity. The traces and memories of passage are retained and plotted within these musical forms. It is to the nature of these global networks that I now turn.

OUTERNATIONAL CULTURE: INDIA AND INTER-DIASPORIC CONNECTIONS

> When I came back from Jamaica, it was just Jamaica, Kingston ... and nothing else mattered. I just wanted to do pure ragga tracks and I wasn't so much concerned with the Indian side. I was in a *ragga frame of mind* (my emphasis).

In the past three years Apache Indian has travelled extensively, performing and recording in some of the significant sites of reggae music production. On 6 June 1992 he performed in Port of Spain, Trinidad with a host of diaspora figures including Heavy D & The Boyz, Lisa Lisa, and his early Indo-Caribbean idol Apache Supercat. He travelled to Bob Marley's Tuff Gong studio in Jamaica to record part of his debut album *No Reservations*, collaborating with such reggae luminaries as Frankie Paul, Bobby Digital, Robert Livingston and Sly Dunbar.[38] The significance of this is partly to do with the process of making these fusions legitimate mentioned earlier. This is reinforced by the way in which Apache Indian's music has featured on Jamaican sound systems. 'Chok There' in particular was a big hit in Jamaica.

38. Apache Indian, *No Reservations*, Island CID 8001/514/112-2.

This tangle of inter-diaspora connections is also present in the political fragments which underpin Apache Indian's music: Mahatma Gandhi's *satyagraha* (literally meaning 'holding on to truth' and the name given by him to the doctrine of non-violent resistance) is coupled with the dread maxims of Bob Marley. What is striking within this music is that stylistics and ideological combinations can be made accessible and comprehended by Caribbean, European and Indian audiences. In Trinidad and Jamaica people of African origin sang along to Punjabi lyrics while in India vast crowds in Delhi and Bombay sang Jamaican patois choruses. Here Apache reflects on his experience of performing the cut 'Moving On' in Adheri Stadium, Bombay.

> There was a problem with understanding what I was trying to say in India. So before every song I would do it a capella so that they would understand what it was all about. I made a big speech before 'Moving On' and I said the Hindu, Muslims and Sikhs must stick together and move on as one people. They stood up put their hands in the air and sang 'Moving on moving and we na turn back!' An Indian crowd singing this in [Jamaican] patois and it was so powerful almost as if they really wanted to move on. Even [Kid] Milo the security said he wanted to cry. 25,000 people singing 'Moving on moving and we na turn back.'

Released in 1993 on the back of 'Chok There' single, 'Moving On' puts forward a clear position on the issue of inter-communal violence.

On the 6th December in 92
In a India there was a curfew
Ca a Mosque get destroyed mon by the Hindu
So the Muslim talk say revenge is due
So them lick down a temple a next one too
People get kill here when me tell you
And you know segregation bound fe follow through
All this have fe stop it cannot continue
... Me say an eye for and eye make the whole world blind.[39]

39. Apache Indian, 'Chok There', Sure Delight SDT 41.

The promotional poster carried a message in Urdu, Punjabi and black English it also stated unity: 'The Hindu, Muslim, and Sikhi brother, live as one and you get further, All of us are bound to prosper, One god, one love and unity, Share the land that god lef fe we.' Here black English becomes the medium for the message – a transcendent, 'one love' human unity. The visit to India in June 1993 is important in understanding the interdiasporic significance of this music. Apache's music is extremely popular on the subcontinent largely due to the exposure of his first Indian single 'Chok There' on MTV Asia transmitted from Hong Kong. The *No Reservations* album sold rapidly in India during the summer of 1993 and went double platinum in a matter of three months. Apache Indian was the first artist to receive platinum records on Indian soil. The June visit caused unprecedented media attention. His arrival was front page news in many Indian newspapers. He performed to a 25,000 strong audience in Bombay's Andheri Stadium and to a similar size crowd at New Delhi's Rabindra Rangshala where he came on stage on a white horse while 4,000 people stood outside unable to get tickets. Apache was invited to meet the Governor of Bombay, Sonia Gandhi and the President of India. This raises some important issues in relation to the cultural politics of diaspora communities.

In a recent essay Ruth Frankenburg and Lat Mani argue that:

> Not all places in this transnational circuit are similarly 'postcolonial'. The active, subjective, inescapable, everyday engagement with the legacies of colonialisation/decolonisation that is part of the British matrix for reggae, bhangra rap ... are not the terms of the theoretical artistic or political endeavours in India.[40]

40. R. Frankenberg and L. Mani, 'Crosscurrents, Crosstalk: Race, "Postcoloniality" and the Politics of Location', *Cultural Studies*, 7, 2, p302.

The political terrain and theoretical language of India and the United Kingdom is far from uniform. However, the spectre of 24,000 Delhites singing a message of interfaith Indian unity in a Birmingham cut of Jamaican patois may signal the potential for the development of a transnational matrix for cultural politics in India. The Africanological notion of antiphony is again useful to describe modest forms of 'postcoloniality'. Apache Indian, answering the call of black music, heralds a subcontinent with a *diasporic triple consciousness* that is simultaneously the child of Africa, Asia and Europe. In the language of black vernacular cultures the music has gone *outernational*, simultaneously inside and beyond the nations through which it passes.

SLACKNESS AND DANCE-HALL CULTURE

The politics of the dance-hall are complex and it would be a gross misrepresentation to present the expressive cultures which are fostered here as unambiguously transgressive. Syncretism is a two way process. While the asesthetics of 'small nationalisms' are parodies and carnivalised within these spaces, one can also identify the cultural traces of imperialism and the echoes of slavery within these styles, dances and sounds. Recent controversies over the celebration of misogyny, homophobia and 'gun iconography' in the culture of the dance-hall provide key moments where the rupture and violence of white supremacy are registered in black culture in seismic proportions. Following bell hooks, one must see these phenomena not as the product of racial alterity but as the assimilation of the modernity inheritance replete with hierarchies of race, class and gender.[41] This inheritance feeds the powerfully critical and transcendent qualities embodied within these cultures. Yet it can also harbour some of the destructive features of racial supremacy within the culture itself. Fanon in his seminal discussion of colonialism suggested that the violence deposited by the coloniser 'in the bones' colonised would be first turned inward against themselves and their peers.[42] The deaths by shooting of almost a generation of Jamaican DJs needs to be seen through the lens of these wise words.

The resurgence of 'slackness' during the late-1980s and early 1990s shifted the agenda on the mike. Jamaican DJs like Shabba Ranks, Lovindeer, Chaka Demus and Buju Banton led the sensibilities of the dance-hall into unparalleled 'sex talk', word-play and controversy. This reached its height in the summer of 1992 when Buju Banton's 'Boom Bye Bye' proposed taking a gun to gay men and Shabba Ranks appeared on British television to denounce homosexuality by invoking the Bible. These incidents feed the British and American media's appetite for racial demonology. The implications of this turn within the culture cannot be easily dismissed as merely another white supremacist moral panic. These attempts to marshall and define the relationship between sexuality and blackness produced a form of authoritarianism aimed to compensate for the devastation being experienced by black people in the Caribbean, America and Europe.[43] Within this line of argument contemporary music, dance and oral cultures are viewed as an 'after shock' of slavery in which the body becomes the prime text of authenticity and recompense for an enduring lack of freedom.[44] Several commentators have warned against the convergence of a militarised machismo, homophobia and racial absolutism.[45]

Others have argued that within the hyper sexualised settings of 1990s ragga one can find a politics of subversion missed by those who see slackness as culturally conservative. The most ardent exponent of this line is Carolyn Cooper who argued that in Jamaica slackness can be seen as a 'down town'

41. b. hooks, 'Gangsta Culture-Sexism and Misogny', in *Outlaw Culture: Resisting Representations*, Routledge, London 1994.

42. F. Fanon, *The Wretched of the Earth*, Penguin, Harmondsworth, 1963, p40.

43. C. West, *Race Matters*, Beacon Press, New York.

44. This point is developed in Isaac Julien's film *The Darker Shade of Black*, Arena BBC2.

45. See in particular P. Gilroy, *Small Acts: Thoughts on the Politics of Black Cultures*, Serpent's Tail, London 1993, and I. Julien, 'Black is, Black Ain't: Notes on De-Essentialising Black Identities', in G. Dent (ed), *Black Popular Culture*, Bay Press, Seattle 1992.

revolt against the pious morality of fundamentalist Jamaican society:

> Slackness is not mere sexual looseness – though it is certainly that. Slackness is a metaphorical revolt against law and order; an undermining of consensual standards of decency. It is the antithesis of Culture. To quote Josey Wales: 'Slackness in di backyard hidin, hidin from Culture'. Slackness as an (h)ideology of escape from authority of omniscient Culture is negotiated in a coded language of evasive *double-entendre*.[46]

Cooper maintains that the moralist critique of slackness misses the power that dance-hall possesses for flaunting the moral conservatism of the Jamaican uptown elite. Such an assessment produces a barren ethical position which merely celebrates everything within the dance as 'resistance' no matter what the consequences. More convincingly, Cooper points to the opportunity that the dance-hall offers women to have control over their bodies and express their sexuality. Sexually expressive forms of dancing like 'wining' allow 'female power to be exuded in the extravagant display of flashy jewellery, expensive clothes, elaborate hairstyles and the rigidly attendant men that altogether represent substantial wealth'.[47] The emergent fame of 'dance-hall Queens' like Carlen Smith provides important examples of where women have achieved status and economic power through such means. For Cooper women's power within the dance lies in the control over their sexuality and men's dependence upon them.

On the other hand it can be argued that women's power lies in their autonomy from men within the dance-hall. Daniel Miller has argued in relation to Trinidad that the auto-sexuality of 'wining' engenders for women something akin to a Hegelian form of absolute freedom. Here sexual fulfilment becomes the dancer's own autonomous object: 'It is an expression of a free sexuality which has no object but itself, and most especially it is a sexuality not dependent upon men'.[48] This momentary and transient individuation produces a self-absorbed and self-sufficient sexual fulfilment in which the dancer is free from everything that binds her to the world. Inge Blackman, director of the film *Ragga Gyal D'bout*, argued further that the dance-hall offers a context for black women to celebrate their sexuality. Unlike any other form of black popular culture, ragga in Britain allowed black women to be sensual with each other beyond narrowly heterosexual terms of reference. The sexual politics of ragga are clearly complex. Opportunistic media racism characterised these forms of music and dance as crudely homophobic and misogynistic, yet these evaluations produce little more than the latest in a long line of racist moral panics. Despite this, serious issues remain in the future regarding the ways in which the echoes of slavery and imperialism re-surface in the loaded plans of dance-hall culture and music.

Before concluding I want to briefly explore the relationship between Apache Indian's music and the gender politics of the dance-hall. In particular, I want to discuss the way his music both reproduces and subverts the masculinities

46. C. Cooper, *Noises in the Blood: Orality, Gender and the 'Vulgar' Body of Jamaican Popular Culture*, Macmillan Caribbean, London 1993, p141.

47. *Ibid*, p155.

48. D. Miller, 'Absolute Freedom in Trinidad', *Man*, 26, p333.

associated with the culture. Apache Indian has been careful to try and explain that slackness is a product of urban Jamaican life, while being steadfast in his resistance to chat unambiguously slack lyrics. On the issue of the Buju Banton controversy he is guarded:

> What Buju Banton chats is reality to him. I have been to Jamaica and seen what has happened there. I am not saying that it is alright to chat slack lyrics and mash [beat/kill] up gay people. I am just saying you have to understand where it comes from – but I am not saying that I agree with it or persecuting gay people.[49]

49. Quoted from a seminar with cultural studies students, Birmingham University, 25 January 1993.

50. Apache Indian, *Nuff Vibes EP*, Island CID 560.

Importantly, his second release of 1993 the *Nuff Vibes EP* includes an AIDS awareness cut called 'Warning' in which he points to the ignorance which characterises AIDS/HIV as a 'gay man disease' and urges collective responsibility for safer sex.[50] There is an ambiguity with regard to his position, reflecting a tension between the way he identifies with figures like Shabba Ranks and Buju Banton, while attempting to subvert elements of dance-hall machismo.

His music also explores contemporary heterosexual masculinities and specific issues which effect young Asian men. A good example is his top twenty hit 'Arranged Marriage'.[51] The tune takes Apache through an arranged marriage. It could be read as an unthinking exercise in masculine bravado, where Apache over and over proclaims 'Me want gal [woman] to look after me'. The crucial point in the tune is where he asks the listener 'But when is the right time to tell my girlfriends'. This signals the point at which the rhetorical chauvinism of the tune is called in to crisis. The tension within the fictional marriage echoes the experience of Apache's male peers who developed relationships with young women and then have to reckon with family marriage arrangements. While realising that many of his white listeners will miss this irony, Apache maintains: 'That is the truth for a lot of Asian people. I am not against arranged marriages but people have to realise that growing up in places like Birmingham, London or Toronto young people are going to have relationships.'

51. Apache Indian, 'Arranged Marriage', Island CID 544.

He is most outspoken when it comes to the question of violent masculine rhetoric and 'gun culture' in lyrics:

> The gun thing is a huge thing. In my first track with Frankie Paul I sang 'Talk what you want but don't touch me beca if you touch me be dead and bury'. And there is an element of dance-hall that involves that 'bad boy' image but now it is getting ridiculous, somebody got shot today in Lozells [an area adjacent to Handsworth]. Someone got shot in his face and I will never, ever, ever chat lyrics like that again. The gun thing is frightening.

There is an ambiguity between the way he locates himself within dance-hall masculinities and his attempts to undermine elements within these gendered codes of presentation and style. This ambivalence runs through all of his music.

The grain of these inflections and the potentially productive tensions embodied within the culture are missed by the moral critics of ragga and dance-hall.

DIFFERENT IMAGINATIONS AND TRUTHS

> Warehouses [unofficial parties] taught young Britons of different classes how to be social together outside of the confines of work, clubs and football terraces. Taught them there didn't have to be rules – or expensive bars or doormen telling you what you could and couldn't wear. We freed people's imaginations.
>
> Norman Jay[52]

> A whole literary fiction of the festival grew up around the plague: suspended laws, lifted prohibitions, the frenzy of passing time, *bodies mingling together without respect*, individuals unmasked, abandoning their statutory identity and the figure under which they had all been recognised, *allowing a quite different truth to appear*.
>
> Michel Foucault (my emphasis)[53]

The expressive musical cultures of Britain's cities provide a context in which political autonomy and self-representation can be realised alongside profound forms of transcultural dialogue. Michel Foucault, in the above epigraph, describes the carnival of transgression that occured during the plagues of the medieval period. There are important similarities between Foucault's telling description and the suspension of the social divisions that is made possible, although not guaranteed, within the alternative public spheres of the dance-hall, club and house party. The liminality of the dance-hall allows a similar potential to transgress and change. Foucault also argues that the possibilities of liberating rupture are met by the capillary functioning of power: '... not masks that were put on and taken off, but the assignment to each individual his "true" name, his "true" place, his "true" body ...'.[54] The musical cultures I have discussed here provide a key site where comparable forms of self-definition and regulation are being contested.

As Kobena Mercer has rightly observed, identity only becomes an issue when it is in crisis, when something assumed to be fixed, coherent and stable is displaced by the experience of doubt and uncertainty.[55] He suggests that preoccupation with talking about identity is symptomatic of the postmodern predicament of contemporary politics. What is alarming about the almost insatiable appetite for 'identity talk' is the degree to which these sentences – in both the grammatical and ontological sense – return to the same subject. The debate on politics and identity in postcolonial and poststructural thinking has become preoccupied with the strategic justification for prime identities.[56] The central issue has been how to reckon with fragmentation and rupture while keeping open the possibility of identity and agency. This is demonstrated in

52. Quoted in C. Rose, *Design After Dark: The Story of Dancefloor Style*, Thames and Hudson, London 1991, p42.

53. M. Foucault, *Discipline and Punish*, Tavistock, London 1977, pp197.

54. *Ibid*, p198.

55. K. Mercer, 'Welcome to the jungle: identity and diversity in postmodern politics' in J. Rutherford (ed), *Identity: Community, Culture, Difference*, Lawrence & Wishart, London 1990, pp43.

56. G. Spivak, *The Post-Colonial Critic: Interviews, Strategies, Dialogues*, Routledge, London 1990.

57. S. Hall, 'Minimal Selves', ICA Documents Number 6, *Identity: The Real Me*, ICA/BFI, London 1987 and S. Hall, 'Cultural Identity and Cinematic Representation', *Framework*, 36, 1989, pp68-81.

Stuart Hall's attempt to navigate between essentialist notions of identity based on a primordial self and the 'anything goes' pluralism of postmodern ideology.[57] His resolution is that arbitrary or strategic forms of closure are required in order to make politics possible. What I want to foreground is that there are other options for cultural politics. In short, a politics of the multiple that refuses the confines of the Subject while avoiding any banal form of assimilationism.

The music of artists like Apache Indian refuses to be located within the either/or ism of 'identity'. This music manifests itself in a connective supplementarity – ragga *plus* bhangra *plus* England *plus* Indian *plus* Kingston *plus* Birmingham. The culture which is produced relies not on entities of selfhood but on the process of becoming more than one. Apache Indian's music demonstrates a quite different truth from the one commentators like Roy Kerridge invoked in the aftermath of the summer of 1985 and what came to be known as the 'Handsworth riots'. Kerridge and members of the media were quick to name the tragic deaths of two Asian shopkeepers as the result of

58. *Sun*, 12 September 1995, see also *Sun*, 11 September 1995, *Daily Telegraph*, 11 September 1985.

a 'race riot', offering spuriously to 'explain' 'Why Blacks hate Asians!'[58] The inter-cultural processes which operate within youthful communities explode these crude discourses which attempt to explain the crisis of urban Britain via a notion of 'race relations'. In this sense these musical cultures offer an important challenge to forms of subjectification which define social groups through invoking racial archetypes and their associated attributes. It is here that Apache Indian's music is most significant. His biography and music demonstrate the fragile but nonetheless profound forms of association and dialogue that have been established around the production and consumption of reggae music. This is not the only story. There are many other forms of youth mobilisation and identity formation occuring within cities like Birmingham. I do not want to reduce the cultural politics of youth to the forms of dialogue described here, or offer this artist as a privileged emblem of south Asian cultural production. A plurality of forms of musical expression needs to be recognised and others more qualified than me are beginning to document and evaluate this culture and music.[59]

59. I am thinking here particularly of the work of scholars like Ko Banerjea, Ash Sharma, and Sanjay Sharma.

60. J. Solomos and L. Back, *Racism and Society*, Macmillan, London forthcoming.

In general the music industry markets limited numbers of south Asian artists and displays the impulse to privilege particular exponents. Cultural hybridity is marketed and re-territorialised to satiate the saccharin desires of corporate multiculturalism.[60] The cultural politics of popular music needs to be qualified through an understanding of the market discipline to which artists and performers submit. The tendency to over-politicise musical cultures on the part of cultural critics needs to be resisted. Yet, it would be foolish to ignore the power and immediacy these forms of expression possess with regard to addressing issues in the vernacular which relate to the experience and plight of young Asians and their associates.

On Thursday 16 September 1993, Derek Beackon, a British National Party candidate was elected as the local political representative for East London's Millwall district. The news sent shock waves through Britain's political culture.

It was the first time that an openly fascist candidate had ever gained the 'respectability of an electoral win. Apache Indian's response to these dramatic developments was to cut a 'Special', the dance-hall equivalent of a news bulletin. This recording demonstrated that these forms of performance have the capability to make interventions which connect subaltern public spheres with a wider audience. Over the weekend that followed he transformed his tune 'Movin' On' from a call for unity in the face of inter-faith violence in India to a pronouncement on events in East London. The tune was built around the bass line from the Willie Williams reggae classic 'Armagideon Time'. The lyric connected the BNP victory with the attack by a gang of white youths on the Bengali youngster Quddus Ali.[61] Like Walter Benjamin's storyteller[62] Apache took his own experience and the practical concerns of young Bengalis and fashioned a collective rebuff to racism. The proceeds from the record were offered to give financial support for a youth led defence campaign.[63] The record owed its form to a tradition of generating popular news within the reggae dance-hall. These creative musical cultures are being forged in a context where the incidence of violent forms of racism is increasing. In Birmingham alone 400 incidents of racist violence occur each year.[64] The significance that music can have in facilitating such interventions should not be trivialised in a situation where young Asians are almost completely excluded from the public sphere of Britain's civic culture.

Sacrificing certitude for fragmentation may bring about new political possibilities. A sensitivity to the politics of inter-diasporic connections may well provide the potential for establishing commonality and association. At an analytical level such an approach promises to remain sensitive to the particularities of 'the local' while being alert to the global matrices of diaspora cultures. Forms of anti-racist agency can flourish which reject both ethnocentrism and the psychic shackles of the 'either/or' model of identity. Finally, I want to return to the metaphor of the crossroads. I suggested at the beginning that the utility of this notion was in the way it captured a sense of convergence, particularly in the wider context of the global passage of cultural flows. The crossroads, however, is not just a place where routes converge, it is also the point where choices have to be made and directions plotted. Something exhilarating is happening in the musical cultures that I have described, which points to new forms of cultural politics and begs a reconsideration of the way in which black music is analysed. Equally, the work of musicians like Apache Indian expands to new limits the utility of concepts like antiphony and diaspora. Returning to Robert Johnson's secular hymn, magic is being worked by young musicians caught and allied in the darkness at the crossroads.

61. Apache Indian, 'Movin' On Special', CID 580.

62. W. Benjamin, *Illuminations*, Fontana Press, London 1992.

63. 'Unity Beat', *The Guardian*, 13 October 1993.

64. L. Back and D. Bains, *Racism Overground: A Multi-Agency Approach to Racial Attacks Monitoring*, Birmingham Racial Attacks Monitoring Unit, Birmingham 1993.

WAR AND PERCEPTION

Trudi Tate

Paul Virilio, *The Vision Machine*, tr. Julie Rose, Indiana University Press and British Film Institute, Bloomington and London 1994, £9.95 paperback. John Taylor, *War Photography: Realism in the British Press*, Routledge, London 1991, £12.99 paperback.

'We have all had enough of hearing about the death of God, of man, of art and so on since the nineteenth century', writes Paul Virilio. These imaginary deaths are actually symptoms of another crisis: the loss of faith in perception. No longer do we rely on the evidence of our own eyes. Vision takes place at one remove, as machines do much of our looking for us. And machines spend a lot of time looking *at* us. In the street, in shopping centres, on public transport, even in the local paper shop, we are scrutinised by automatic cameras. And at the same time, we live out a fantasy of seeing everything, of complete knowledge, a 'totalitarian ambition' of omnivoyance (p33). Everything must be investigated, illuminated under bright lights. Virilio locates this development in the French Revolution, a period obsessed with lighting. 'The general public, we know, craved artificial lighting. They wanted lights, city lights, which just involved man illuminating himself' (p35). The public sphere was lit up; the revolution tried to make the private sphere equally visible, through investigation, the secret police, and a terror based on looking. A tragedy, says Virilio, 'brought about by an exaggerated love of light' (p34).

From self-illumination, we have come to live in a culture of surveillance, surrounded by objects which look at us. This produces both comfort and paranoia. Who is it that is watching us? Often there is nobody, just the machine, impersonally recording. The perception of our surroundings is now split between the gaze of the human subject and the gaze of the object (p59).

Lacan, too, argues that it seems as if the world (and its objects) are always looking at you.[1] Virilio criticises Lacan for 'passing prudently from image to language, to the linguistic being' (p23), and for paying too little attention to the function of images. For Virilio, the loss of faith in perception has produced a crisis in our social and psychic organisation. 'In the West', he argues, 'the death of God and the death of art are indissociable'; linked through changes in perception. We are left with *'the zero degree of representation'*, fulfilling a prophecy of a thousand years ago: 'If we remove the image, not only Christ but the whole universe disappears' (p17).

Virilio's vision machine is partly real, partly imagined. Much of his discussion refers to what already exists; to changes in the act of looking produced by photography, film, computer-generated images. But the book also strives to

1. Jacques Lacan, 'The Eye and the Gaze', *The Four Fundamental Concepts of Psychoanalysis*, tr Alan Sheridan, Penguin, Harmondsworth 1979, p75.

imagine where this is leading. Virilio quotes Paul Klee's statement, 'Now objects perceive me', and asks: 'What will be the effects, the theoretical and practical consequences for our own "vision of the world" of Paul Klee's intuition's becoming reality?' This is more than simply the 'proliferation of surveillance cameras in public places' of recent years, but a 'doubling of the point of view', shared between subject and object; between person and machine. And this has significant consequences for the very structure of perception, for our understanding of human subjectivity. More than this: we are on the verge, says Virilio, of *synthetic vision*; of the machine itself producing the thing seen.

> Although we know that the imagery from video cameras in banks and supermarkets is relayed to a central control-room, although we can guess the presence of security officers, eyes glued to control monitors, with *computer-aided perceptions* – visionics – it is actually impossible to imagine the pattern, to guess the interpretation produced by this sightless vision (p62).

The Vision Machine is an apocalyptic book, compelling if often confusing, and drawing on a fascinating range of historical and theoretical material on the displacement of looking in the twentieth century. Some of the ideas in *The Vision Machine* are set out (rather more clearly) in Virilio's early work, *War and Cinema*.[2] Much of his argument is based on technical developments in modern warfare, and here his work is most instructive.

Virilio argues that the First World War radically altered the cultural uses of photography. War photography moved into mass production, 'like a factory':

> it was not a matter of images now, but of an uninterrupted stream of images, millions of negatives madly trying to embrace on a daily basis the statistical trends of the first great military-industrial conflict (p48).

Aerial photographs were vital in the First World War, though with mixed results, for they could be out of date within hours, and it was not always possible to get new information to the front lines. This was a particular problem for the early tanks, which often relied on aerial photographs for navigation. Photography played a significant part in the development of modern warfare; of organising battle at one remove. And it was equally important in the management of civilian responses to the war, through propaganda. 'Immediately after the war', Virilio argues, 'Britain decided to abandon classic armaments somewhat and to invest in the logistics of perception: in propaganda films, as well as observation, detection and transmission equipment' (p49). After the war, military filming continued and was to become vital in the planning and execution of the next war. Virilio describes this as the 'continuation of the First World War by other means' (p50).

Photography and film have become vital elements of warfare, both for military planners and for the civilian public. British and American

2. Paul Virilio, *War and Cinema: The Logistics of Perception*, tr Patrick Camiller, Verso, London 1989.

photographers made a significant contribution to the defeat of Nazism; 25 years later, photography was instrumental in America's defeat in Vietnam.

> Once the military twigged that photographers, steeped in the traditions of the documentary, now lost wars, image hunters were once again removed from combat zones. This is perfectly apparent with the Falklands war, a war that has no images, as well as in Latin America, Pakistan, Lebanon, etc (p56).

Photographers and television workers are now at risk of imprisonment or even murder in many of the world's war zones. In others, they have become, wittingly or not, a valuable part of the military propaganda machine, as we saw (or rather could not see) in the Gulf War of 1991.

John Taylor's book, *War Photography: Realism in the British Press*, looks at the use of newspaper photography from the First World War until the Falklands, with a chapter devoted to press reports on terrorism. Where Virilio's argument is dazzling, if disorganised, Taylor's is well organised and clearly written, if somewhat unadventurous. The book draws upon a limited but useful range of historical material; the chapter on the First World War, for example, places research on popular photography and the family snapshot in the context of well-established arguments about the culture of the war (pp28-34). Taylor summarises current historical views of major wars and gives a concise account of the function of the press in each case.

Like Virilio, Taylor demonstrates that the use of photography transformed the structure of the First World War, though he does not take up the theoretical implications of his material. He notes that the commanders derived much of their knowledge of the war indirectly, through reading photographs, while some journalists saw the war at first hand, watching the battle from a vantage point, 'almost like the generals of old'. However, the journalists could see almost nothing, and were reliant upon official military communiqués for their own reports (p22). This peculiar circularity inverts the whole structure of *seeing* the war. Those who are present see almost nothing; the real view is available only to people miles away, whose looking is done for them, by machines. Taylor documents this remarkable shift; Virilio explores its consequences.

The problems with seeing serve the complex propaganda machine of the time. Journalists who are present at the bloodbath on the first day of the Somme, for example, have no idea what is going on. Their articles, based on misleading military reports, suggest a successful day of battle with light casualties. The appalling suffering of that day is simply rendered invisible (p22). Here and in later wars, the reporting produced the 'truth' of the conflict; photographs were used to endorse the written material in the press, producing a kind of evidence which Taylor suggests seemed incontestable to many readers. Taylor notes that journalistic 'realism' is itself a set of conventions, and he looks at how those conventions determine what is photographed, how the picture is composed, and how it is used by editors in setting up the page. This is useful, but needs to be argued further. Taylor often assumes that the conventions of realism produce only one meaning, and he makes too little allowance for other meanings and other possible ways of reading. Part of the problem lies in his tendency to treat the population as a unified readership, and to locate oppositional voices outside the discourses of the time. So when he looks at pacifism during the Great War, for example, he refers unquestioningly to 'popular resentment at the actions of pacifists', and writes as if pacifists were somehow not part of the general public. A more persuasive view would take more account of the fact that several different discourses were in circulation at the time. Pacificism might have been a minority position, but it was a potent discourse which seriously challenged popular support for the war; that is why such drastic measures were taken to suppress it.

Similarly, key terms such as 'patriotism' need to be argued through, and not merely assumed as a single, monolithic way of thinking. Taylor's attempts to explain everything at a fairly simple level leaves too much unquestioned, and sometimes leads to some rather troubling statements. In a brief discussion of British anti-Semitism during the Second World War, for example, Taylor argues:

> We should remember that the British antagonism towards rich Jews was not translated into death camps. Anti-Semitism was part of a groundswell of hostility towards the rich in general (p65).

'Jews' and 'the rich' become elided in this argument (as also occurred in Nazi propaganda). This airy remark covers up the question of British anti-Semitism, rather than engaging with it. The book would be stronger if it questioned some of its own assumptions, and did not try to explain away complex historical and ideological issues in a few terse sentences.

Taylor makes extensive use of the notion of 'common sense' during various wars, and indicates that a good deal of ideological work – censorship, propaganda, and so forth – was required to keep it afloat. This is a crucial aspect of the book, and needs to be explored further, for it renders the very notion of 'common sense' precarious. How it has been sustained, in various forms, up until the present day, is an ideological question which requires more analysis. As Slavoj Žižek argues, it is not a matter of people not knowing what they do; the real problem is that we know quite well what we are doing, but we do it anyway, pretending that we do not know.[3] That is how ideology works, and we need to understand it much better if we are to grasp why we continue to fund and support wars (and sell large quantities of armaments) whilst claiming that we oppose them.

3. Slavoj Žižek, *The Sublime Object of Ideology*, Verso, London 1989, pp30-2.

HEROES AND VILLAINS

Sean Nixon

Graham Dawson, *Soldier Heroes, British Adventure: Empire and the Imagining of Masculinities*, Routledge, London 1994, £14.99 paperback, £50.00 cloth. Michael Roper, *Masculinity and the British Organization Man Since 1945*, Oxford University Press, Oxford 1994, £25.00 cloth.

The production of powerful public narratives around, on the one hand, the Falklands/Malvinas War and, on the other hand, economic regeneration emerges as a strong framing presence within Graham Dawson's *Soldier Heroes* and Michael Roper's *Masculinity and the British Organization Man*, respectively. Given the importance of both these narratives in giving shape and direction to the Thatcherite project of 'regressive modernisation' in the 1980s, it should not surprise us that they surface in these two fine, scholarly books researched during this period. Both books, however, have, tangentially, something new to tell us about this recent history; namely the way images of national decline, the national past and the revitalisation of the nation were powerfully linked with representations of masculinity within a range of public discourses.

The Falklands/Malvinas War provides the immediate context for Graham Dawson's enquiry into the place of the soldier hero in representations of the imperial and post-imperial British nation. As he notes early on in his account, the starting point for his study was the ambition to make sense of the popular support for the war and the language of Britishness aggressively celebrated within this. In a post-imperial moment, asks Dawson, how could a language of Britishness forged in the heyday of Empire and reaccented by the experience of the Second World War still give shape to the sentiments and sense of identity of a large swathe of the population? In answering this question, what emerges strongly in Dawson's book is the centrality of military men to the modern imagining of the British nation and the resonance of these heroic soldier's tales in more recent invocations of the national past and national greatness; invocations guided – as in the case of Thatcherite discourse – by the ambition to reverse what was simultaneously imagined as a process of national decline.

A version of this story of national decline also emerges strongly in Roper's book. Specifically, it is an account of economic decline and the positing by business historians and other commentators (notably the advocates of enterprise culture) of a decline history. Roper quotes a vociferous exponent of this history – the military historian and conservative revisionist of the post-1945 years, Corelli Barnett – reviewing Martin Weiener's influential book *English Culture and the Decline of the Industrial Spirit*. What was so striking about Barnett's review, as Roper suggests, was the way Barnett amplified the gendered metaphors of Weiner's decline history. For Barnett, like Weiner, Britain's economic crisis stemmed from the way the British education system – especially in its elite institutions – had drained the manly virility of England's middle class men and shorn its industry, as a result, of the necessary levels of 'industrial spirit'. Instead, then, of reproducing the aggressive desire for profit and the spirit of enterprise of their fathers, the British education system had turned the sons of the great British entrepreneurs into men disdainful of industry and more interested in pursuing the genteel and cultured lifestyle of the aristocracy. In a prescription which echoed that of the advocates of enterprise culture, the solution for Barnett was the reinstilling of enterprise in the making of 'aggressive and acquisitive capitalists'.

The importance of this decline history for Roper's book concerns the way it impacted on the generation of career managers in UK manufacturing firms who form the focus of his account. In fact, as Roper demonstrates, the gendered narrative of economic decline very pointedly challenged the business culture which the post-war generation of managers he discusses had been forged within and had partly helped to create. Roper argues that this critique of the generation of post-war managers was often made in terms of a battle over competing versions of masculinity and caste by the advocates of enterprise culture; as a struggle to install a superior version of masculinity in business (the creation of new business heroes like Lord Weinstock of GEC, notorious for his ruthless cost-cutting, was prominent in this process).

It is in the context of this critique of post-war British management practices, as well as the declining economic significance of the sectors in which they worked, that the managers interviewed by Roper reflect on their careers. One effect of these conjunctural factors, together with the fact that most of the men interviewed by Roper were either on the edge of retirement or had recently retired, is to produce an 'end of an era' feeling in their accounts. It is these factors, however, which clearly propel the stories these men offer to Roper and which furnish him with a particularly rich set of testimonies from which to piece together the subjective dimensions of the masculinity lived by this group of men.

Roper develops his account through a life-history method. This means, as he notes, encouraging the men (and the few women he interviewed) to largely structure their own stories. From these accounts Roper then draws out, as he puts it, the 'mythical and symbolic aspects of the account as much as its factual content'. At the heart of this form of life-history method deployed by Roper is an attention to the forms of transference operating between interviewer and interviewee. In reflecting on this process, Roper perceptively argues that his own identity – as a young, single Australian graduate student interested in business history – had important consequences for the kinds of accounts produced by the managers. In particular, he notes the way the strong emphasis in his interviewee's stories on the early parts of their careers, and the motifs of youthful omnipotence and freedom from domestic responsibility, were likely to have been shaped in part by what he represented to them.

The central pay-off from using a life-history method for Roper's book is the way it offers up to him a sense of the emotional investments made by these men in their work. This allows him to explore the fractures between the dominant public image of this generation of managers as rational 'organisation men' and their own subjective experience of this identity. What emerges strongly in his account – and it is one of the book's most important arguments – is the way that far from operating as rational managers along the lines set out in the management textbooks they themselves helped pioneer, these men continued to draw on the repertoire of the owner-manager's emotional and intuitive investment in the company. Most important within this, Roper argues, was the persistence of forms of patrimony within organisational culture and its structuring around homosocial desire between men at work.

Roper notes the way his presence in the interview situation brought into play aspects of these forms of desire between men: the dynamics of seduction and succession and forms of aggression and hostility. Drawing on Freud's essay 'Family Romances', Roper gives considerable weight to comments made by all his male interviewees concerning their relationship with mentor figures. He reads these relationships as romances, in which his managers idealised these older men. For Roper this amounted to more than the repetition of father/sons relationships and strongly suggested the organisation of desire and seduction in these relationships. One striking claim that he makes is that these relations between older and younger men might mimic the dynamics of normative heterosexual relations. Underpinning this, he argues, was the importance of family symbolism within the work-environment in mediating relations *between* men.

It was not only in relations between men at work that this family symbolism was important. The marked separation of the spheres of home and work reproduced within management during the formative years of his career managers had profound consequences itself for how managers viewed secretaries. What loomed large amongst the men interviewed by Roper was both the dismissal of the servicing work done by secretaries in comparison to their own heavy-weight contributions and the casting of these functionaries in the role of 'office wives'. Negotiating this particular gendered regime was just one of the problems faced by women attempting to move into management positions within this sector.

If relations of affection and desire operated between men at work and were central, as Roper claims, to the processes of succession within management (and key to the exclusionary practices which faced women attempting to move into management), then relations of aggression also surfaced in relations between men. Succession might not be a smooth process in management. Younger men might decide to 'take on' and aggressively challenge their superiors.

Bright young men armed with new ideas about business were certainly not protectively nurtured. Change in management might just as easily be driven by aggressive unseating of older men by younger men.

A valorisation of an assertive masculinity and toughness was also a distinctive component of the self-representation of the managers interviewed by Roper. This took particular forms. A celebration of what Roper christens a 'cult of toughness' based upon hands-on experience gained in the early years of their careers figured prominently amongst his interviewees. Anxieties about their largely desk-bound and cerebral role in organisations also led these men to emphasise their technical know-how and valorise the products produced by their companies. What also loomed large was the generational experience of national service and its importance in underpinning the sense of superiority with which these men viewed their masculinity when compared to a younger generation of business school trained managers.

A clue to the valorisation of this experience of soldiering by Roper's career managers emerges in Graham Dawson's *Soldier Heroes*. As he states in the introduction, the soldier represents a quintessential and idealised figure of masculinity with deep roots in Western cultural traditions. In his book, Dawson explores the figure of the soldier hero in relation to representations of the British nation and the way in which images of the nation itself were gendered through public representations of great men and within the cultural forms of boy culture. As he notes, soldiers have historically occupied a central place in the representation of English-British national identity – from heroes like Drake and Wolfe to Nelson and Wellington. This link between the imagining of the nation and masculinity was made particularly strongly within the configuration of British identity forged in the period of Empire and it is the legacy of this formation of English-British masculinity which centrally preoccupies Dawson.

What emerges strongly in Dawson's account of these imperial and post-imperial soldier heroes is the way the consolidation of a modern mass media and associated leisure and entertainment industries provided key conditions for the telling and retelling of these heroic soldier's tales. In relation to Dawson's first case study – Sir Henry Havelock, hero of the 1857 relief of Lucknow in the Indian rebellion – it was the speeding up of trans-imperial communications, and with it the new intensified sense of excitement introduced into war reporting, which was a condition for the representation of Havelock as a soldier hero. In Dawson's second case study – T.E. Lawrence – it was the American journalist Lowell Thomas's multi-media events (using slides and film to accompany a lecture) first brought to London in 1919, which constructed the heroic figure of 'Lawrence of Arabia'. In the third case study – an autobiographical reflection on his own childhood investment in the boy culture of war – it is mass produced toys and periodicals which make possible the imaginative playing out of heroic military deeds.

Getting to grips with the process of narration or story-telling involving soldier heroes, and the way the adventure form in particular furnished a specific range of attributes in the figure of the soldier hero, is at the heart of Dawson's account. In an impressively lucid exposition, Dawson draws out the importance of narrative forms for not only the creation of masculinities in widely circulated public forms of culture, but also as an everyday cultural practice through which (in this instance) men inhabit and compose for themselves a sense of masculinity. Dawson makes good use of the double meaning of the verb 'to compose', emphasising both the way it refers to the creative cultural work of producing or fictioning stories and as signalling the process of subjective composure: the creation of a position for the self which orientates it in relation to the norms of a cultural milieu.

The most striking conceptual presence in Dawson's development of the notions of narrative composition and narrative composure is that of Kleinian psychoanalysis. Dawson mobilises Kleinian concepts to open up the place of phantasy in the processes of cultural production and cultural consumption and to furnish him with a model of the psychic economy underpinning the distribution of figures within narrative compositions. His deployment of Klein is far from doctrinaire and Dawson offers a carefully delimited reading of what Kleinian psychoanalysis can deliver to his analysis. Where this works best is in relation to his analysis of the racialised nature of the distribution of figures within the soldier's tales. In his analysis of the reporting of the relief of Lucknow by the British troops led by Havelock, for example, Dawson emphasies the split within the reporting between the brave heroic Havelock and the abject brutality projected onto the perpetrators of the 'mutiny' and the counterposing of images of innocent Christian women and children with that of maniacal 'cruel Hindus'. These psychic dimensions of the telling of Havelock's story in the press, Dawson argues, in turn drove a series of revenge fantasies in which a highly-charged form of story-telling called for retribution for the 'mutiny' and the reimposition of British rule.

The historical context of each of his three case studies – the era of high Empire, the beginning of the erosion of confidence in the imperial ideal in the post-1918 years and the post-Suez years of decolonisation – throws different light on the narration of the soldier heroes tale for Dawson. An important finding of the book in this regard is the change in the rendering of the soldier hero across these periods. The contrast between the public lives of Havelock and Lawrence is particularly striking. The triumphalist story of Havelock's 'exemplary life' is not mirrored in Lawrence's most ambivalent public representation as the 'Blond Bedouin'. Thus, while the stories of both men are 'imbued with power and imagine the continuing dominance of Britishness' (as Dawson puts it), Lawrence is a different kind of soldier hero to Havelock. Subsequent retellings of the Lawrence myth have made this differentiation in the figure of the soldier hero even clearer.

In his account of the Havelock and Lawrence stories, Dawson concentrates on the process of cultural production. In the third and final section of the book, he turns to a discussion of how these public stories of the soldier hero might be inhabited by real historical men and boys. In exploring the consumption of these soldier tales, Dawson turns to an autobiographical mode of analysis, exploring his own investments in the figure of the soldier hero through an analysis of his childhood participation in the boy culture of war. This section represents some of the most original passages of the book and certainly for me (as a boy of the *Airfix* generation) is deeply evocative. Drawing strongly on Klein in these sections, Dawson explores the ways in which comics, toys (notably, model soldiers) and childhood war play open up key ways of composing a masculine identity that can be lived in relative psychic comfort.

Dawson ends *Soldier Heroes* by posing a set of questions about how it might be possible to come to terms with the figure of the soldier hero as it resides in both individual and larger collective representations of masculinity and English-British identity. Dawson's central contention is that any adequate strategy of reparation must insist on not simply forgetting or repressing these tales of heroic soldier deeds – whether in the figure of Havelock, Lawrence or boyhood self-imaginings as a soldier hero. Rather, he suggests the need to develop more integrative ways of retelling these stories that would be based around

> the heroes of Imperial British adventure [being] brought into dialogue with the colonized peoples whom they once triumphed over, and if the dichotomous narratives of adventure and domestic life could be brought into creative tension and enabled to speak and argue with each other, then it might become possible to acknowledge the historical damage that has accompanied heroic idealization and to readjust our conceptions of others accordingly (p291).

A concern to refigure the divide between domestic life and adventure – in this case between the servicing work performed by wives and secretaries and the adventures played out between men at work – also emerges as a part of the practical politics of masculinity advocated by Roper at the end of his book. Both books propose a politics of masculinity based around the specific configurations of power operating within the cultural forms and institutions they focus upon. In one sense this is a perfectly proper position. It certainly has the advantage over more recent grandiose versions of a politics of masculinity informed by cultural politics. These have tended to produce overblown (and in practice, largely rhetorical) models for transforming masculinity tout court drawn from a reading of the progressive currents in popular culture. However, I remain convinced – in line with this version of sexual politics informed by cultural politics – that it is necessary to go on thinking about a broader based politics of masculinity because (as the tropes of military masculinity in both these books suggest) there are social hegemonies operating across discrete versions of masculinity. Given the arguments, however, about the differentiated nature of masculinity well evidenced in both these books, this broader-based politics cannot be built around only one version of a reconfigured masculinity. Rather it must recognise a gender future based around a plurality of different formations of masculinity and femininity. This ambition to reconfigure the relations between masculinities and between masculinity and femininity, must necessarily retain from cultural politics the concern with representation (like that evidenced in Dawson's injunction to cultural practitioners to reinvent the soldier's tale).

Some clues to the strategies for transforming masculinity, however, might also be found in the model of how one thinks about the relationship between cultural languages and lived identities. I have problems in this regard with the psychoanalytically driven model deployed by both Dawson and Roper. Leaving aside other difficulties with psychoanalysis for social and cultural criticism, it does locate both the persistence of specific cultural identities and the grounds for their transformation within what goes on inside people's heads. This attention to an ideational account of identity formation – the way in which, as Graham Dawson puts it, identities are fashioned in the imagination – fails to recognise the 'dull compunction' of non-ideational techniques and practices through which forms of conduct and subjective composure are produced and reproduced. It is these techniques of the self which provide the conditions for forms of agency and individuation and which are themselves associated with specific technologies of government across a range of compartments of social life. Reconfiguring masculinities, then, needs to lay bare these technologies of government and offers proposals for transforming these governmental technologies. Such a project might have little to do with what is going on in men's heads. Such a project is not advanced by these books. However, in elucidating key problems with contemporary formations of English-British masculinity, both books facilitate the task of thinking beyond the contemporary range of masculine heroes and villains.

1992 – THE YEAR QUEER BROKE

Michael Wyeld

Paul Burston and Colin Richardson (eds), *A Queer Romance – Lesbians, Gay Men and Popular Culture*, Routledge, London 1995; £12.99 paperback. £37.50 cloth.

In the run-up to the London Lesbian and Gay Pride Festival in June of 1992, Britain's *Guardian* newspaper published an article headlined, 'The politics of the new queer'. The tone of the article was simple – picking up on a new trend. Melanie Phillips wrote about queer for *Guardian* readers to digest, 'It's punk, it's anarchic, it's dangerous, it's gesture politics. It's also very confusing.'[1] Who were these queers? And why weren't they happy, for example, that one of Britain's most respected queens, Ian McKellen, had been knighted and had had tea with John Major? What more could they want?

Over the next weeks and months, a variety of media outlets and cultural institutions, including the ICA, *Sight and Sound* magazine and *The Guardian*, as the daily newspaper that includes lesbians and gays more than any other, explored these (seemingly) new ideas. The September 1992 edition of *Sight and Sound* picked up on queer with a twelve page supplement on Queer Cinema[2] with contributions from Cherry Smyth and B. Ruby Rich, who *The Guardian* noted as 'one of the first to spot the trend'.[3] The ICA hosted *The New Queer Cinema Conference* in September of 1992 that featured a talk from film producer Christine Vachon who, again in September of 1992, *The Guardian* called 'American cinema's queen of queer'.[4]

These initial discussions of what queer meant, at least in cinematic terms, defined some of the new players, spokespeople and their interests, but did little to define a history of this new curiosity. Director Dave Markey's 1993 film, *1991 – The Year Punk Broke* went back to 1991, exploring the unparalleled success of a different 'new' phenomenon – grunge – and revealed it as punk's greatest apology, not only because of the popular success of bands like Sonic Youth and Nirvana, but because of a pervasiveness among a certain group of people of the ideas coded in that music. Like that film, *A Queer Romance* goes back – to 1992 – and finds some of the players who helped formulate queer in Britain and allows them a more formal attempt at defining the ways that a new generation of lesbians and gays perceive the world.

> The real trouble is that we have rescued a word not allowed to our kind.
>
> Jeannette Winterson[5]

Actor Michael Cashman, a founding member of the lesbian and gay lobby group Stonewall, in the same Melanie Phillips' *Guardian* article, dismissed the

1. *The Guardian*, 23 June 1992, p19.

2. *Sight and Sound*, September 1992.

3. *The Guardian*, 15 September 1992.

4. *Ibid*.

5. Jeanette Winterson, 'The Poetics of Sex' in *Granta 43, Best of Young British Novelists 2*, Granta, London 1993, p318.

6. *The Guardian*, 23 June 1992,

new ideas as he bitched, 'The New Queer politics is a metropolitan phenomenon of media queens.'[6] And media queens the writers of *A Queer Romance* are. Co-editor Paul Burston is the opinionated, much talked about editor of the gay section of London listings magazine *Time Out*. Likewise Burston's partner in crime, Colin Richardson is the Assistant Editor at *Gay Times*. Both Richardson and Burston are notorious for their public squabbles and fisticuffs with other journalists and writers. The evidence of these squabbles and the alliances formed as a result are apparent in *A Queer Romance*.

7. *The Guardian*, 17 December 1993.

8. *The Guardian*, 22 December 1993.

In December of 1993 *The Guardian* ran an article on a new movement within the indie-pop music scene that was getting a lot of attention – queercore – a kind of music that was as important to the gay scene as it was to the music scene.[7] The article was critical of the lesbian and gay press and in particular *Gay Times* for ignoring queercore. In response Colin Richardson wrote back, 'There's a good article to be written about queercore. Sadly, [*The Guardian's*] was not it.'[8] Contained within *A Queer Romance* is the article about queercore to which, presumably, Richardson referred. Written by one of queercore's founding dissidents, film-maker Bruce LaBruce, it is an article that is set apart from the remaining contributions to this collection, not because it is any different in quality from the remaining articles, but because of its dissent. Writes LaBruce, 'I don't feel I have a lot in common with a bunch of rich kids with degrees in semiotic theory ... I've never felt comfortable with the new 'queer' movement, never attended a Queer Nation meeting or participated in any marches or protests or actions' (p194).

So Bruce LaBruce's inclusion in this work was not merely because he is an interesting character with something to say about his fascinating corner of the world or because he fits in with queer ideology, but because of the strange nature of queer theory in Britain at the moment. It is a scene rife with great gossip and some good stories, and the players in this new queer theory, like the characters in some as yet unmade Robert Altman's film, have their histories and their axes to grind. All of this goes to make *A Queer Romance* a trendy, sexy, happening and compelling read. But does it say anything true about the world, or some small section of it?

Obvious to anyone regularly browsing through the more urbane book shops, the last few years has seen an explosion in titles explaining the lesbian and gay bent on the world. Some of the material is less than well thought out, as though publishers had rushed to print to cash in quickly. The recently published book *Queer Noises*, written by John Gill (Cassell, London 1995), presents a rather silly look at lesbians and gays in popular music. Despite the disclaimer on the jacket to the contrary, the entire book is dedicated to outing lesbians and gays involved in the music industry. *Queer Noises* amounts to not much and leaves you thinking, 'who cares?' *A Queer Romance* is thankfully concerned with the more legitimate and interesting question of the ways that lesbians and gay men engage with popular culture despite the fact that acknowledging a lesbian or gay spectator in most film and television is rare.

'Reading mainstream films subversively, lesbians have constructed heroines who do not officially belong to them, not only by disrupting the authority of the heterosexual male gaze, but also by appropriating the heterosexual woman as a homosexual object,' writes *A Queer Romance* contributor Cherry Smyth (p123). In this most succinct explanation of why lesbians bother to pay the price of a cinema ticket, Cherry Smyth also sums up the project central to this collection. In revealing the existence of a queer gaze most of the contributors use film and televison and the framework set out in Laura Mulvey's essay 'Visual Pleasure and Narrative Cinema',[9] to show how a variety of readings and positions are available to lesbian and gay spectators, allowing them the opportunity to take pleasure in works that don't speak directly to them. The question remains about whether a queer gaze will suffice to do what the contributors to *A Queer Romance* seem to want it to do – unify lesbians and gays in an approach to looking at the world.

9. Laura Mulvey, 'Visual Pleasure and Narrative Cinema' in *Visual and Other Pleasures*, Macmillan, Basingstoke 1989.

On the one hand these writers want to avoid dictating how the world is read by lesbians or gays, to show that it is possible, for example, that many lesbians enjoy Hollywood cinema, maintaining that there is plurality among a group of people who were once imagined homogeneous. On the other hand there is the desire to formulate a shared reading of popular culture by lesbian or gay spectators. As Cherry Smyth writes (p125):

As we feel freer to be ourselves, the useful organising fiction of the past – that a person's politics could be determined by his or her sexual orientation (or some other salient feature of identity) – no longer serves. We need a new way of thinking about identity, or at least a new application, one that preserves the promise of sexual liberation. It isn't enough to become parallel to straights – we want to obliterate such dichotomies altogether.

So if sexual orientation can't explain a person's politics, why then, according to another of this collection's contributors, Steven Drukman, can it explain why gay men prefer George Michael to Iron Maiden? Or do they? Steven Drukman wants to define how a generalised gay man can watch MTV, which doesn't specifically speak to him, and still enjoy it. In so doing Drukman makes the same assumptions about gay men that the old school gay scene has made – they like Madonna, they don't like heavy metal. Why is it necessary to define out of existence the possibility that there are lesbians and gay men who position themselves as spectators in all sorts of ways to enjoy all sorts of artistic works?

Here is a passage from Drukmans piece:

Although the antics of the [heavy metal] band members are often replete with stroking guitars and inventive uses for the microphone, [heavy metal] videos are not the ideal sit of application for the gay gaze. The reason may lie in the bands' uses of their 'to-be-looked-at-ness'. More often than not, the performers work to subvert the spectator's pleasure, usually through methods of visual distraction. Often this involves constant cutaways to adoring (usually female) fans in the 'audience', allowing for a shift in gaze to diffuse the one-on-one relationship of MTV spectator and spectacle ... (p191)

If it is possible to use this argument to show why gay men don't like these videos, how can he explain how heterosexual women can enjoy them or are they, too, excluded from enjoying these videos? Drukman uses a very limited number of examples to prove this point and has missed a variety of heavy metal, punk and noise music videos that do court the kind of gaze for which he argues. Among those readily memorable are Van Halen's *Pretty Woman*, in which singer David Lee Roth – dressed as Napoleon – makes advances to a man in drag. There are also the videos of Metallica and Soundgarden, which are often as homoerotic as Drukman claims George Michael's videos are. It is increasingly evident that a large number of lesbians and gay men do enjoy all sorts. There are gay men and lesbians who like heavy metal or whatever – but they don't talk about it while on the dance floor at *Heaven*.[10]

10. 'Heaven' is a (mostly) gay London nightclub owned by Richard Branson.

In the light of this, it is perhaps Bruce LaBruce's writing that, despite lacking an explicit intellectual framework, is the most challenging and exciting. Writes LaBruce, 'I've never been able to surrender my mind to prefabricated dogma, or reduce my politics to a slogan, or even situate myself in a fixed position on the political spectrum. No, I'm not "queer," and I don't know why they had to go and ruin a perfectly good word, either' (p194).

Preferring to remain the perpetual voice of disagreement, LaBruce is in the privileged position of never having to produce limiting ideas on anything – continually looking for a new way of looking, merely for the sake of looking. LaBruce's writing is part of a larger picture of his career, '... when [I] find any kind of foothold into being legitimised or institutionalised [I] drop it and turn on it and move on to something else.'[11] This is either very irresponsible or a license to continually enjoy the world as you come in contact with it. To borrow a line from *The Guardian* back in 1992, 'It's punk, it's anarchic, it's dangerous, it's gesture politics. It's also very confusing.' If that's queer, then count me in.

11. 'The bitched is back', an interview with Bruce LaBruce *Gay Times*, January 1995.

International TechnoCities Conference

Culture & Political Economy of the Digital Revolution

Coventry University 29–30 March 1996

The much heralded arrival of the 'information society' is built on assumptions of exponential growth rates amongst users of computer-mediated communications, and general interest in the potentials of computer networking. Cultural and commercial interest has attracted the attention of policy-makers at all levels of government.

This unique international conference will move beyond the prevalent discourses of technologically-driven utopias and dystopias. Employing a measured response to the rapidy developing desire to create new epistemological approaches it will:

- Examine the ambiguities and ambivalences of this technocultural revolution.
- Promote discussion based on theoretical, and empirical research.
- Exchange perspectives on policy approaches at all levels of government.

Speakers include:

Simon Bell, UEA Development Studies; Simon Davies, Essex, Law, Specialist on Surveillance & Policy; Leen d'Haenens, University of Gent Communications; Stephen Graham, University of Newcastle, Centre for Urban Technology; Ursula Huws, Analyctica; Douglas Kellner, University of Texas, Philosophy; Celia Lury, University of Lancaster, Sociology; Mel Read MEP, Labour Spokesperson on New Information Technologies; Judith Squires, Editor *New Formations*; Julian Stallabrass, Deputy Editor *New Left Review*; Liesbet Van Zoonen, University of Amsterdam, Communications; Frank Webster, Oxford Brookes, Sociology.

**For further details and booking arrangements, please contact
Mike Walford, Centre for Communication Studies,
Coventry University, Priory Street, Coventry, W. Midlands CV1 5FB.
Telephone: +44 (0) 1203 838536/224965 (24hr) Fax: +44 (0) 1203 838667.
e.mail: techcity@vide.ac.coventry.uk**

new formations

New Formations is published three times a year.
Forthcoming issues for 1996 are:

SPRING (No 28)
CONSERVATIVE MODERNITY
Edited by Cora Kaplan and David Glover
Contributors include Paul Gilroy, Peter Osborne, Bill Schwarz, Lynne
Segal and Janet Wolff.

AUTUMN (No 29)
TECHNOSCIENCE
Edited by Jody Berland and Sarah Kember
Contributors include Rosie Braidotti, Neil Tenhaaf and Jan Marchessault.

WINTER (No 30)
CULTURAL MEMORY
Edited by Erica Carter and Ken Hirschkop

Why not SUBSCRIBE?
Make sure of your copy

Subscription rates, 1996 (3 issues)

Individual Subscriptions		*Institutional Subscriptions*	
UK	£35.00	UK	£70.00
Rest of World	£38.00	Rest of World	£75.00

- -

Please send one year's subscription starting with Issue Number _____

I enclose payment of _____

Please send me _____ copies of back issue no. _____

I enclose total payment of _____

Name _____

Address _____

Please return this form with cheque or money order (sterling only) payable to
Lawrence & Wishart and send to:
Lawrence & Wishart, 99a Wallis Road, London E9 5LN